Painting Landscapes

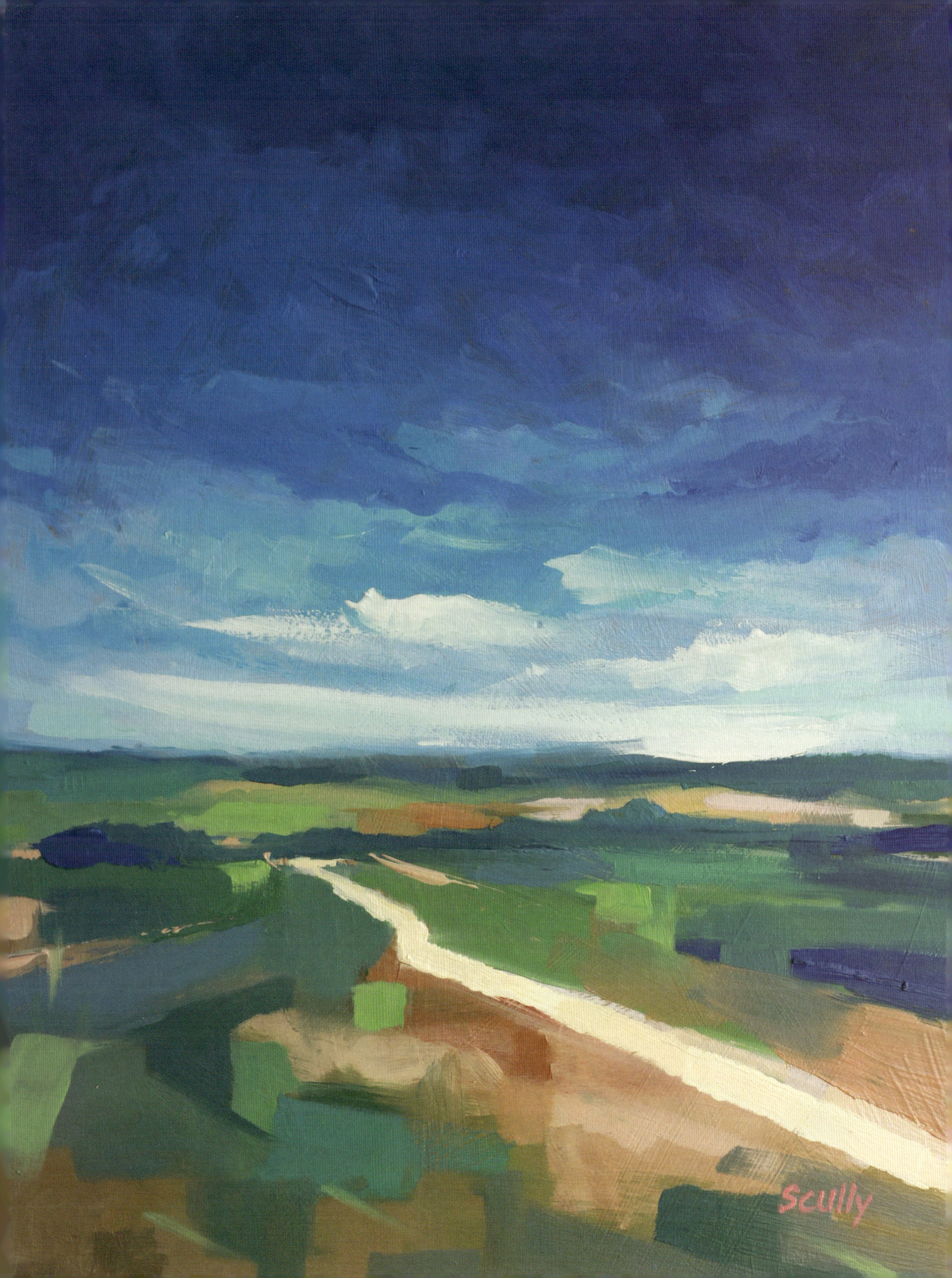
Scully

Painting Landscapes

Kevin Scully

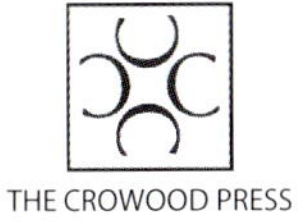

THE CROWOOD PRESS

First published in 2018 by
The Crowood Press Ltd
Ramsbury, Marlborough
Wiltshire SN8 2HR

www.crowood.com

British Library Cataloguing-in-Publication Data
A catalogue record for this book is available from the British Library.

ISBN 978 1 78500 383 7

Frontispiece: *From Beacon Hill*, Kevin Scully, oil on board, 12" × 10". An oil sketch, painted *en plein air*, in preparation for a larger painting to be produced later in the studio.

Graphic design and layout by Peggy & Co. Design Inc.
Printed and bound in India by Replika Press Pvt Ltd

Contents

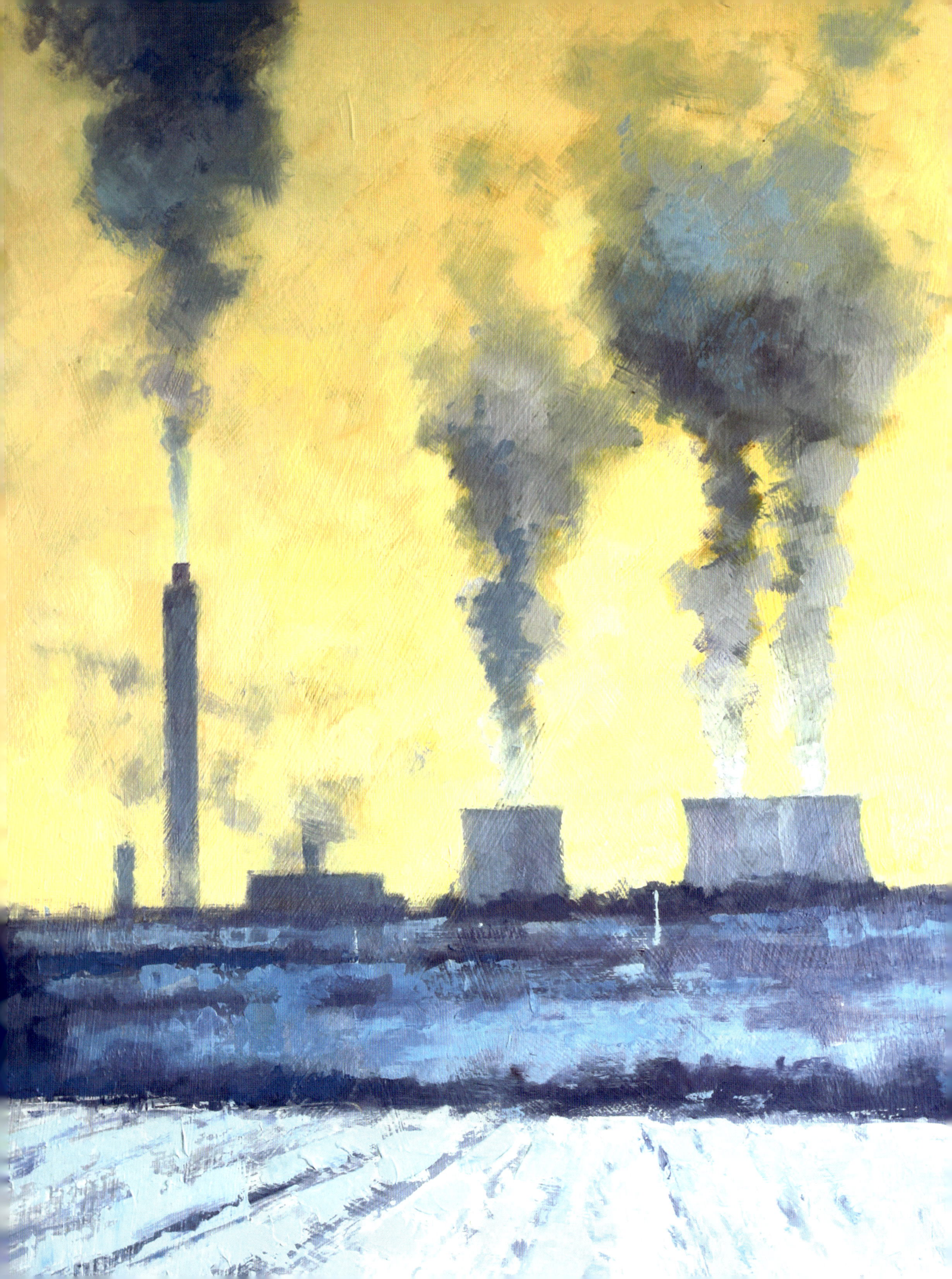

Introduction

When you go out to paint, try to forget what objects you have before you, a tree, a house, a field or whatever. Merely think here is a little square of blue, here an oblong of pink, here a streak of yellow, and paint it just as it looks to you, the exact colour and shape, until it gives you your own naïve impression of the scene before you.

CLAUDE MONET

All painting is an illusion. When we produce a painting, we are attempting to recreate the sensation experienced when viewing something in three dimensions, into a two-dimensional representation. The physical process of applying paint to a support is something that will always be totally unlike creating an image by any other mechanical or digital means. It is deep in our DNA to want to make symbols of those things that we see around us by using an ancient physical process. Ever since *Homo sapiens* began making representational marks on cave walls, we have been striving to do the same in ever more sophisticated ways. It is a means of self-expression, together with the need to communicate with others that which we see around us.

For painters, the click of a button and the manipulation of the photographic image will never be enough to satisfy the desire to reproduce what he or she experiences when being confronted with the complexities of nature. Why do we bother to paint the landscape, when we can far more easily photograph it? There are many obstacles

Vapour Clouds at the Power Station, Kevin Scully. (12" × 10", oil on board)
The water vapour emitted from the chimneys at this power station takes on some spectacular colours, depending on the atmospheric conditions and the colour of the sky at certain times of the day. To obtain the full impact of this, the chimneys are best viewed from a distance. The white area at the bottom of the painting could be mistaken for snow, but is in fact several acres given over to growing *papaver somniferum*, the opium poppy used in the pharmaceutical trade. The choice of contrasting colours – orange and blue used in this image – add a sense of drama to the unusual subject matter.

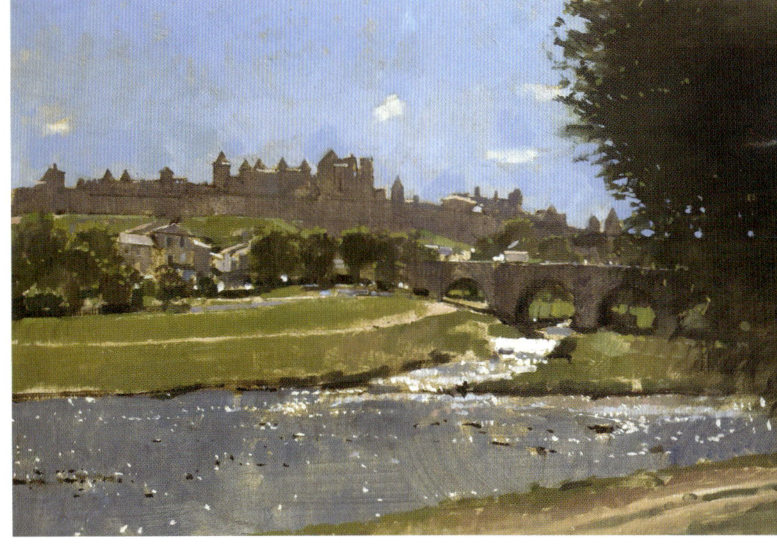

The Old Bridge at Carcassonne, David Sawyer. (16" × 24", oil on board)
Contre-jour, or painting against the light, is an excellent way of working, especially if you want to avoid getting bogged down in too much detail. The complex architecture of the medieval city and bridge has been reduced almost to a silhouette. The large, dark tree on the right gives a degree of cohesion to the whole composition and keeps the attention focused in the centre of the picture. The whole painting was completed in less than three hours, and all painted on the spot. With a minimum of brushwork and a limited colour range, the artist has produced a very successful and convincing painting. When in doubt, it always pays to keep it simple!

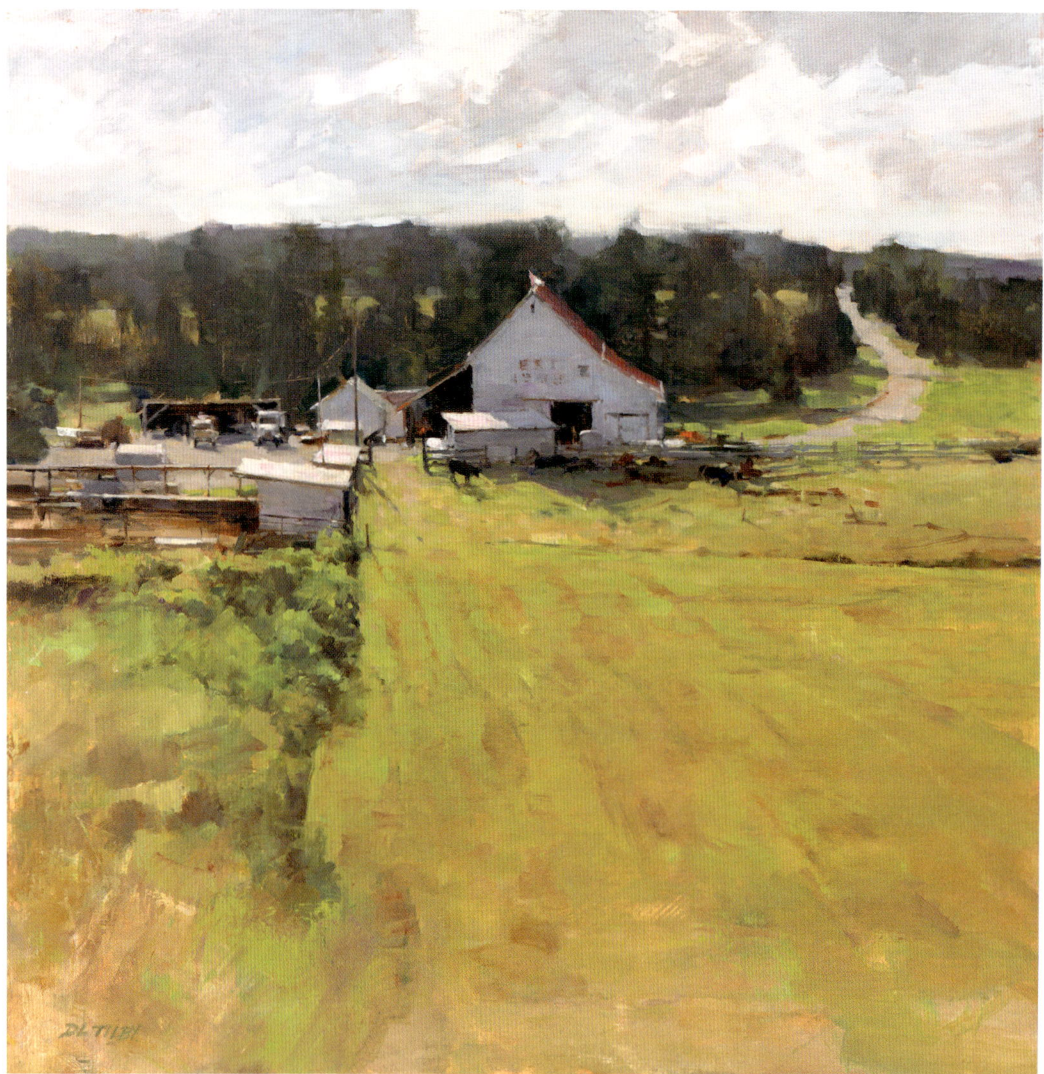

High Oaks Farm, Deborah Tilby. (18" × 18", oil on board)
Subjects such as this are fun to paint – all the paraphernalia that is found in a farmyard has been painted loosely and without any definition, merely suggesting what it all might be rather than actually stating it. The large, fairly plain expanse of yellow/green field on the right of the painting creates a strong design element. The narrow strip of foliage and fence on the left divides the composition vertically, and this has been counterbalanced by the road on the right. The scene is backlit with simple clouds painted with very little detail, but just sufficient to suggest the backlighting. The warm, golden colour with which the board has been prepared has been allowed to peek through in certain areas, which unifies the whole painting.

to overcome, and the methods employed in translating what we see into a painting are countless and sometimes tortuous. But it is this journey that we make, with all of its complications and twists and turns, that gives the most satisfaction. It is something that has to be worked at, to be fretted over and eventually to be honed into the finished article that actually makes a statement about why we chose the subject in the first instance.

There are often underlying patterns and arrangements in the landscape that appeal to us in a subconscious way, and it is by understanding and analysing these systems that we can begin to reproduce an image that appeals to us. However, by simply basing our paintings on long-established rules, and underpinning them with trusted compositional structures, we will only be able to tell half the story. But there are no limitations when it comes to using our imagination and desire to reproduce in paint that which initially inspired us.

But there are limitations to what can be reproduced using just paint. For example, it's impossible to replicate the brilliance of pure light by simply placing pigment on canvas, but by employing certain devious means, the sensation can be simulated by the manipulation and juxtaposition of colour in its various tones.

Not everything in nature is perfect, and just because something is there, it doesn't necessarily mean we have to reproduce it exactly as we see it. A few adjustments might have to be made when translating the natural world into an agreeable composition. The challenges set by nature are immense and complex, and ultimately the way in which we represent them as painters is an individual one. We should strive to look beyond simply copying what we see, and instead we should attempt to make a statement about the sensation that drove us to paint that particular scene in the first place.

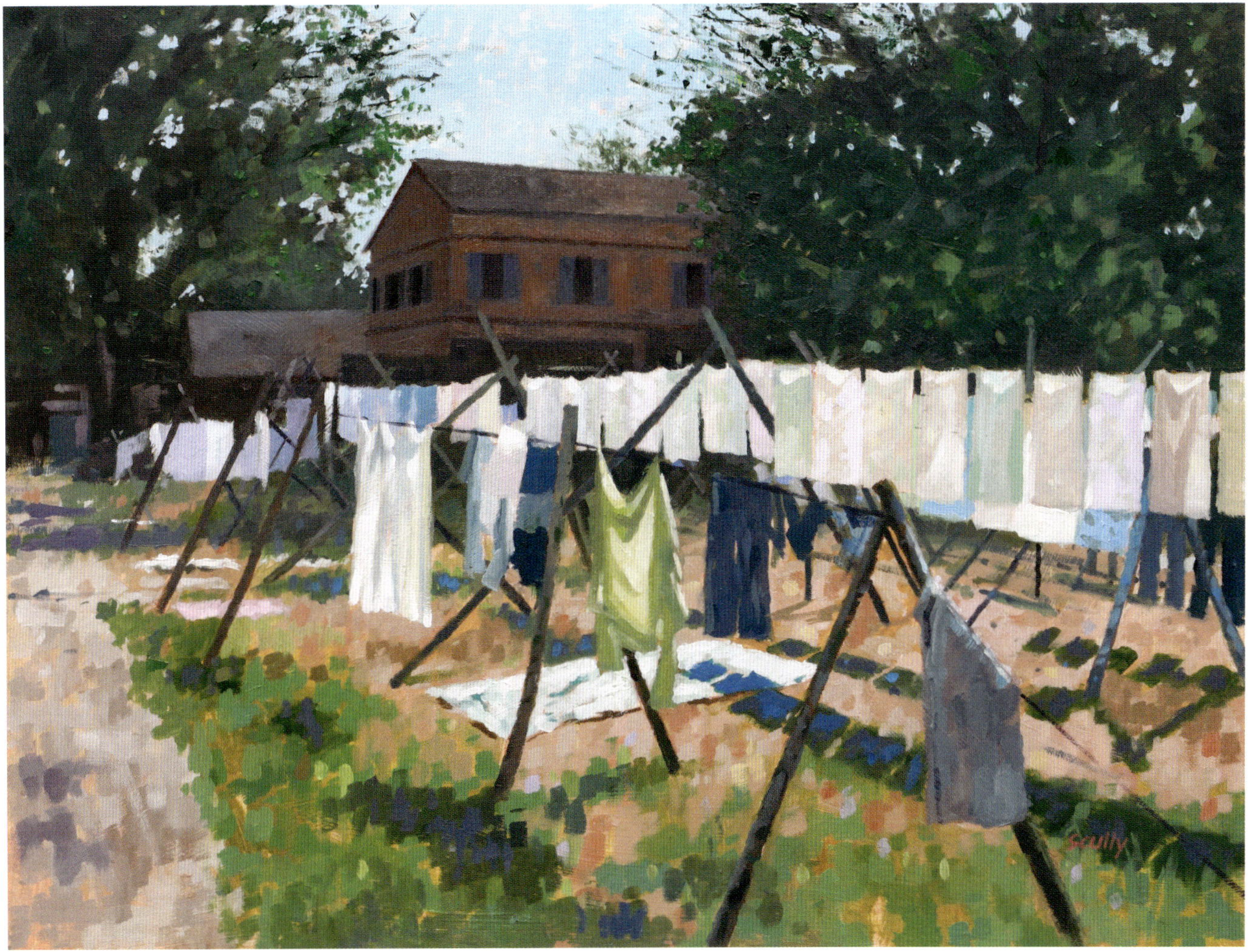

Village Laundry, Kerala, Kevin Scully. (20" × 27", oil on board)
Although by no means an uncommon subject for a painting, the sheer volume of washing on display perhaps excuses its inclusion in this book. This was also just a small section of ground that the laundry occupied in this village in the region of Kerala in southern India. The sheer volume of washing has been emphasized by the viewpoint taken, showing the lines at an angle, and the washing diminishing in size as it moves across the composition. To add interest to the image, small patches of colour seen in the washing have been scattered around the rest of the painting. The main focus has been strengthened by the dark background.

The term 'landscape painting' can also encompass other categories of subject matter, and there is much justification for overlapping one with the other. Although it definitely excludes portrait and figure painting, as well as interior scenes and traditional still-life subjects, there is good enough reason to include certain river and seascapes as well as urban and industrial landscapes. In its broadest terms, it could be described as painting anything that exists outside.

Inspiration and Motivation

There is nothing so exciting for an artist than to be able to pick up their brushes and paints and dive headlong into painting a scene that has fired them into action. Inspiration leads to motivation, and as a general rule we are inspired by the things we like to look at. By consistently placing ourselves in front of those scenes that delight us, inspiration will eventually shine upon us and keep us enthused during our painting sessions. This may be the early morning mist rising from a deep valley, or perhaps the lengthening shadows of winter trees on a sunny, snow-covered hillside at dusk. What inspires one person may not necessarily inspire another. A simple path leading into a wood may not seem to be the most exciting of subject matters, but if you have chosen to paint it for whatever reason first stirred you, it is the way in which you convey your interest in the scene to others that is the challenge.

Seeking inspiration can be a frustrating experience. If you feel the urge to paint, and nothing that presents itself inspires you, it is very easy to become dejected, especially if you end up painting something just for the sake of it. This approach usually leads to a very unsatisfactory outcome. Nobody can be inspired all of the time, but when that moment arrives you must be prepared for action.

Virtually every landscape subject has been tackled by another artist at some time or other, but this doesn't mean that you can't interpret it in your own, individual way. Within this book there are a number of paintings by different artists, each possessing a particular, unique style. Some of them will undoubtedly appeal to you more than others, but they have been chosen because they each have qualities to be admired. Because you may be drawn to the style in which some of them have been painted, this doesn't necessarily mean that you wish to paint in that way. With experience your own handwriting will emerge, usually in spite of adopting some of the techniques of another painter. Although a highly realistic image may have been executed with great skill, and may contain all of those elements that combine to reproduce a great painting with faultless technique, it may not be appropriate for you. Your natural instinct may require the same scene to be painted with looser, less descriptive brushwork. Your approach may be a more expressive response to the landscape that you have chosen to depict.

However, inspiration can be drawn from those paintings that appeal to you; it may be the low horizon line, or the way in which the image has been unconventionally cropped, or perhaps the muted colour palette that the artist has used. It's very difficult to work in isolation, and even the greatest painters will have been influenced by others that have gone before them, and often perhaps by some of their contemporaries. Even those artists whose work has been influenced by others will at some stage put their own thumbprint on the paintings that they produce.

The greatest source of inspiration is of course the landscape itself. Who couldn't help but be motivated by a misty, early morning scene gradually lit by a pale winter sun, or the deep, rich shadows cast by the summer sun at dusk? To experience these wonders of nature does require a degree of effort though, and you may have to rise early, or travel further afield to experience that which isn't on your immediate doorstep. By observing nature in the raw, you will eventually be able to train your eye in detecting what it is that makes a scene visually pleasing. It may be the repetition of certain elements in the landscape, for instance a row of trees, or a line of fence posts disappearing into the distance. Or conversely it may be a single element, such as a solitary tree on a barren hillside, or a lonely farmhouse deep in a hidden valley. Different seasons provide us with some spectacular subject matter; skeletal trees silhouetted against a cloudless sky, the rich, warm colours of autumn, or the blue shadows across a snowy, winter landscape, illuminated by brilliant sunlight.

Mediums Covered

This book is primarily concerned with oil and acrylic painting, and the necessary materials and equipment associated with these mediums. Although the majority of paintings in this book have been executed in oils, the underlying principles of composition, perspective, tonal variation, form and colour can be applied to any other medium, whether it's watercolour, pastels, mixed media or simply drawing. An artist may choose a medium because it suits the way in which he or she likes to work, and in the case of oils this may be because of the appearance of a finished oil painting, with its richness and depth of colour. It may also be the medium's versatility that appeals. A painting can be built up in stages with careful consideration to produce subtle effects, or it can be applied with gusto and bravura to create an expressive work of great dynamism.

One of the major advantages of using oils when painting the landscape is their fairly slow-drying nature. A painting can be adjusted and tweaked as lighting conditions change during the painting process. Colours can also be blended with each other or removed altogether with the wipe of a rag, and corrections can be made at almost any stage during the development of the painting.

There are very few rules that need to be adhered to when using oil or acrylic paint, but there are numerous applications and techniques to be aware of that will enable you to exploit their qualities fully when using them to develop a sound foundation for painting the landscape.

Acrylic paints have the disadvantage of drying rather quickly and tend to have a more 'plastic' appearance, but they will appeal to those artists who favour a more hard-edged, modern look to their work.

The way in which you work will undoubtedly dictate which medium you prefer, and perhaps your preferred medium will influence your own painting process. The qualities of each will be described later in this book.

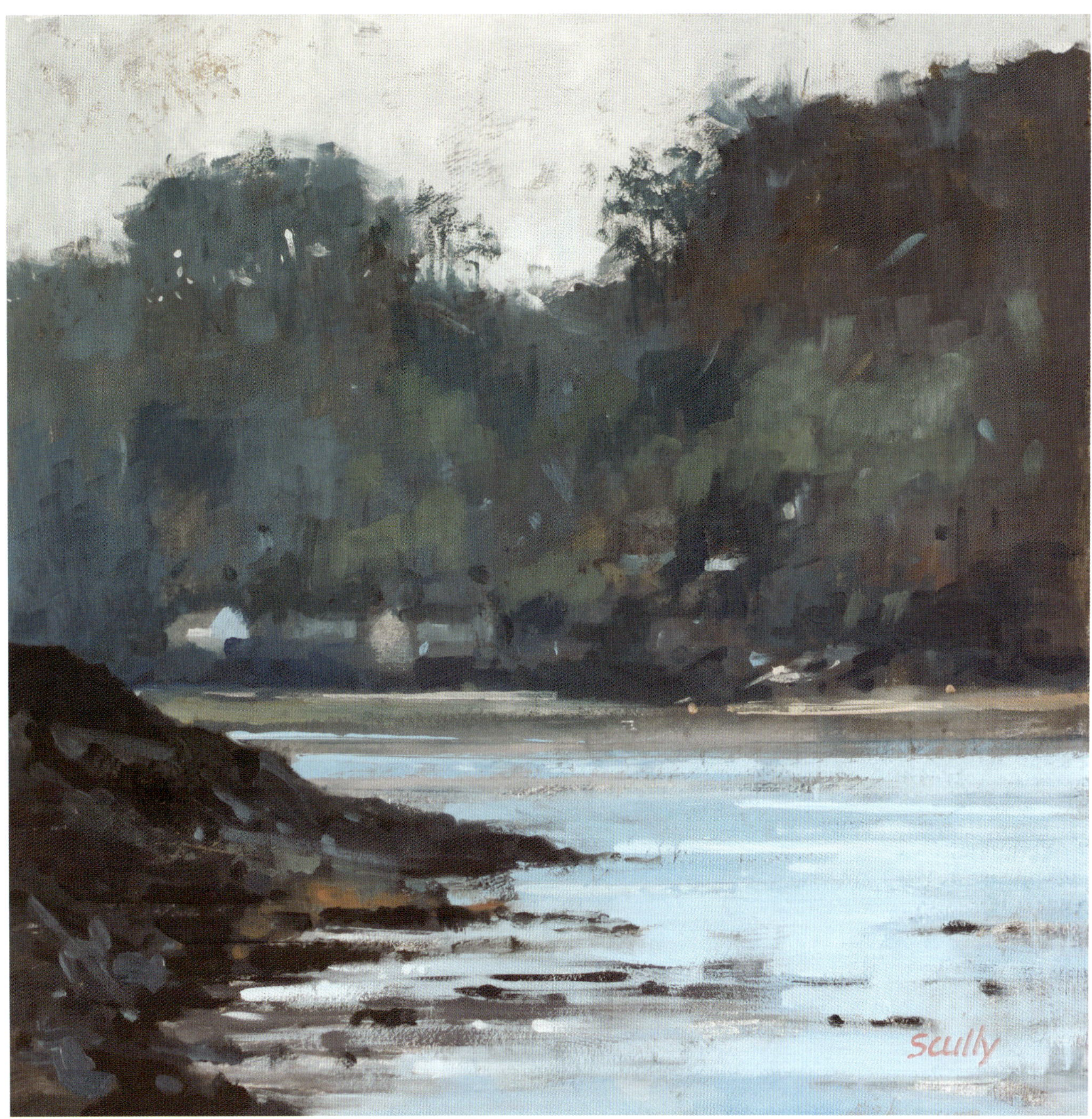

Out of Summer, Kevin Scully. (12" × 12", oil on board)
The water level of this river has been placed low down in the image to emphasize the height of the wooded hill in the background. The four main shapes in the painting, the sky, the woods, the water, and the rocks, are each different in the way that they have been treated. The sky has been rendered in random, alternate brushstrokes, the woods in vertical ones, the water in horizontal ones, and the rocks in predominantly diagonal ones. The whole painting has retained a sense of cohesion with similar colours appearing in each separate element.

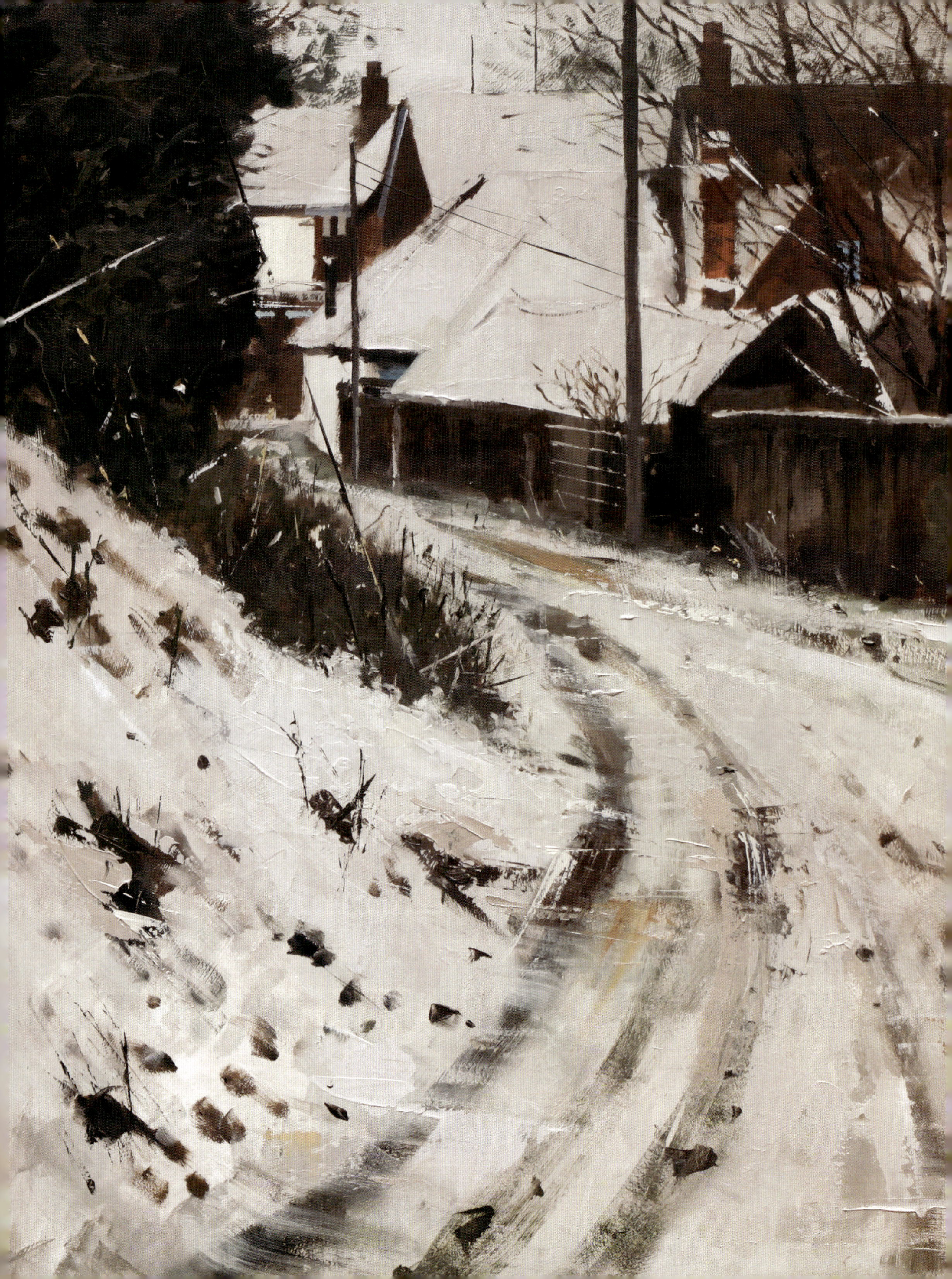

CHAPTER 1

Initial Planning

If you fail to plan, you are planning to fail!

BENJAMIN FRANKLIN

Before you leap head-first into a painting, it's wise to take some time out to consider a few things. What is it that you are hoping to achieve? Will you be content painting a simple landscape that may just contain some fields in the foreground, perhaps some trees in the middle distance, some hills behind and a cloudless sky? Or will you be attracted to a more complex composition that might include some buildings and even people? If you are fairly new to landscape painting, it would probably be rather unwise to embark on a vast, panoramic scene filled with layer upon layer of complicated detail receding into the distance. It would be far better to set your sights a little lower, and begin with a more modest scene.

If you haven't yet developed your own style, I see nothing wrong with gathering together some images of the kind of paintings that you not only like, but those that have been painted along the lines of the kind of paintings you hope to produce. There may be many paintings that you admire, but this doesn't necessarily mean that you want to paint in that style. Having a few paintings around that resonate with you can act like a springboard when it comes to settling on a composition, a format, or a colour scheme. Sometimes it's possible to detect in another artist's work a kindred spirit, and it may be that by experiencing that sensation you were inspired to paint in the first place. It might not be immediately obvious why this is so, but by studying that work and

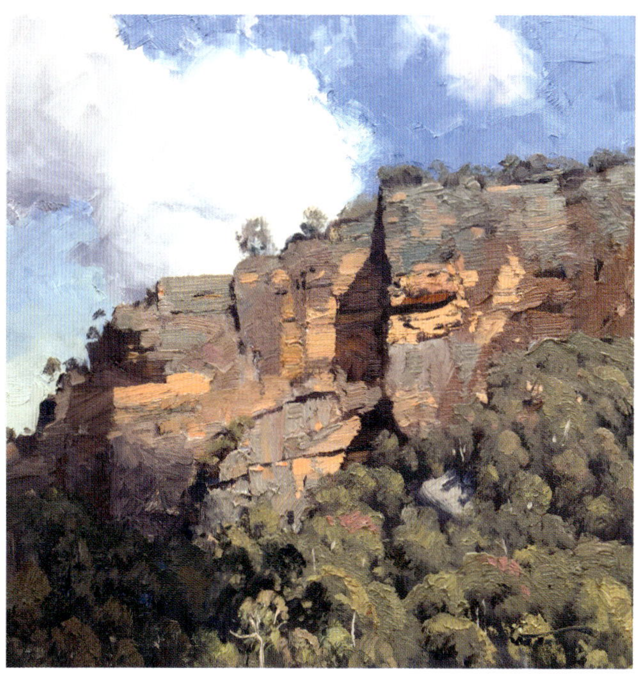

Towers of Stone, Capertee Valley, Warwick Fuller. (18" × 18", oil on canvas, stretched onto board)
The technique employed in executing this powerful painting lends itself perfectly to the subject matter. After an initial wash of thin oil paint, the artist has painted the rock and foliage with gusto, laying the paint on with bold directional strokes that describe the strata of the rock, and the rounded form of the foliage. The billowing clouds and sky have been painted with slightly thinner paint, which prevents this area of the painting from overpowering the main subject matter. The painting was completed on site from the shelter of the artist's camp below the bluffs, in one and a half hours.

White Hart Track (detail), Kevin Scully. (22" × 24", oil on board)

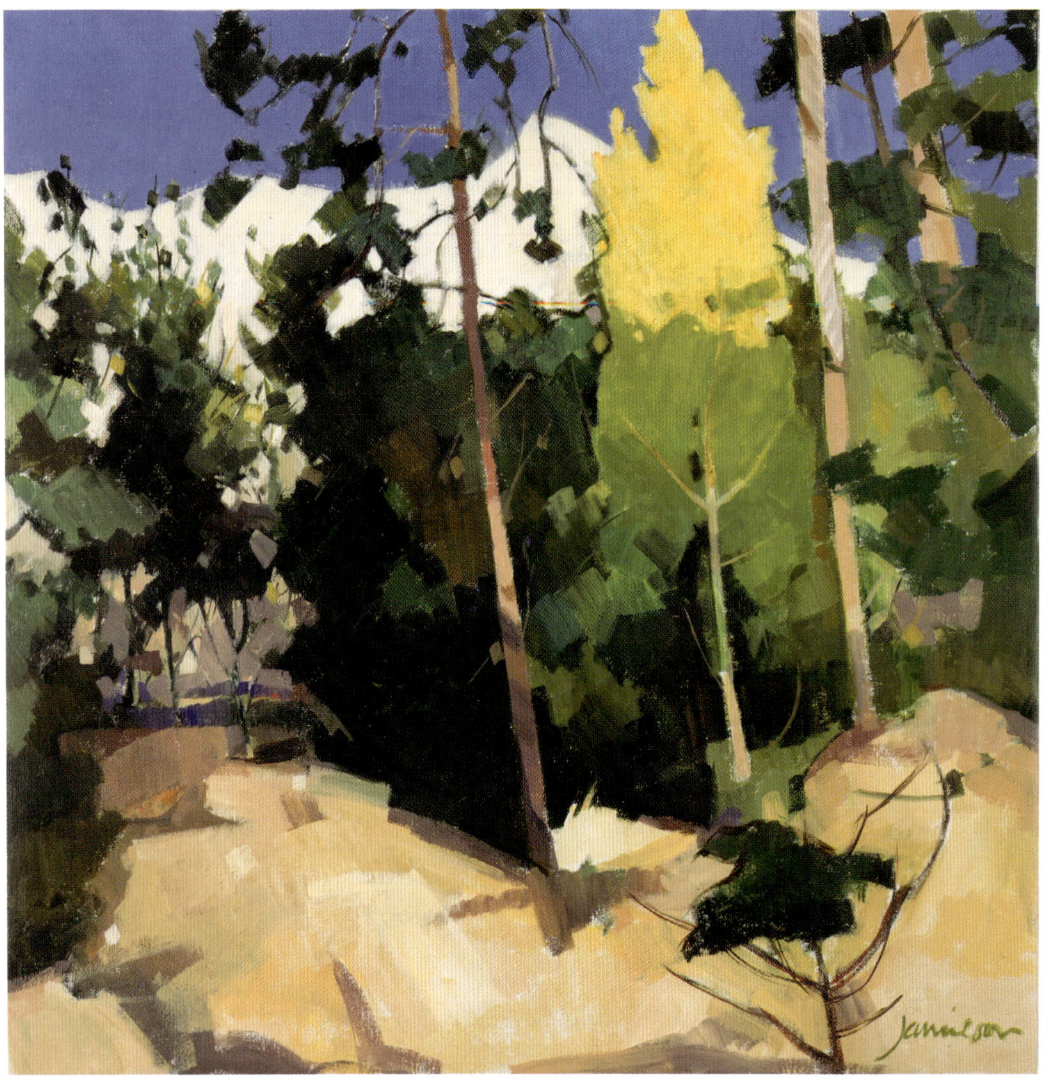

Gorge at Cundiyo, New Mexico, Charles Jamieson. (25" × 25", oil on linen) This painting contains two separate focal points. On the left, the eye is drawn towards the gap in the undergrowth and into the more subtle shadowed areas. The other focal point is on the right, where the sun has crept over the edge of the gorge and splashed a highlight across the upper part of the tree. The artist uses the weight and depth of colour in the lower area of greenery to lead the eye into both these places. This sensation is reinforced by the strong horizontal shapes of the sky, the sun-bleached rock face in the background, the mass of the foliage, and the bare earth in the foreground. The verticals are as strong as the horizontals, particularly the two tree trunks framing the sun-drenched tree. In this painting, the eye is encouraged to travel around both horizontally and vertically.

trying to read beneath the surface to discover exactly what the artist was trying to say about the subject, and why it evokes in you such exciting responses, may lead to some stimulating discoveries.

Your aim when painting anything should be to make a statement about why you chose to paint it. Hopefully, it should be obvious to the viewer that you have done so, whether this is immediately apparent or perceived more gradually, or even subliminally, is less important. Your painting should be about something, and not just a literal interpretation of what you see in front of you.

You have to accept that not all of your paintings are going to be masterpieces, and instead regard each as a warm-up, and an exercise in learning the skills and techniques that you need to be able to eventually produce successful paintings. With experience you will be able to tell whether or not a scene is going to make a good painting, as certain things that we see in nature might look beautiful to us, but that doesn't mean that when we replicate the scene in two dimensions, it always works as a painting.

An experienced landscape painter might make the task look easy, but the truth is, it is difficult. If it were easy, anyone with the necessary skills could do it, but it is only with practice, patience and sustained persistence that we reach our goals.

Subject Matter

The possibilities for a landscape painter are infinite, and for the inexperienced painter, often just too overwhelming. Unlike other subject matter, the landscape by its nature is immense and complex. It is its own master, and what you see is what you get. It can't be physically rearranged or altered as can the elements in a still life set-up, or a model posing for a portrait painting.

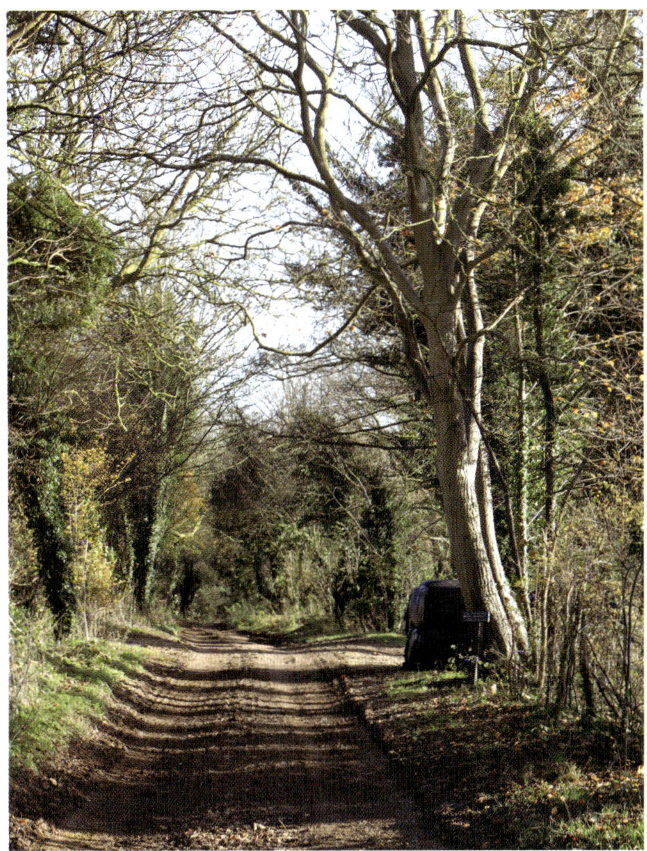

This is the kind of photograph an inexperienced artist would probably choose to paint from, and very soon would find themselves in difficulty. The main problem with tackling this kind of picture is the absence of sufficient distinction between the various layers and shapes of the receding landscape. In its three-dimensional state it would probably have appeared as a good enough subject to paint, but the photograph has reduced much of the scene to a jumble of greenery. The two trees on the right appear to be too close to each other, and even if it were one tree with two trunks, it doesn't look right. The stripy shadows are too dominant, and are at odds with the direction that the path is taking. The hay bales wrapped in black plastic block the view of a path leading off to the right, and the sky stops too abruptly along the treetops in the distance. So to compose a more acceptable arrangement, these things will need to be addressed.

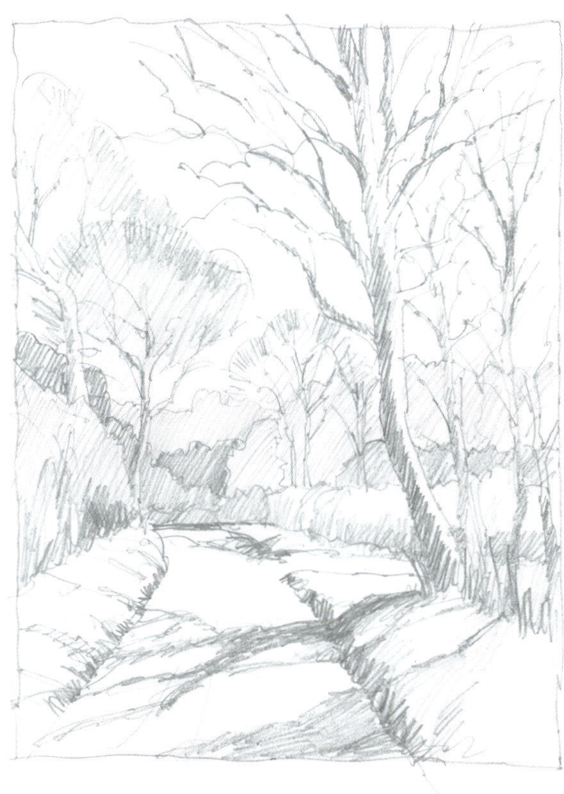

In this compositional sketch, the elements in the landscape have been rearranged and separated by shape and tone, making more sense of the way in which the image can be understood spatially.

We all have favourite subject matter that appeals to us more than others, and this would be a good starting point when contemplating what to paint. You may have some photographs that you took because you thought one day you would like to paint that scene, and perhaps some of them would indeed translate into successful paintings. You may be struck by a particular location that you feel has all the ingredients to make a spectacular painting, and as long as you feel the urge to paint it, the chances are pretty good that it will have possibilities.

There are of course enduring scenes that have been painted a thousand times, but this doesn't mean that they can't be painted a thousand times more. Some typical examples of this are views of lakes and rivers with trees and hills reflected in the water, or the Tuscan farmhouse with its terracotta roof, perched on a hill backed by Cypress trees and flanked by golden fields beneath a clear, cobalt sky. Sunsets and sunrises are always appealing, but should be approached with caution, less you are lulled into producing a rather clichéd pastiche. Another typical image shows a road or track disappearing and reappearing across a landscape punctuated with hedgerows and copses, whilst the majestic grandeur of a mountain range offers great scope for a painting of great dynamism.

It's unwise to tackle subject matter that doesn't really appeal to you simply because it's popular. If you have a passion for something, it will be far more likely to succeed than one that leaves you a little cold and uninspired. Sometimes the simplest of scenes can provide excellent subject matter for a painting, and conversely a highly complicated scene when rendered in paint can be rather confusing to the eye unless it has been composed and approached with care.

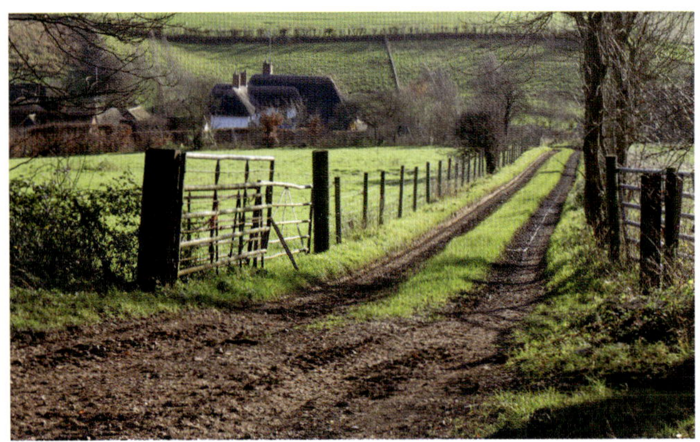

This image contains some interesting elements, but too many of them don't sit comfortably together. The thatched cottage is a fairly dominant feature, but the track veers off in a different direction, leading the eye out of the picture instead of into it. There are too many lines going in different directions, and the whole image would need some serious editing to establish an acceptable arrangement. It's also quite difficult to produce a well-balanced landscape composition without showing any sky.

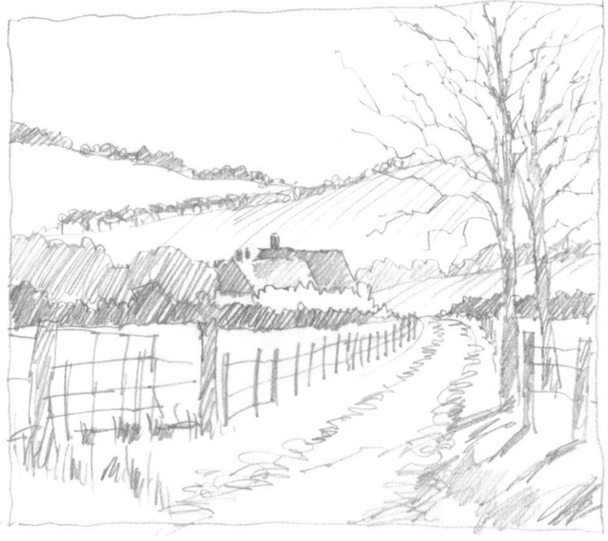

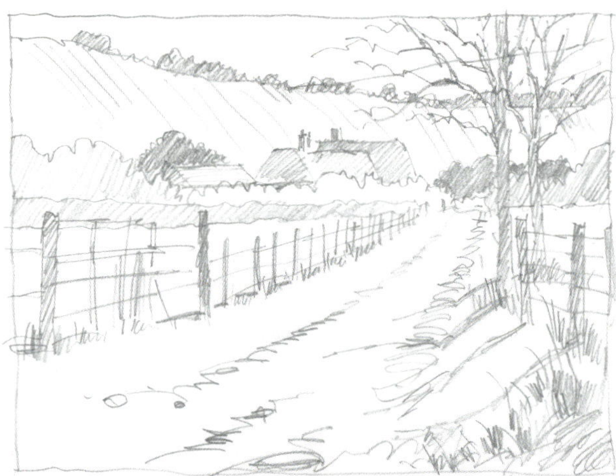

These two sketches show possible alternative formats, where the positions of the different elements have been relocated.

Preparing a Strategy

There is much to consider before embarking on a landscape painting, and this is perhaps one of the most important aspects of the painting process. To some, this first stage is considered as an irritation, but it can't be emphasized enough how essential it is, especially if you are inexperienced. A careless approach at this stage could lead to disappointment or even worse, disaster later on.

Although these initial decisions are important, they can be altered and adjusted during the early stages of your planning strategy, but rather more difficult to change once you have started to paint. A technically and beautifully painted picture may be irredeemable if any one of a number of mistakes has been made at an early stage.

Having chosen your subject matter, there are now certain decisions that have to be made. If you are working from a photograph, it's likely that when considering compositional issues, you will need to crop the image somewhere. Having taken a photograph of a scene that appealed to you and then printed it out, you may now begin to wonder if the automatic format that the camera uses suits the subject. It is always worth considering a different format, and this could be portrait, elongated landscape, or even a square. The size of canvas or board that you choose to work on is probably of less importance, and more a matter of personal preference. A dramatic painting of doom-laden clouds casting shadows across a vast landscape can look just as dramatic on a small canvas as one painted on a much larger scale.

The next thing to consider is composition. When you took the photograph you may have consciously or subconsciously composed your image, but you should reflect now on whether or not to crop it. The temptation when taking a photograph is to include everything that you see, and this can result in an image with no strong focal point. You may now decide that the horizon line needs to be raised or lowered to shift the emphasis slightly between sky and land. If a group of trees on one side of your image is too dominant, it may need to be cropped slightly, or even entirely. What we should be doing when we are painting is to instil into our pictures that which the camera is unable to.

Another way of approaching your compositional decision is to produce a number of quick sketches, which rather than being simply linear, should be tonal. These will very quickly demonstrate what is going to work and what is not.

An arrangement that falls short as a thumbnail sketch, will also fail as a completed painting. It's important to evaluate the tonal variations in your image. If there is little

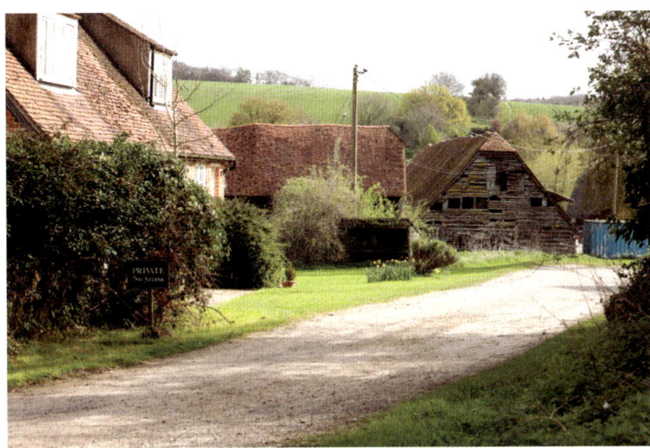

There is a section of this photograph that has the potential for the basis of a good painting, but there are a few grey areas that need to be addressed.

distinction between the dark, middle and light tones, your painting may lack the impact that you were hoping for, and these tonal variations need to be adjusted. Even in a subdued painting, it will be necessary to have some variance between the lights and darks, and to have them distributed throughout the painting in a balanced and cohesive manner.

Having established your tonal arrangement, you must now think about colour. More often than not, the colours of a photograph can be rather disappointing, and don't in any way reflect what you saw when you took it. The bright colours that you initially perceived have become diluted, and the deep, rich shadows appear as colourless dark holes. You may have to organize your own colour scheme, and this may be based on a system of complementary colours, a warm/cool relationship, or a monochromatic range of tones.

The Limitations of Two Dimensions

Because of its complexity, what we observe in nature has to be amended so that it sits comfortably within the constraints of two dimensions. We have to devise devious means by which to suggest spatial divisions. This visual code can create the illusion of three dimensions, and can be suggested by differences in tonal value, aerial and linear perspective, and also colour differences. We will never be able to replicate the brilliant light emanating from the sun, and there has never been a painting so startlingly bright that we need sunglasses to look at it, but we can suggest its intensity by tweaking other colours in our painting.

We can hint at spatial differences by overlapping different elements in our landscape paintings, so that one contour appears to be behind another. This device can be further

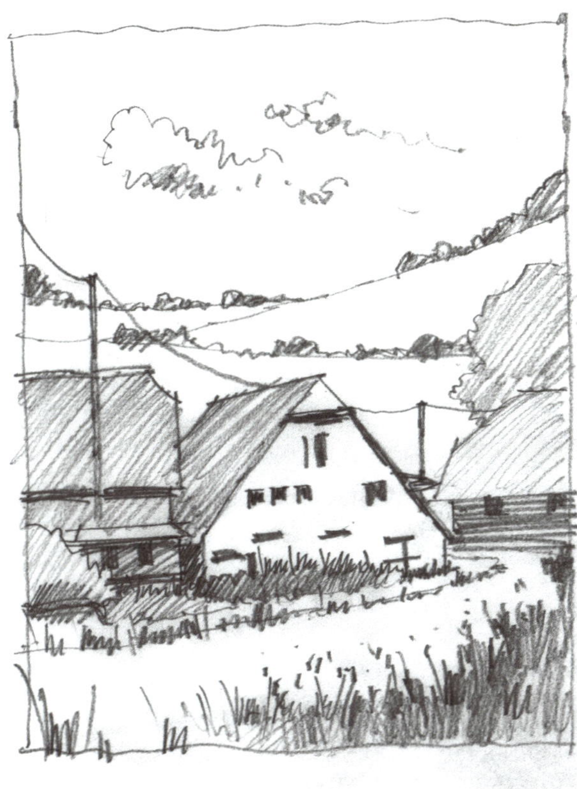

As an alternative format, the image has been changed from landscape to portrait, and the building to the left-hand side has been removed.

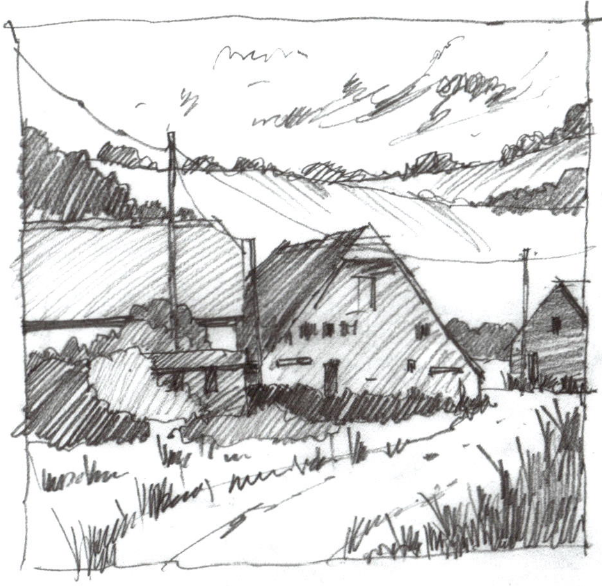

The square format would also work well, and in both sketches the building to the right has been altered, and the contours of the fields in the background changed to create a better balance of movement.

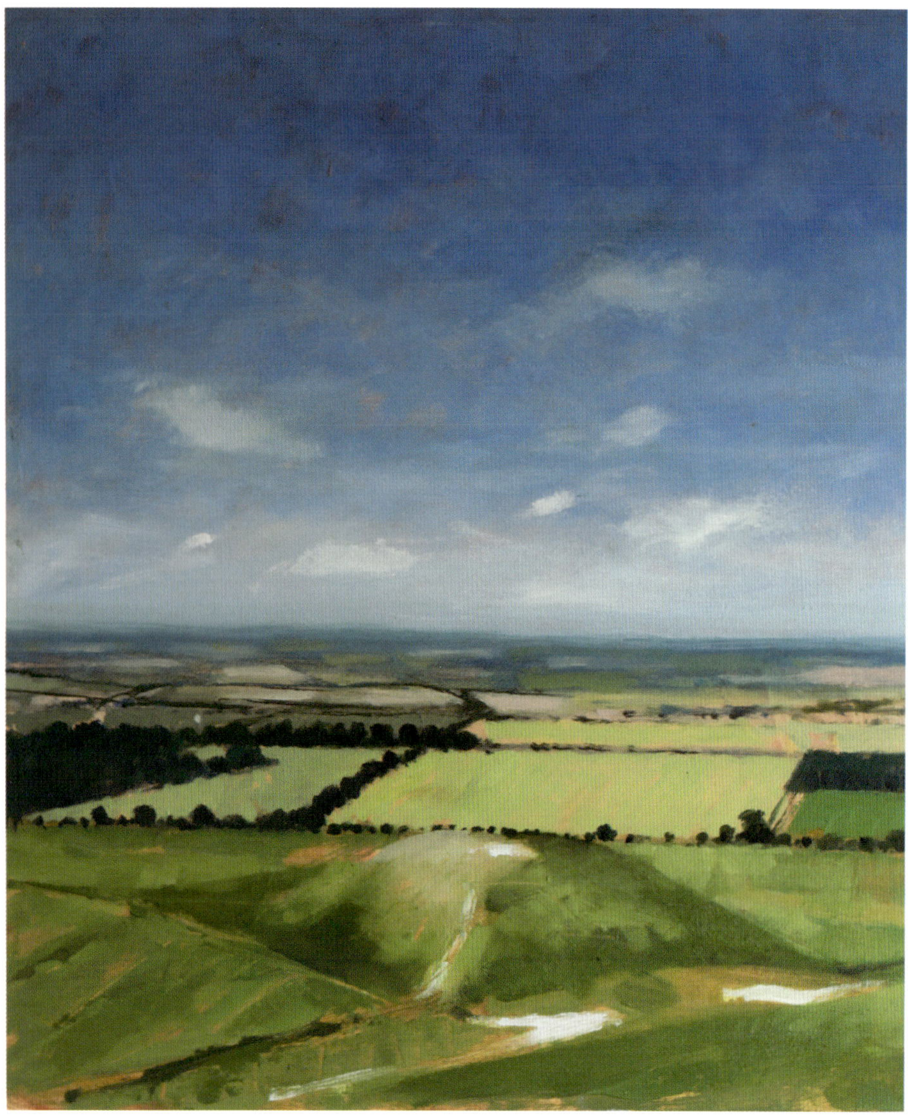

Dragon Hill, Oxfordshire, Kevin Scully. (16" × 14", oil on board)
Painted on a Raw Sienna ground to suggest a warm and clear summer day, the image uses both linear and aerial perspective to create a sense of distance across this open, flat landscape. The hedgerow boundaries diminish in size and tone as they recede into the distance, and the sky is gradually lightened as it meets the horizon. The fields in the far distance take on the blue haze of the atmosphere where the clouds can be seen to diminish in colour, intensity and size.

emphasized by a variation in tone or colour. Even in landscape painting, linear perspective plays an important role, where objects of a similar size appear to be smaller the further away they are. This is a useful device when painting clouds, where those closer to the horizon are depicted as smaller than clouds of a similar size, higher in the sky. The difference in the size of these clouds can also be exaggerated to emphasize the illusion of distance even more convincingly.

Aerial or atmospheric perspective can be used to suggest distance by rendering those elements seen in the distance in a more subdued colour range, and with a lack of strong contrast, texture and detail. A common trap that the novice painter falls into is trying to include everything that they see. When we focus on single elements in a scene, it is certainly possible to detect individual leaves on a tree, or blades of grass in a field, but by painting them as such, it usually detracts the viewer's eye from that part of the picture that we want them to look at. It would be far better to paint the tree and the grass as a series of shapes of varying tones and colour, which is what we see in our peripheral vision when we are focusing on a bridge across a stream, or a dilapidated barn in the middle distance.

Minimizing Nature's Complexities

We are all confronted with too much information when we place ourselves in front of nature, so we have to extract the essential ingredients from her complexities, and through a process of reduction and simplification, we must organize her various elements into a series of coherent forms. The most important part of producing a landscape painting is first to establish the general masses. It can be all too tempting to start indulging in unnecessary detail at this early stage of the painting before the foundations of the subject

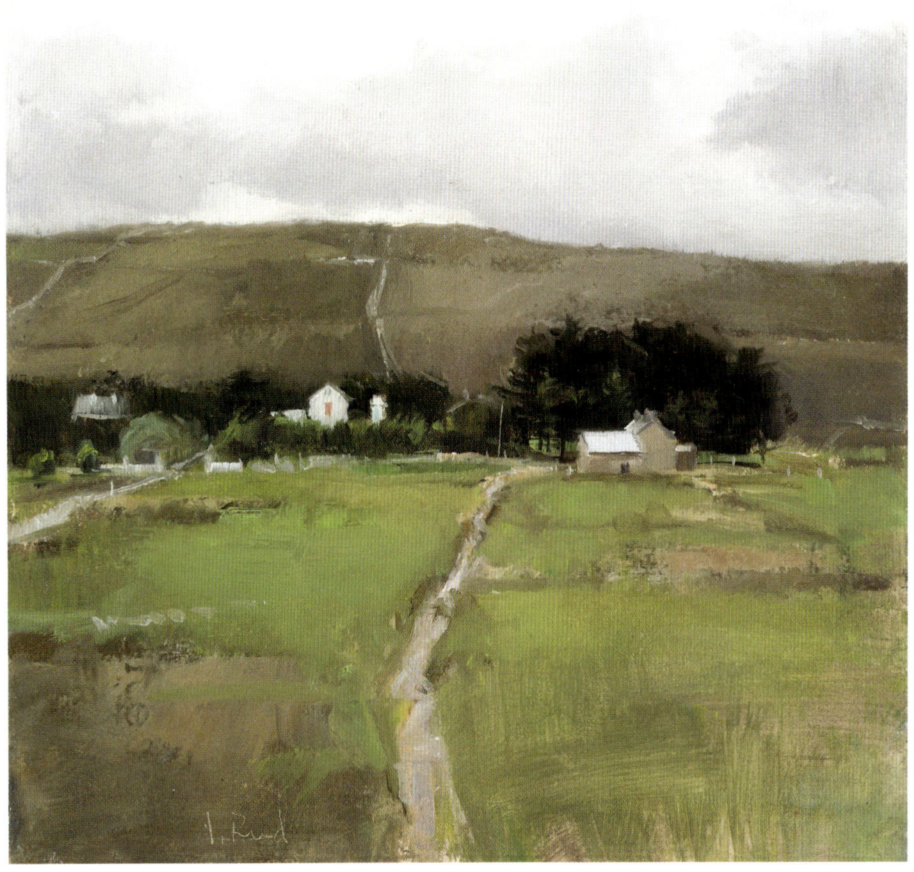

Belderg Farm, Jeffrey Reed. (10" × 10", oil on canvas)
Using a very limited palette of muted colours, the artist has created a painting that describes perfectly the space that the farmhouse occupies in this open landscape. There is a strong but not obvious design element holding this composition together, where the picture is divided roughly into three sections, with the centre section being anchored by the line of foliage and farm buildings, focusing the viewer's attention on the middle distance. Rough tracks lead the eye both to the farm, and also away from it. Overlapping the various sections has created a sense of distance, and the painting has been injected with atmosphere by adding the pale grey clouds that appear to drift across the sky in a gentle breeze. In this surprisingly small painting, just 10" × 10", so much has been said with so few brushstrokes. Painted on location in County Mayo, Ireland.

matter have been laid. The first thing that the viewer of a painting sees is not the detail, but the overall shapes. There may well be more descriptive detail within these areas, but this is subordinate to the overall shapes. Remember also that paintings are supposed to be viewed from a certain distance, as on the wall of a gallery, so it's important to regularly stand back from your work to establish whether or not the overall shapes are strong enough, and not overwhelmed by extraneous detail.

In this simplification process, the fewer shapes that you can break the scene down into, the better. These shapes can then be fine-tuned and embellished at a later stage if necessary, to a degree that describes the landscape as it is, or to leave a certain amount to the viewer's imagination. A sound approach to organizing these shapes is to imagine them as a series of flat cardboard cut-outs, lined up one behind the other. They can be distinguished from one another by changes in tonal value and colour. Viewing the landscape through the zoom lens of a camera or binoculars also has a similar effect of separating its various components into separate, flat planes.

As well as leaving certain things out, remember too that we should also be adding things to our paintings. We shouldn't be simply copying what we see, but instead we should be striving for originality, and our own original response to nature.

SIMPLIFYING SHAPES

To determine basic shapes when looking at a scene, it helps to screw your eyes up so that the image becomes less distinct. What happens is that many of the mid tones are eliminated, leaving just four or five discernable variations. This variation in tones and simplification of shapes become even more apparent if you take a photograph of the scene, and print out the image in black and white.

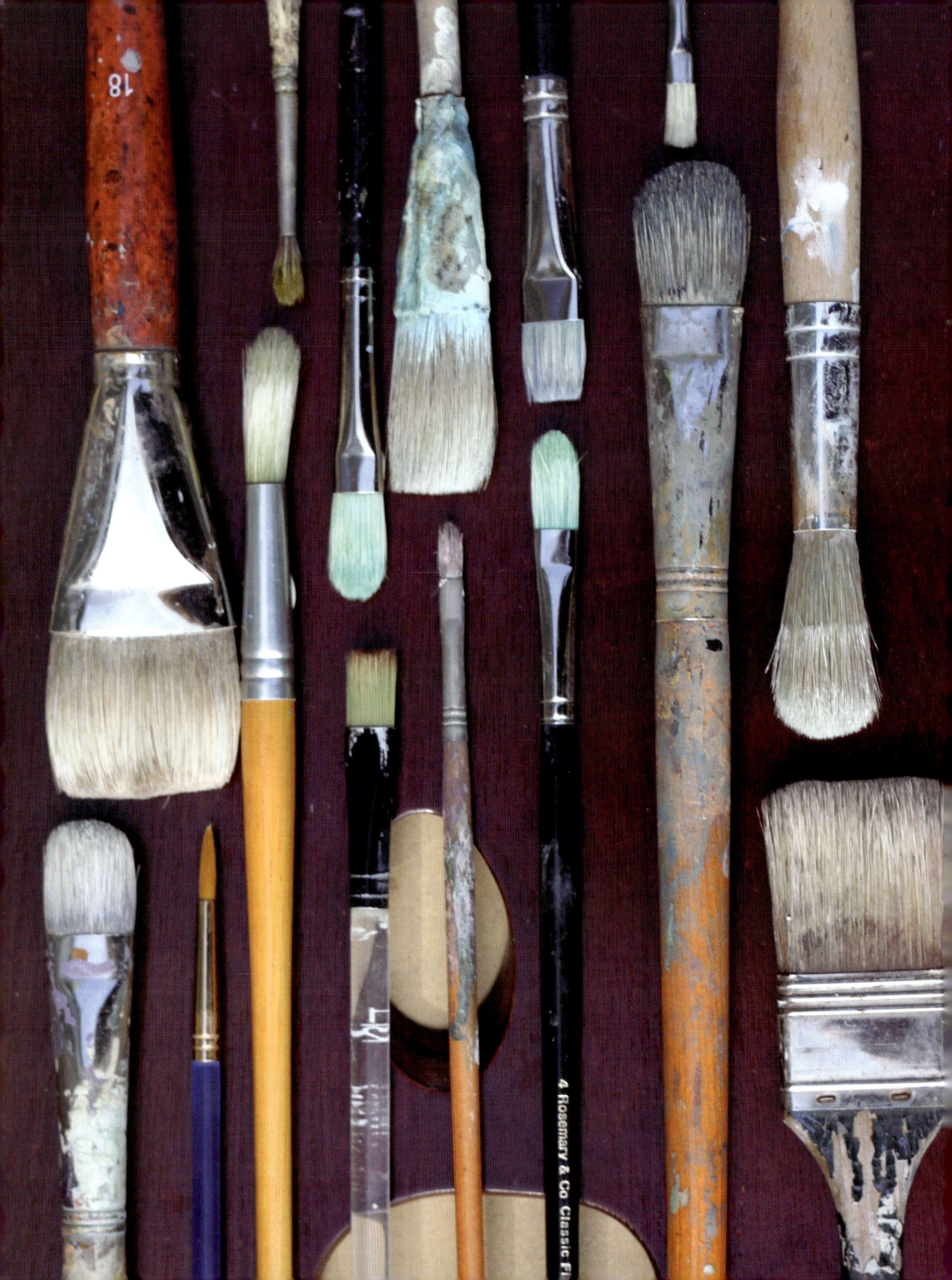
18
4 Rosemary & Co Classic Fi

CHAPTER 2

Materials

Do not just pick up the brushes you used and cleaned yesterday because they are there. Put those back, look at all of them, and then choose your weapon, like a type of gun or a certain type of sword. You are going into battle and you want the best weapon for the job.

RICHARD SCHMIDT

To begin with, no one painting medium is superior to another. It's simply a matter of personal preference. There are brilliant artists who will extol the virtues of watercolour, and for them no other medium possesses its intrinsic qualities. But this is purely because for them it suits their way of working and performs in a manner that produces the end result that they are striving for. And so it is with oil and acrylic, which are the paints that we concern ourselves with here. Each has its virtues, and each its potential shortcomings.

OILS

Perhaps the major advantage that oils have over all other mediums is the fact that the colour doesn't alter during the drying process. They will lend themselves to a variety of applications from transparent glazes to heavy impasto. Colour can be built up in stages, or applied wet-in-wet. Most artists who use oil paint adore its buttery consistency and its ability to be blended and workable over an extended period, because of its relatively slow drying time. As with

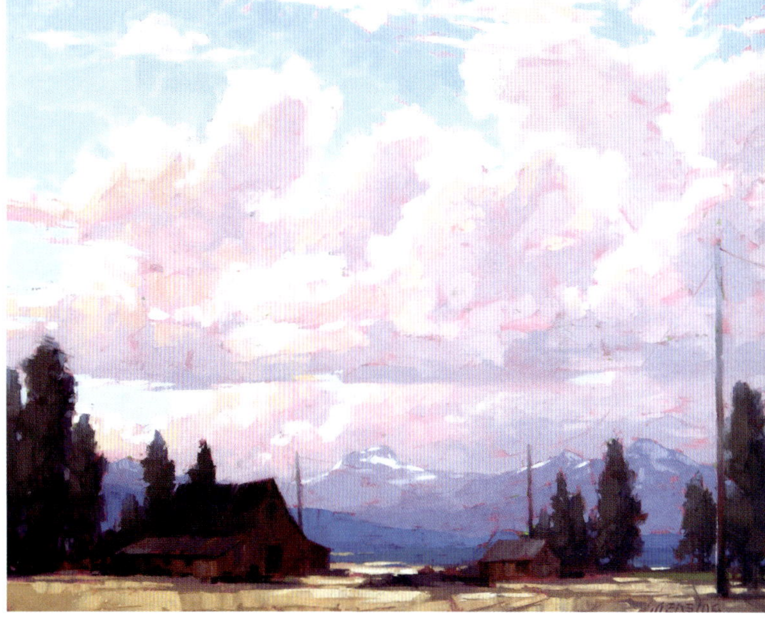

Faith, Hope and…, David Mensing. (30" × 40", oil on canvas)
This dramatic thundercloud is swelling over 'The Three Sisters', near Bend, Oregon. The title of the painting is derived from the nicknames of the three mountains: 'Faith', 'Hope' and 'Love'. The buildings in the foreground have been painted in exaggerated, dark tonal values, to increase the illusion of depth, and to emphasize the intensity of the distant clouds. The powerlines strung from the vertical posts create interesting diagonals, which lead the viewer's eye into the painting.

The Good, the Bad, and the Ugly
Whilst it is good practice to keep your brushes in good condition, at some stage it's inevitable that they will deteriorate, but even when they have become worn, they will have their uses. It may be that they are perfect for scumbling or any other technique that requires rough treatment, or simply for mixing paint.

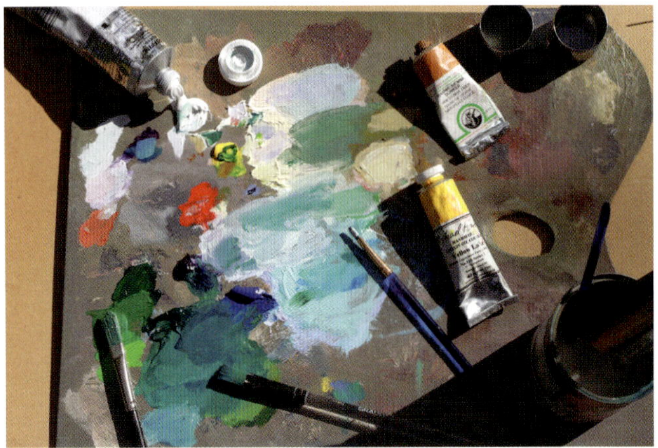

When things get a little out of hand on the palette, and you run out of space to mix up new colours, it's time to clean everything off with a palette knife and rag, and start again afresh. Although incorporating some of these neutral mixes into your painting can create a harmonious effect, sometimes these colours can eventually turn into mud.

all paints, the price you pay for them usually indicates the quality that you can expect. 'Artist's quality' paints from reputable manufacturers are what they say, and are superior to cheaper products sometimes described as 'student's quality'.

The oil in which the pigment is suspended, commonly linseed, walnut or poppy seed oil, is harmless, but the fumes given off from the traditional turpentine that is used to thin the paint and the white spirit, or turpentine substitute used for washing brushes, can cause problems for some people, because of its toxicity. There are those who simply don't like the smell of oil paint and its traditional solvents, but there are others who just adore it. There are low-odour, non-toxic, alternative solvents available, but these can be expensive, especially when using the relatively large quantities required for washing out your brushes. If using traditional solvents, be sure to work in a well-ventilated area and dispose of the waste material with consideration for the environment.

If you are affected by any of the solvents and are worried about their effect on you, you can wear latex gloves when using them.

Some of the pigments used in the manufacture of traditional oil paint are toxic, notably lead and cadmium, but the levels are now relatively low, so unless you intend consuming your oil paint, or inhaling pure cadmium pigment, you are safe. There are now substitute paints available containing no toxic pigments, and the manufacturers are constantly improving their products with the health and safety of artists in mind.

Even if you are new to oil painting, be sure to buy the best paints you can afford, and these will be described as 'artist's quality'. Other cheaper, lower-grade paints will almost certainly give you disappointing results, and to buy these will be false economy. They will contain artificial fillers rather than pure pigment. Amongst the better, professional grade brands are Old Holland, Winsor & Newton, Michael Harding, M. Graham, Vasari, Schmincke Mussini, Williamsburg, Sennelier and Gamblin. As with all paints, the different brands will vary slightly in the way in which they behave. Some of them will have a slightly stiffer consistency, whilst others will contain more oil, and therefore be more creamy in texture.

Although each artist has their own favourite colours, here is a list that will cover the basic needs of the landscape painter: Titanium White, Cadmium Yellow Pale, Cadmium Red Medium, Phthalo Green, Cobalt Blue, Cerulean Blue, French Ultramarine, Raw Sienna or Yellow Ochre, Burnt Sienna, Raw Umber, Burnt Umber, Dioxazine Purple and Permanent Rose.

Alkyd Oils

Alkyds are similar to traditional oil paints, but are faster drying. They are diluted with similar solvents and can also be mixed with standard oils. A painting completed with alkyds, providing the paint hasn't been applied too thickly, will normally be dry to the touch the following morning. If the paint has been applied fairly thinly, it will be dry in a matter of hours. This makes them ideal for painting outside, as you will be able to transport your work back home after a painting session without getting smothered in paint. They are especially popular with those who struggle when painting wet-in-wet with traditional oils, because their fast-drying qualities allow you to paint over areas that are partially dry, and therefore to finish a painting in one session without having to wait too long for the paint that has already been applied to dry.

It could be argued that because they dry faster than standard oils, they may become slightly sticky during the drying process. This can be alleviated with the addition of a painting medium such as Liquin.

Many artists, and particularly those who like to paint *en plein air*, use traditional oil colours, but include an alkyd white in their palette, such as Titanium White, to mix with their other colours when necessary, which helps to speed up the drying process. An alternative strategy is to use a small amount of alkyd medium as an additive when mixing colours.

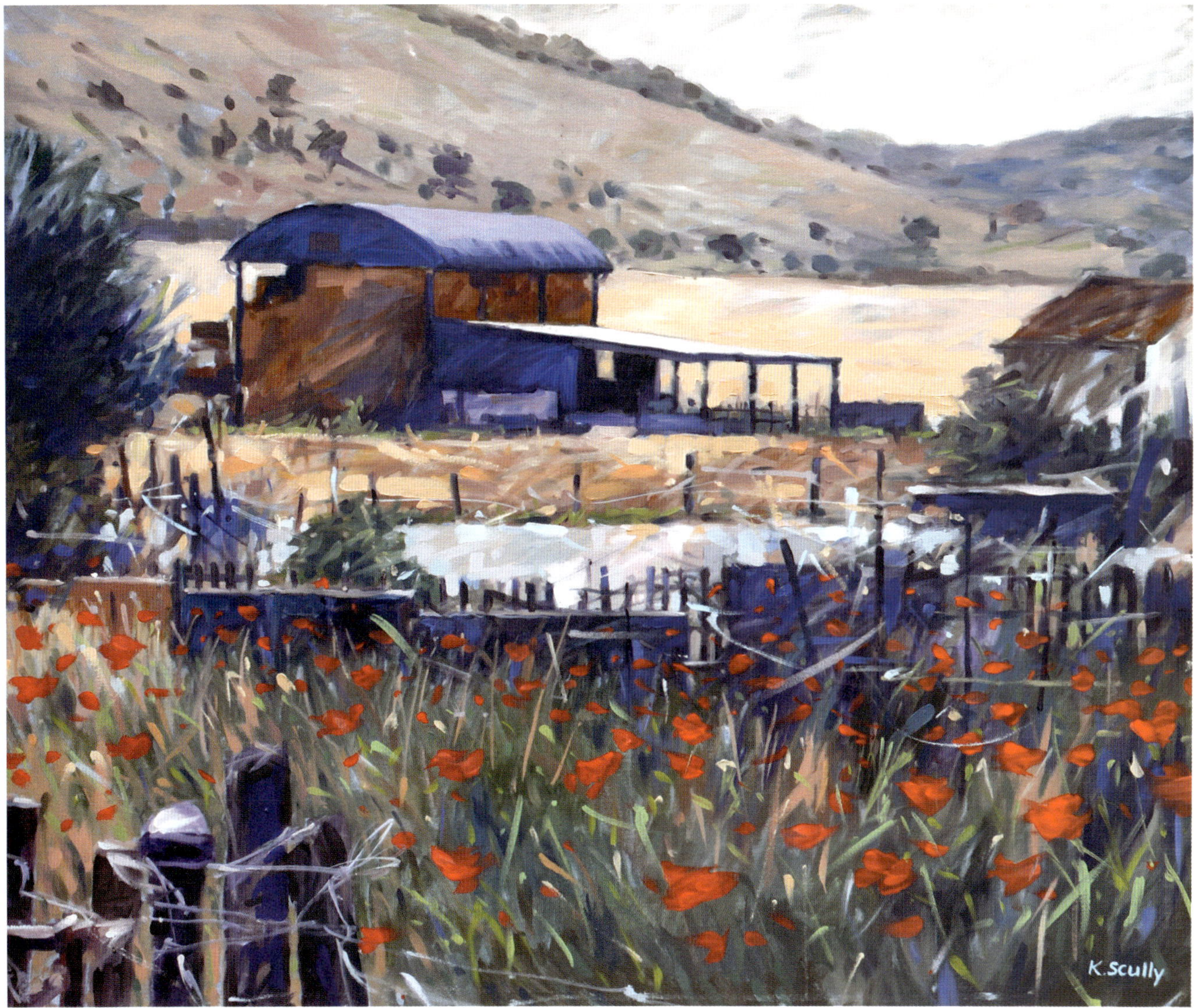

Warren Farm, Kevin Scully. (30" × 36", oil on canvas)
A painting displaying two separate areas of contrasting colours. The top half is based on an orange and blue complementary pair, whilst the bottom half pairs green with red. However, all of these colours except the red appear in other parts of the picture, which helps to tie everything together. The poppies didn't exist, but were added later to inject some extra colour into the composition. The colour scheme doesn't necessarily follow any laid-down laws of colour theory, but seems to work nonetheless.

Water-soluble Oils

The main advantage of these paints is that although they resemble traditional oils in many respects, they dispense with the need for any toxic solvents. The paints can be diluted with water, and even mixed with acrylics. However, their drying time, although quicker than traditional oils, is slower than that of alkyds. As yet, they don't seem to have established as much of a following as the other alternatives, and there are conflicting views from many artists regarding their handling qualities, consistency of texture and drying times. When first introduced, they were regarded by some as a product aimed primarily at the amateur artist rather than the professional, and this notion seems to have rather stuck as a general opinion. More recently though, as these paints have developed in recent years, improvements have been made and there are now a limited number of colours available in ranges by some of the established paint producers including Winsor & Newton, Jackson's, Talens, and a larger range of colours by Holbein.

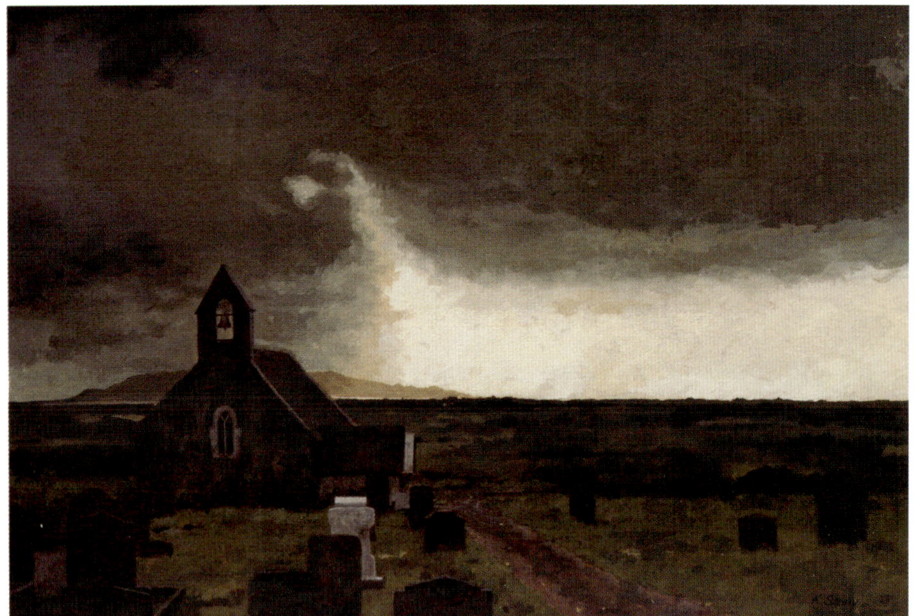

Storm on Anglesey, Wales, Kevin Scully. (20" × 30", acrylic on board)
By recording the church and foreground in a restrained range of tones, the bright light shining on the landmass in the distance becomes the main focus of the painting. As a sub plot to the dramatic scene, the eye is taken along the path to the church and from there up into the sky. The composition combines three separate photographs from different parts of the island, so the location doesn't exist in this form. The result is a painting created from both photographic reference and imagination, most evident in the cloud formation in the sky, where the colours of the surrounding landscape are echoed. The entire painting comprises just four colours; Titanium White, Yellow Ochre, Payne's Grey and Burnt Sienna.

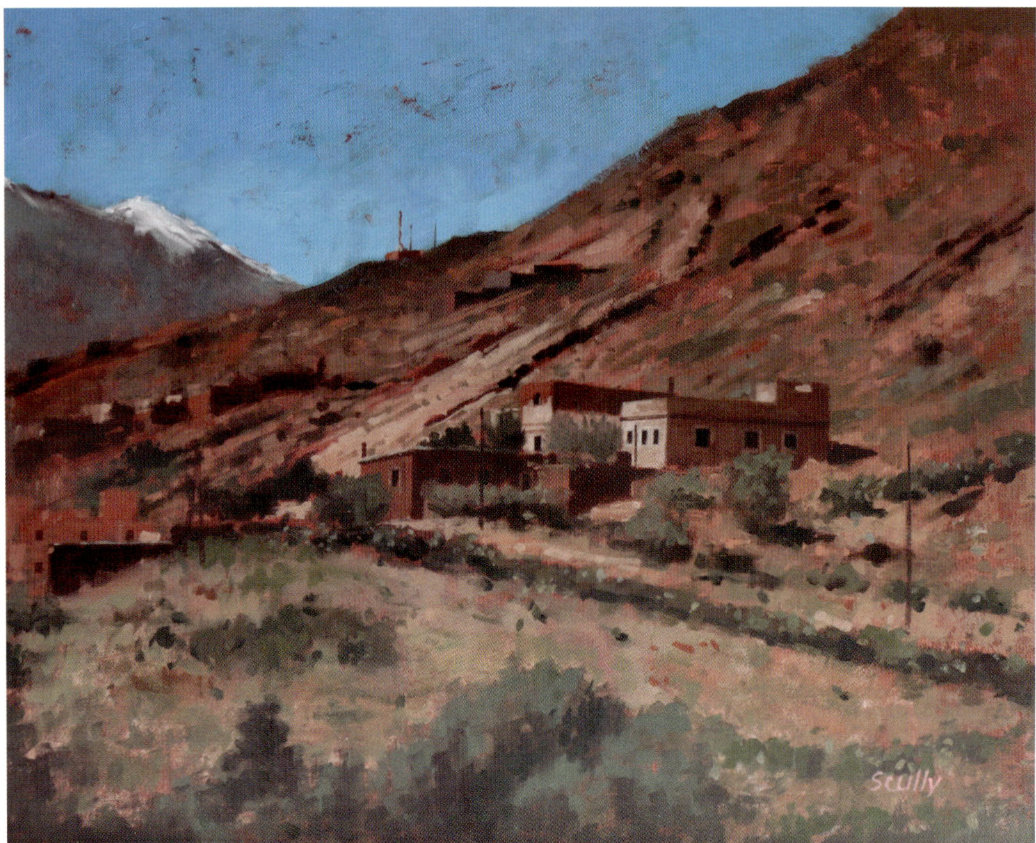

High Atlas Mountains, Kevin Scully. (14" × 18", acrylic on board)
The earth in this part of the world is a rich, red ochre colour and is used extensively in the construction of buildings. As such, the starting point for this painting was to tone the surface with that same colour, so that during the painting process the buildings slowly emerged from their background, and still remained part of it. In the intense blue colour of the sky, which was a fairly accurate match tonally, some of this red earth colour can still be detected. The detail has been restricted predominantly to the middle distance, and the foreground has been rendered in loose and imprecise brushstrokes.

ACRYLICS

Acrylics are water-based, and therefore more popular with artists who have trouble with the solvents associated with oil paints. Being fast drying, one of their characteristics is their immediacy, which will appeal to certain painters who favour a more graphic, hard-edged look to their work. Generally, they dry rapidly to a matt finish, although they may also have a rather plastic appearance, which isn't to everyone's taste. There are acrylics that are full-bodied, and these will suit impasto applications, and there are others that are fluid to the extent that they can be poured.

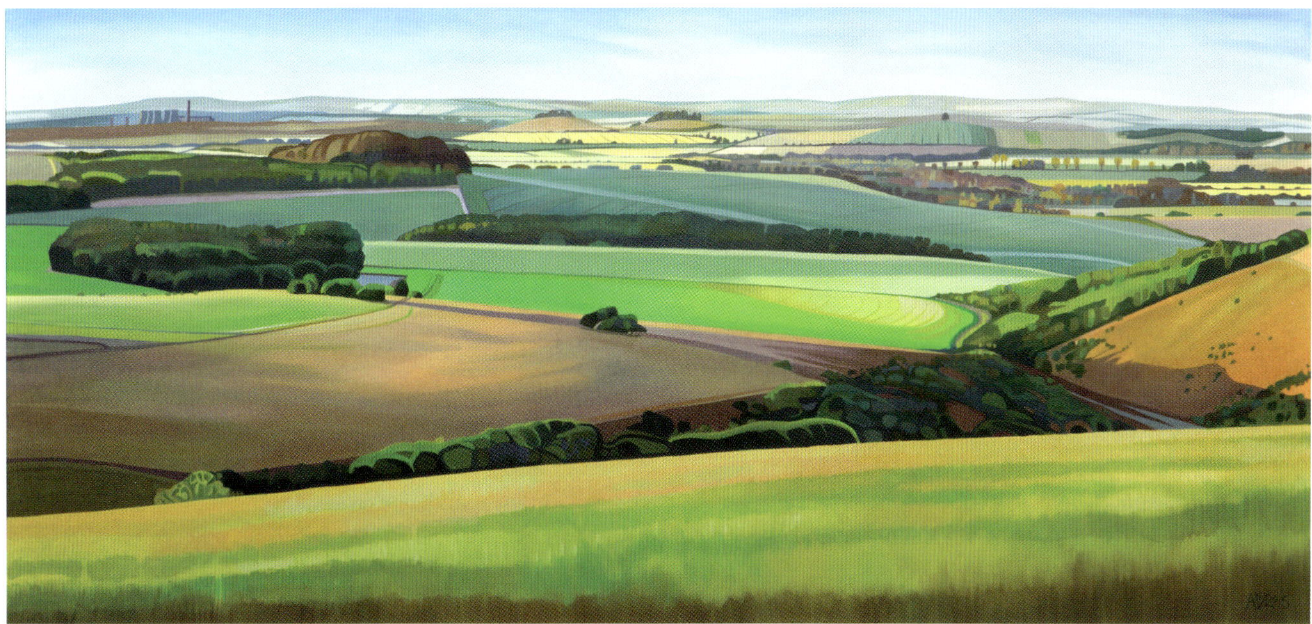

Happy Valley from Lowbury Hill, Anna Dillon. (31" × 67", oil on board)
A large and dynamic commission of the Berkshire Downs, looking out over the South Oxfordshire Plain. A series of diagonals and horizontals bisect this view of the vast, mainly flat landscape stretching across many miles into the distance and low hills beyond. The artist has given us a clue as to her viewpoint, by painting the valley below the immediate foreground in shadow, and the grass-covered spot on which she was standing in bands of colour in diminishing tonal values, suggesting a curved and steeply sloping hill. Groups of trees overlap fields to indicate distance, as do the paler tones of the landscape that retreats into the distance.

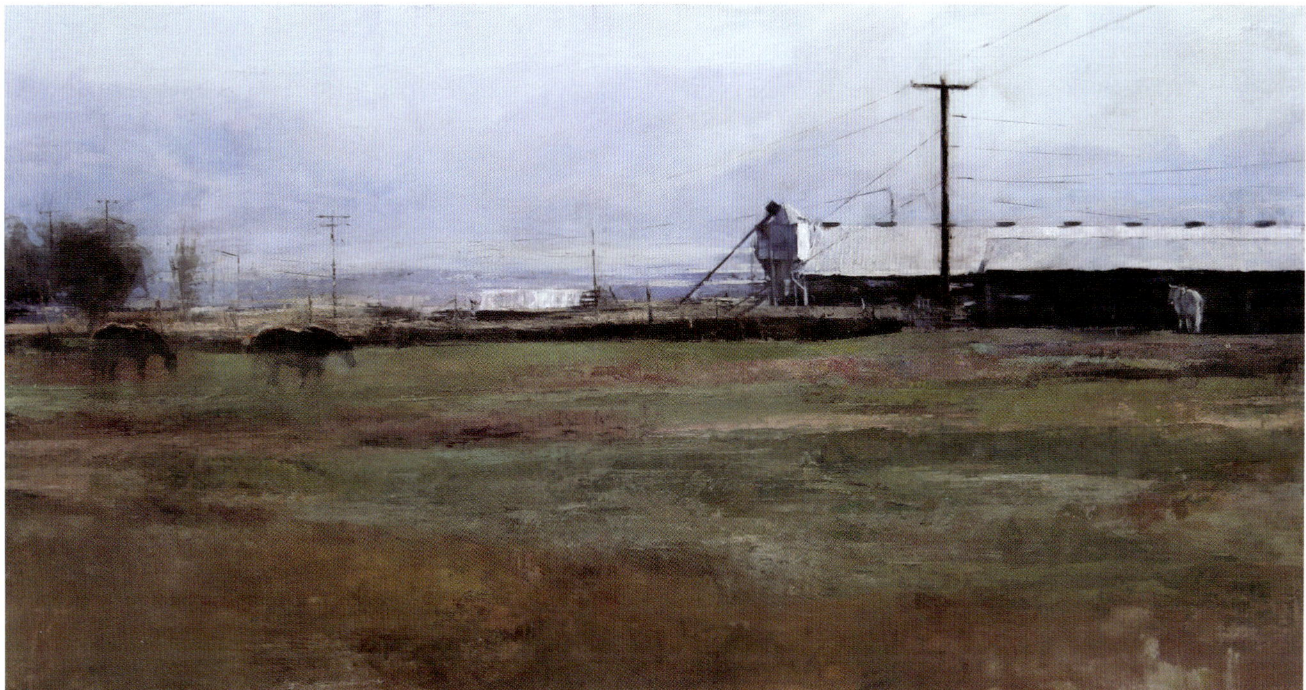

North Valley Farm, Douglas Fryer. (15" × 30", oil on panel)
The success of this painting relies on the simplicity of its composition, and contains three basic elements: horizontals, verticals and diagonals. This is further reinforced by the subtle transitions of colour and tone within these shapes. There is also a strong sense of balance, harmony and repetition of shape. This is perfectly demonstrated by the artist having painted the dark horses against a lighter background to the left of the image, and the light horse against a dark background on the extreme right. The shapes seen in the clouds and mountains are not dissimilar to those in the foreground field. The horses, grass and clouds add a sense of what is alive and moving, which contrasts well with the static rigidity of the architectural elements. But even these are not entirely rigid and sharp-edged, and are only relatively more structured than the organic elements around them. To prevent the dark horses on the left from becoming too dominant, a glaze has been cast over them, which has the effect of allowing them to be glanced at in marginal vision only.

CHOOSING YOUR MEDIUM

Each medium has its advantages. There are generally those who sit in one camp or the other, and there are a very few artists who use both oils and acrylics in equal measure. Struggling to master one medium is difficult enough, but to get to grips with two that are seemingly poles apart is to be burdening yourself with difficulties twofold. Each requires a different mindset and technique, and you must choose which suits your working method.

Depending on the type of pigment used in their manufacture, these paints may be opaque, whilst other colours may have a rather transparent quality. Some brands have a range in which various colours dry rather darker in tone on the canvas than they appear when wet, so a certain amount of adjustment has to be made when mixing colours, and particularly when trying to match colours that have already been applied, whilst other brands claim that there is no colour shift from wet to dry. The fast-drying characteristic of these colours can be counteracted with the addition of a retarder, which will allow a greater degree of manipulation of the paints when working, especially when blending colours together.

There are paints available from a variety of reputable manufacturers that should satisfy every fan of acrylic, and the way in which they like to paint. If you like to use acrylics, you can choose among brands such as Golden, Winsor & Newton, Talens, Sennelier, Liquitex, Daler-Rowney, and many others. There is now a range of paints on the market produced by Atelier that have the ability to be re-worked once dry by spraying them with water, and during the painting process they can also be sprayed to compensate for the loss of moisture, extending the length of time the paint can be manipulated. In theory, these 'interactive' paints allow the artist to have complete control over the drying speed of the work in progress.

MEDIUMS AND SOLVENTS FOR OIL PAINT

There are a bewildering number of mediums, solvents and additives on the market, and each possesses slightly different characteristics.

Turpentine

At some stage you will need to dilute your paint, and to either speed up or slow down the drying process. You may also need to alter the paint's consistency to allow it to flow more easily. One traditional way of diluting your oil paint has been the use of turpentine as a solvent, and this was used primarily for the lean under-painting employed as the basis for the finished work.

The most common painting medium has traditionally been a mixture of distilled turpentine and linseed oil in equal proportions. This mixture provides a good, general-purpose medium. Turpentine, when used on its own as a medium, will make colours appear rather flat and dead.

Linseed Oil

When used without any further additives as a medium with oil paint, linseed oil will give colours a high gloss. It will also slow down the drying time, and when compared to some other oils, it has a tendency to make colours a little yellow over an extended period. This is an excellent medium to add to your colours if you like to use glazing techniques.

Stand Oil

This oil is a faster-drying alternative to linseed oil, which reduces the paint's consistency and brush marks, and improves its flow.

Poppy Oil

A fast-drying oil, pale in colour for adding to white and lighter colours.

Experimentation will allow you to choose which oil is ideal for you, and it may even be that a mixture of two different oils added to turpentine is your preferred choice.

Ready-mixed Mediums

Rather than mixing your own mediums by adding turpentine to one of the previously mentioned oils, there are proprietary mediums available, too numerous to mention by name, which will either increase or reduce gloss or transparency, slow down or speed up drying times, or increase or reduce the paint's consistency. As a general guideline, your medium should be no more than about 20 per cent of your paint mixture, which is usually achieved by just picking up a small amount with your paintbrush and adding it to your paint mix on the palette.

These mediums will of course thin your paint slightly, and although you may not want to thin your paint at all, during the painting and drying process it may be

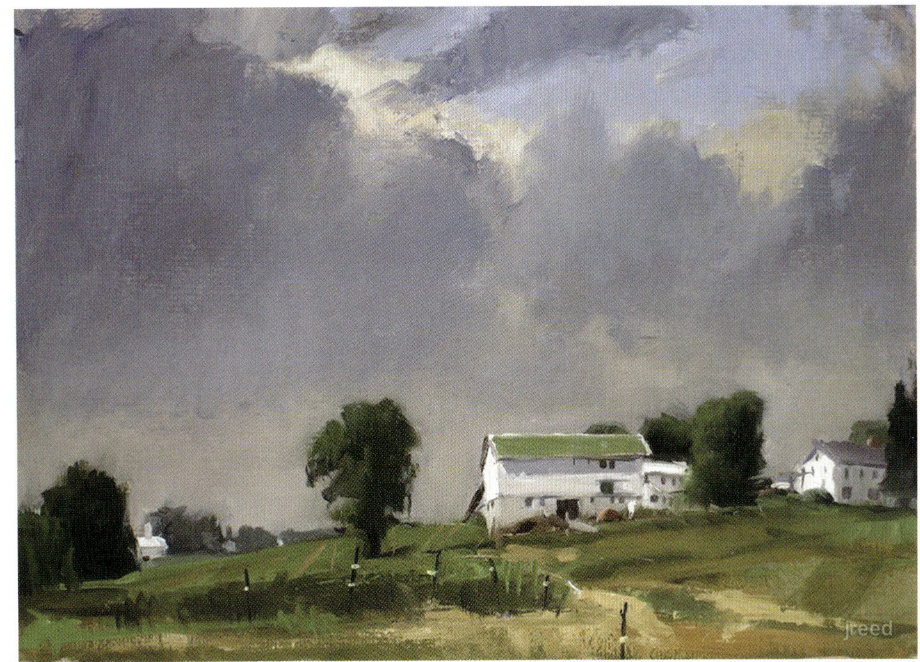

Oxford Farm, Jeffrey Reed. (8" × 10", oil on paper)
The dark mauve-grey sky adds a sense of drama to this scene, and as with all things we perceive, there are touches of this colour reflected in other parts of the painting, notably on the roof of the building on the right-hand side, and the shadow under the eaves of the central white farmhouse. To emphasize this, the main components of the painting have been positioned in the lower quarter of the composition. To suggest distance, a hint of this mauve-grey colour has been added to the foliage along the horizon. A visually balanced painting has been created by combining the curved shapes of the clouds and undulating fields, with the horizontal elements of the farm buildings. The trees and posts for the electric fencing provide a contrast with their strong vertical forms. Painted on location in Lancaster County, Pennsylvania.

necessary to increase the paint's fluidity with the addition of a little medium. If your style of painting leans towards heavy impasto, you may wish to make your paint even thicker, in which case there are mediums on the market that will do just that, such as Roberson Oil Medium Impasto, Pip Seymour Beeswax Impasto and Sennelier Thickening Medium.

Solvents

White spirit is the most economical solvent for oil paint, and consequently ideal for cleaning your brushes. It is, however, rather toxic, so an alternative to this is the slightly more expensive low-odour white spirit or thinners (not to be confused with cellulose thinners, which are highly toxic). There are also odour-free, non-toxic alternatives made from a variety of substances, including citrus fruits, but these can be expensive when used in the quantities needed for washing out brushes.

Solvents are generally used for mixing with oils to produce a painting medium. When used on their own as a dilutant, they can cause the oil paint to become rather dull and lifeless, as it sinks into the painting surface more readily. The solvent will also reduce the binding ability that the oil in the paint provides, and as a result, when subsequent layers of paint are applied, the underlying diluted paint is liable to taint the colour that is applied on top of it.

Unless you already have a favoured painting medium, to keep things simple, use a 50/50 mixture of refined turpentine and linseed oil for mixing with your paint when necessary, and use a low-odour white spirit for washing out your brushes. You can experiment with other medium concoctions at a later stage, if you find that this recipe isn't entirely satisfactory, or doesn't suit your way of working. If you want to speed up your paint's drying time, there are a variety of alkyd-based mediums to choose from, such as those produced by Winsor & Newton, Gamblin and Lukas. These mediums tend to increase the paint's transparency and gloss.

If you are both environmentally and frugally minded, you can cut down on the amount of white spirit you use by filling an empty bottle with white spirit that has been used for cleaning brushes. Over a period of time the paint will form a sediment at the bottom of the bottle, leaving the white spirit relatively clear although a little yellow. This can then be poured off into another container and re-used for cleaning your brushes. This process can be repeated two or three times before it becomes unusable. The old spirit and sediment should then be safely disposed of at a recycling centre.

Once your painting is completely dry, and the drying time will depend on a number of factors including the type of medium you have used, and how thickly the paint has been applied, you may wish to varnish it. Traditionally, all oil paintings were varnished as a means of protection against the elements, but this has become increasingly unnecessary due to the durability of modern pigments and mediums, as well as now being seen as rather unfashionable. But if you like the effect of a varnished painting, there are plenty of varnishes to choose from, and they don't all produce a glossy finish. There are occasions when applying a varnish can certainly be beneficial, particularly when some areas of the painting appear to have a rather matt appearance, as opposed to other sections that have more of a glossy finish. A couple of coats of varnish will rectify this, unifying the finish of the entire painting.

You can choose between matt and gloss varnish, or by adding different quantities of two varnishes together, providing they have the same chemical make-up, you can produce varying degrees of semi-matt, satin or gloss finishes.

Retouching varnish will revive any dull areas caused by paint sinking into the canvas or board, and should you wish to alter a small section of the painting after it has dried, you can touch-up this area by mixing some retouching varnish with the new oil colour, and after this has dried, the painting can be given a further coat of retouching varnish. Many varnishes can be removed with white spirit or other solvents specified by the manufacturers, if you then decide that you don't like the finished effect.

Mediums and Additives for Acrylics

As with oil paints, there are various ways in which the consistency, appearance, drying time and texture of acrylics can be modified. There are numerous gels and mediums that can be added to produce many different effects and finishes, including impasto, glazing, moulding and crackleure. Gloss can be increased or reduced, and one additive will allow the paint to be poured, which may be of some use when tackling large landscapes.

Acrylic paintings may of course also be varnished with a gloss or matt finish if required, and as well as a brush-on varnish, Golden produce one in an aerosol can.

BRUSHES

Choosing your Weapons

The people's choice of brushes for oil painting has traditionally been Chinese hog bristle. This is a natural material that is ideal for the relatively tough business of applying paint to canvas, canvas boards, or panels. An acceptable alternative to natural bristle brushes is the cheaper, synthetic brushes made from polyester or nylon. Worth mentioning also are those made from a combination of both natural and synthetic materials.

It is generally accepted that the larger the brush you are comfortable using, the better the results are likely to be, and

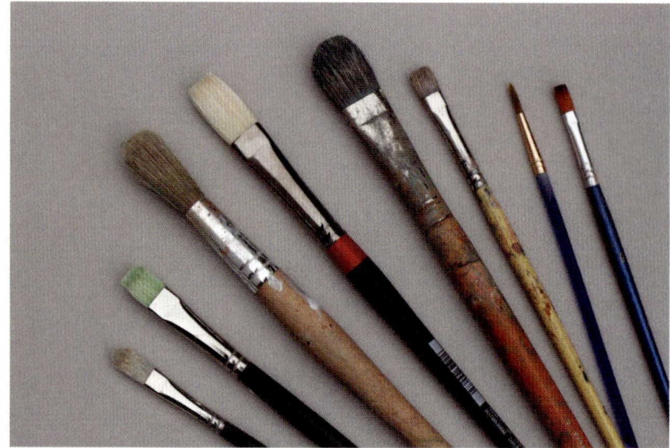

You will need a selection of hog hair brushes for oil painting, together with a few synthetic brushes for smaller detail. Sizes 3, 6 and 10 in flats and filberts would be a good starting point, and a 2 and a 3 in rounds. Acrylic brushes tend to be sold in either a hog hair/synthetic mix, or pure synthetic, as they don't need to stand up to the punishment that oil brushes are subjected to.

this is especially true when it comes to landscape painting, where there will relatively large areas to be covered in the initial laying-in stages. As the painting goes through its various stages of progression, some smaller brushes will be required. If you work on a very small scale, there may be a point where hog brushes are a little unwieldy, so for finer detail, synthetic and semi-synthetic brushes are the answer and some artists even use sables.

In general terms, there are four main types of brushes for oil painting, although they come in a variety of shapes and sizes, which may differ from manufacturer to manufacturer. There is also a slight degree of crossover between the different shapes, and some makes may call a particular brush a short filbert whilst others may call the same shape a 'bright'. The brushes with the shorter length of bristle will be good for vigorous scrubbing strokes, and those with longer hairs for a smoother application of paint.

Filberts are possibly the most commonly used brushes, as they are able to produce a variety of strokes. Due to their slightly curved edges, they can create rounded and thin marks, as well as large, flattish strokes. Having fairly long hairs, they can also be charged with a lot of paint, and so cover larger areas than some of the other brushes. They are flat in shape, but because of their rounded edges, they will leave a fairly soft, smooth edge.

Flats, as the name suggests are flat with a squared-off end, ideal for making square, chisel-shaped strokes.

Brights are also flat, with shorter bristles than flats, and consequently hold less paint.

Rounds have fairly long bristles set in a round ferrule, which gives them a look similar to watercolour brushes. The bristles come to a point at the end, which makes them suitable for producing long thin strokes, and finer lines for detail. Traditionally, most brushes designed for painting in oils or acrylics have fairly long handles, but some are available with short handles.

Princeton now make a synthetic brush called a Polytip that behaves like hog bristle, but claims to be able to hold more paint due to each individual hair being split into two or three different hairs. As well as the standard oil painting brush shapes, they include an 'egbert', which is an extra long-haired, narrow filbert, a fan brush, and a bright, which is cut across its tip at an oblique angle.

There are other brushes that aren't strictly meant for oil painting, but they too have their uses. A soft hake brush, or a fan brush, can be used for blending colours together once they have been applied to the canvas. A synthetic rigger can be used for painting long, thin lines, and a sword liner for a variety of strokes. Old, worn brushes may also be useful for scrubbing-in colour where required as well as for scumbling techniques, where you might not want to ruin some of your newer or more expensive brushes. For really large paintings you could also use inexpensive household brushes made from nylon or some other synthetic material.

All of these brushes come in a variety of sizes, so a good starting point would be to buy the best you can afford in sizes 3, 6, and 10. You will soon find that you get along better with some shapes than others, at which point you can then add some intermediate sizes to your arsenal.

Having advised all of this, there are no hard and fast rules to follow, and everyone is different. There is one artist I know of who paints wonderful pictures with just two brushes, one large flat, and one small round.

It's important to clean your brushes thoroughly, as oil paint and acrylic are particularly hard on them if paint is allowed to accumulate in the ferrule. Oil brushes should be cleaned in white spirit and then washed with either a proprietary brush cleaner or soap, or failing that, a mild detergent or even washing-up liquid.

Brushes for Acrylics

There are brushes manufactured that are marketed as being suitable for both oils and acrylics, and there are brushes made specifically for acrylics. These are synthetic, and as acrylic paint is water-based, the paint flows from these fibres more readily than it does with bristles. They are available in a range of sizes and degrees of stiffness and flexibility. If you like to use thick paint, you will need brushes with stiffer fibres, which will allow you to move the paint about more easily. For smaller, finer work, you can of course use sables or brushes that are a natural/synthetic mix.

PAINTBRUSH CARE

You should never leave your oil painting brushes standing upright in solvent for prolonged periods as this may damage the hairs, and although in theory the solvent should prevent the oil paint from hardening, this isn't always the case. The paint trapped at the base of the hairs and in the metal ferrule may begin to solidify and will be difficult, if not impossible to move. Similarly with acrylics, brushes left standing in water will not stop the acrylic emulsion from solidifying and eventually rendering them useless.

Other Weapons

Palette Knives and Painting Knives

A palette knife is designed for both mixing paint on your palette, and cleaning excess paint from it at the end of a painting session.

A painting knife is one that is used for applying paint to your canvas, and has a cranked shaft to prevent paint from getting on your knuckles and smearing your painting, but now it seems that some manufacturers are using the term 'palette knife' for both types. Indeed, there are now so many different shapes and sizes of knife to choose from, that it's almost impossible to tell one from the other. Some of the shapes available wouldn't look out of place in a painter and decorator's toolbox. In fact, some of the knives sold in hardware shops turn out to be an excellent addition to the artist's toolbox. A glazier's putty knife, and a flexible filling knife will be very useful if you go in for a more robust form of painting. The filling knife in particular is an excellent tool for mixing up large quantities of paint on your palette, and it can also be used for painting bigger areas on your canvas.

The best knives are made from carbon steel, or polished stainless steel. The blades are thin and flexible, which allow for greater precision when applying paint, unlike the cheap plastic variety, which are more suitable for a slightly less refined style of painting technique.

For those who like to make their own equipment, rather than cutting your credit cards in half and throwing them in the bin, you can fashion them into tools for applying paint. They can be cut into specific shapes, and although very flexible they are quite a bit thicker than the blade of a

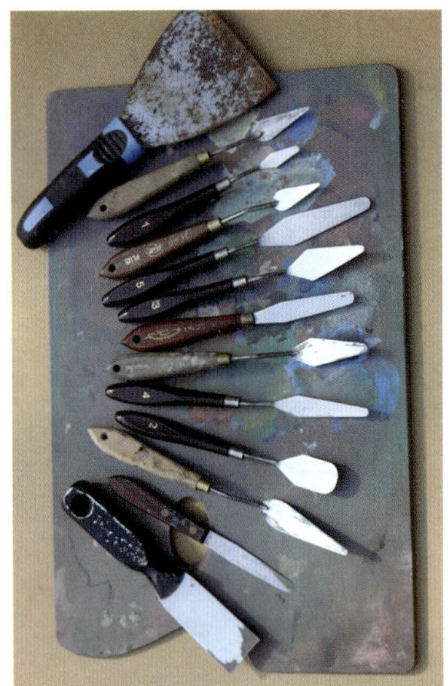
A selection of palette knives, painting knives and filling knives. As well as being useful for removing paint from your palette, the filling knives can also be used for painting, and in particular for spreading paint over larger areas.

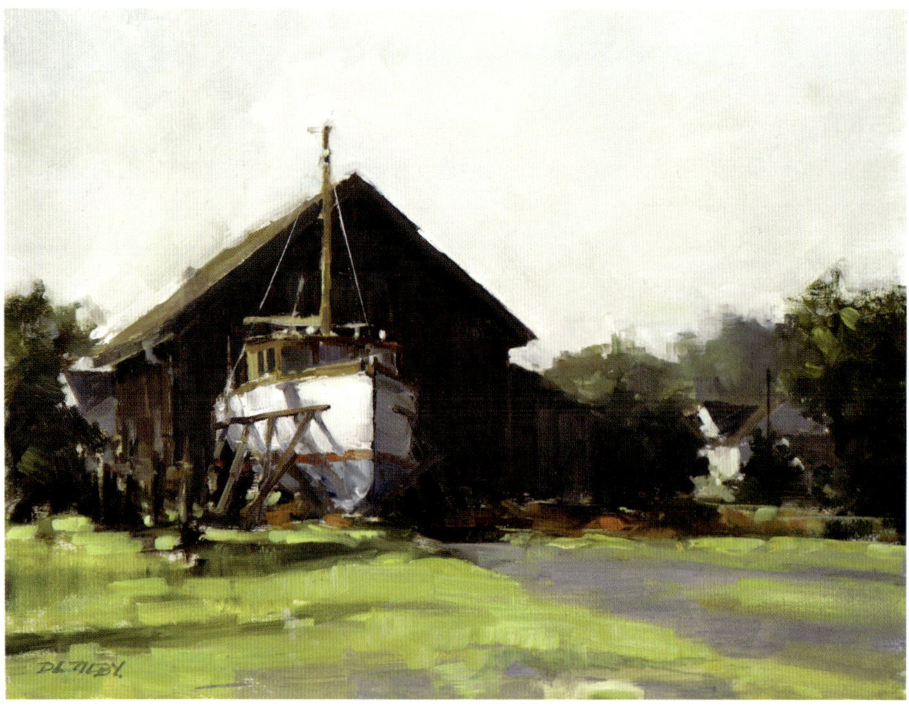
Boat in the Farmyard, Deborah Tilby. (9" × 12", oil on board)
The attraction of this scene for the artist was the juxtaposition of the boat with the farm buildings, in a landscape setting on Vancouver Island. The subject matter is slightly unusual in that there is no suggestion of any water, but instead a landscape rich in colour, further emphasized by the golden hue of the sky. The entire picture has been painted in warm colours, except for the lower part of the boat's hull, the cool tones on the walls of the buildings, and the farmyard track. The lively brushwork prevents the painting from becoming too 'pretty', and adds vibrancy to the static scene.

painting knife, but this can be rectified by sanding down the edges with a fine grade glass or carborundum paper. Not as effective as painting knives, but these are perhaps useful for very occasional use.

If you don't mind getting in a mess, some of the most versatile tools are of course your fingers.

PAINTING SURFACES

The perceived traditional support for oil paintings has always been canvas, but throughout history artists have always used panels of various kinds. Before canvas became the norm, due to its light weight and ease of transportation, panels made from various types of wood were the favoured support. A large painting on wood could be particularly heavy and difficult to transport, whereas a picture painted on canvas could be removed from its stretcher when dry, rolled up and then sent off to whoever had commissioned it. The stretcher could then be re-assembled on site and the painting framed.

Canvas

There are two different materials used in the manufacture of canvas for artists, namely cotton and linen. Cotton is the least expensive of the two, and therefore the most popular surface for oil and acrylics. It has the ability to be stretched tighter than linen, but may become slack over a period of time due to moisture incursion. Linen is more expensive and is less likely to expand or contract, and the natural flax oils within its make-up help retain the fibre's flexibility, which helps prevent it from becoming brittle. Both types of canvas are made in a variety of textures and weights.

You can buy canvases ready-stretched and primed, or you can prepare your own by buying it in lengths, cutting it to size and stapling or tacking it over a stretcher. It can then be primed with a good quality acrylic gesso.

Painting on a fine-textured canvas is certainly a pleasurable experience, as the paint slides over its surface, which has just enough 'tooth' to allow the paint to be deposited where required. There is also something delightful in the way in which it yields to the pressure of a brush on its surface.

But painting on canvas on location can have its

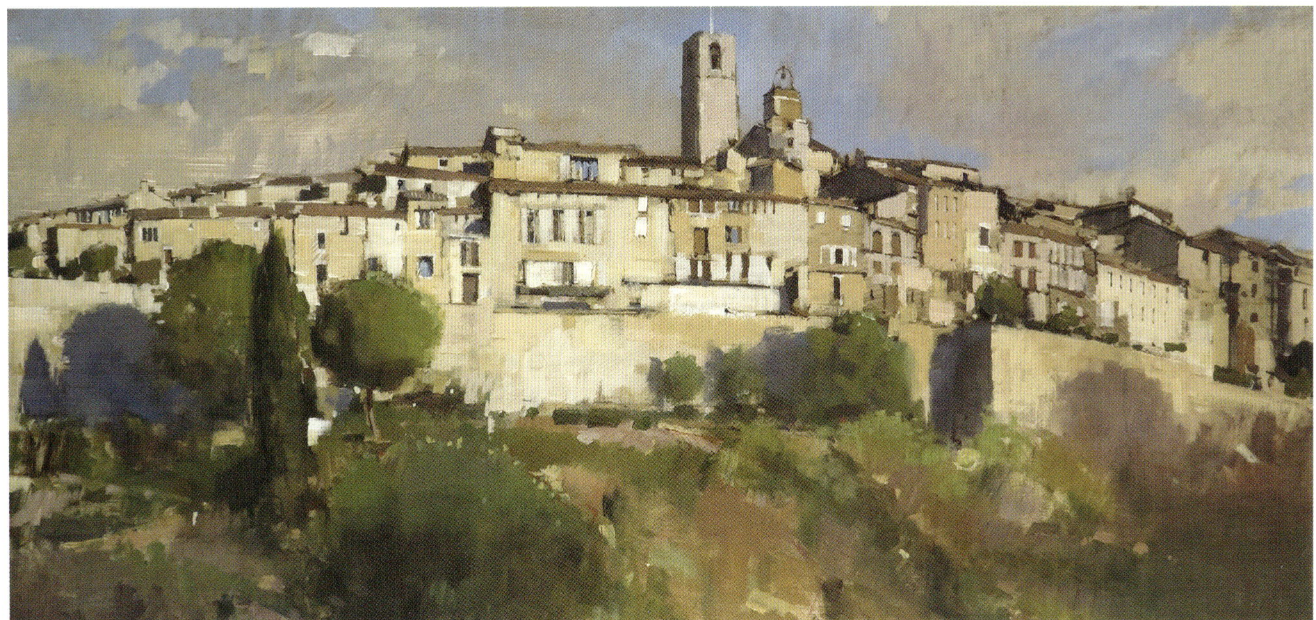

Across the Ramparts, St Paul de Vence, David Sawyer. (20" × 40", oil on board) A large studio painting produced from studies and drawings made during a particularly turbulent week of spring weather in the South of France. The artist has tended to be quite broad and vigorous in the handling of the brushwork and has not gone in for too much architectural detail. Despite the Mediterranean location, there is little evidence of the typical Azure skies, and in fact much of the colour here is feeding into the stone of the buildings. The foreground has been painted very loosely so as not to detract from the buildings, but enough change in colour and tone has been introduced into this area of the painting to provide the necessary interest.

drawbacks, and its relative fragility is its main drawback. It can be dented rather easily, which can be a problem when carrying a wet painting back home. If you still like to paint on canvas you can cut some to the required size, allowing a couple of extra inches all around, and then tape it to a rigid, lightweight board. Back at home and once dry, it can then be either tacked onto a stretcher, or dry-mounted or glued onto a sheet of MDF board. There will of course be a different sensation experienced during the painting process, as the canvas won't succumb to your brushstrokes in the same way that it would with a stretched canvas.

Some artists like to paint on canvas, but prefer a rigid support, so they prepare their own by gluing linen onto MDF, and then priming it with acrylic gesso.

Painting Boards and Panels

There are several alternatives to canvas now on the market. Lightweight, rigid painting boards are ideal, and there are a great many to choose from. You might like to try canvas panels that are mounted onto either thin plywood, hardboard or MDF. These boards are lightweight, rigid and

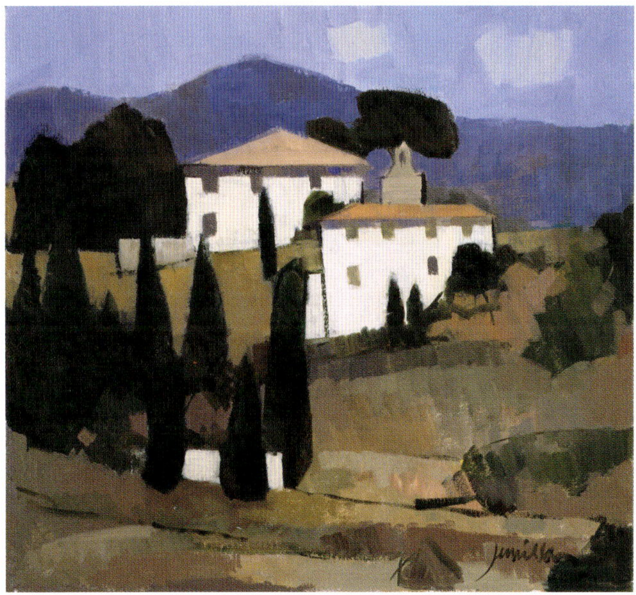

Gréve in Chianti, Charles Jamieson. (18" × 20", oil on linen)
This is a fairly simple painting, and more about mood than anything else, with its slightly sombre disposition reflecting the feeling of the day. The shapes of the fields and hills in the landscape, together with the placement of the trees help to focus the eye around the buildings. The artist uses the dark greenery to emphasize the light buildings that are already holding their own amongst the toned-down colours of the earth and the hills beyond. The left-hand side of the painting fixes the buildings in place, leaving the right-hand side more open and allowing the eye some freedom. The dark V-shape travelling left to right gives that open airy feel to the right-hand side whilst letting the eye play between the two buildings, and by overlapping the trees and buildings the artist has created a sense of linear perspective. The shape of the background hills complements the building in front of them, and the two clouds to the upper right give balance to the overall composition.

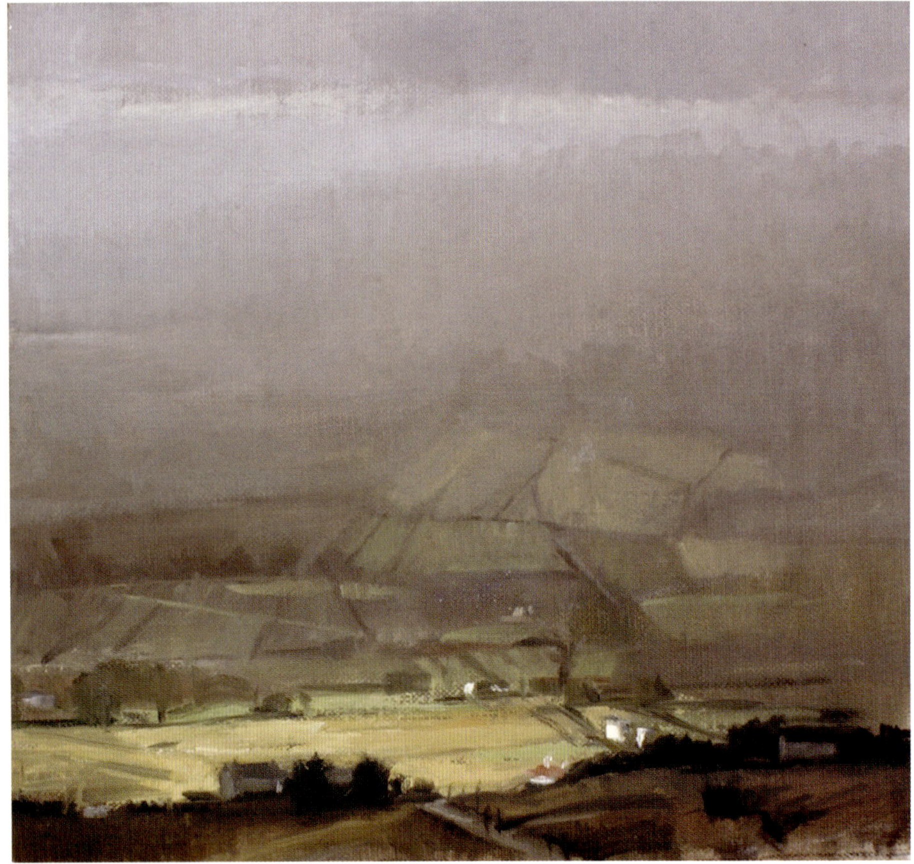

Gold Field, Jeffrey Reed. (10" × 10", oil on canvas)
In this low-key painting, aerial perspective has been employed to suggest the high viewpoint adopted by the artist. The stronger range of colours used in the immediate foreground suggests a steep drop from here to the valley below. Jeffrey Reed has avoided using too much detail here, as it prevents the eye from travelling into and around the picture itself. In the area below, the colours become brighter where an unseen sun casts a golden light across the fields, but there is little detail to be seen here even though it is the focus of the painting. A red roof and a few touches of white add a sparkle to the scene. As the eye travels up the painting, the landscape disappears into the sky where the atmospheric conditions produce a violet haze. Painted on location in County Mayo, Ireland.

durable and can be bought in many sizes, with surfaces graded from smooth to medium.

These degrees of surface finish will vary depending upon which brand you choose. The most expensive ones have a fine linen surface, which is ideal for painting on, especially if you like to paint in detail. Slightly cheaper, are the panels that use cotton canvas of a heavier grain, usually referred to as medium.

These are more suitable if you are painting larger pictures, as the rougher grain of the canvas will be more noticeable on smaller panels. These panels come ready-primed in either oil or acrylic gesso, which acts as a sealant to stop the oil paint from sinking into the support. Some are double-primed which makes them less absorbent than those that have simply been primed once. The primer is sprayed on, so the finish is smooth and there are no brush marks. It is also possible to buy MDF boards that have been given a couple of coats of acrylic gesso primer, sanded down between each coat. If you don't especially like the surface of these panels, you can always sand them down a bit more, or apply another coat of gesso primer.

There are cheaper painting panels made from a composite material or compressed cardboard, which have a rather mechanical texture stamped onto their surface that attempts to simulate the appearance of real canvas, and are probably best avoided. These are often quite thin which means that they are prone to warping, especially if used outside in strong sunlight or damp conditions.

Ampersand is a company that produces Claybord panels, which consist of 3mm hardboard covered in a kaolin clay formula that imitates the clay gesso grounds used by Renaissance artists. The surface is sanded down to a smooth, absorbent surface. There are also aluminium painting panels on the market that have a specially treated surface that paint adheres to. These panels need no priming.

You can buy wooden panels of finely sanded plywood, attached to and braced by a slim wooden frame to prevent warping. These come as bare wood, ready for priming.

Cradled panels are constructed from multi-layered aspen hardwood topped with a smooth, maple hardwood veneer, held rigid at the back by a timber frame. The panels are usually 10mm thick and can be hung on a nail or a screw, without the necessity of a frame. As they are so thick, they are fairly heavy and rather difficult to frame in the standard way.

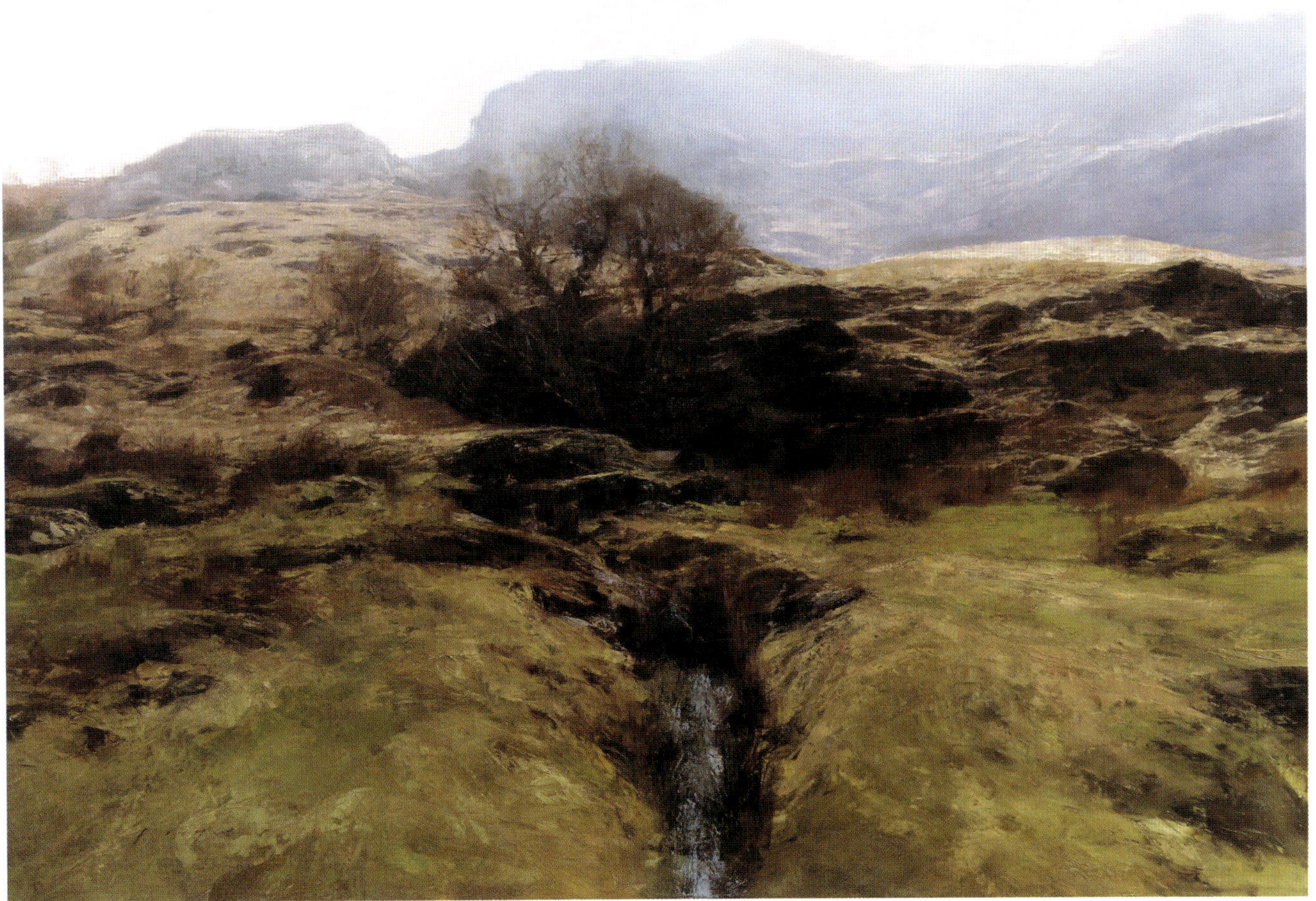

Ancient Hills, Douglas Fryer. (24" × 36", oil on panel)
The subject matter of this painting is the beautiful Lake District near Ullswater, Cumbria, where the light rakes across the surface of the land in a magical way, inviting the artist to produce paintings that lay bare the very bones of the hills. In this simple composition, Douglas Fryer has created variety and interest in the spaces that divide the different sections of the landscape, where there appears to be great distances between them, when they are in fact just feet apart. The colour range is also simple, and the structure of the painting relies on the stark relationship between light and shadow, not only in the fore and middle ground, but also in the distant blue peaks. The artist's working method is to produce a drawing in charcoal on his support, which can be made from adhering muslin, canvas or linen onto a cradled panel with acrylic gesso. This stage is then followed by a thin underpainting or imprimatura. He works from dark to light, so the first stages may be two or three shades darker than those seen in the finished painting. He tries to block-in the entire painting in one sitting with fairly generous amounts of paint using a variety of tools, including bristle and nylon brushes, painting knives and trowels. He adds a heavy, quick-drying medium to his paints, which gives them plenty of body and 'drag' during their application. On subsequent sittings he follows the same method, sometimes painting over the entire piece two or three times until it starts to feel resolved. Elements may be obliterated and substituted at will, and at some stage the marks will begin to feel both natural and complex, just as they do in nature.

Natural wood art panels are similar, but have no bracing at the back and are usually available in both 10mm and 6mm thicknesses.

Although labour intensive, but with economy in mind, you can make your own painting panels from sheets of 3mm MDF bought from a hardware shop. These can be cut to the required size and sanded down. Paint the panels with three coats of acrylic gesso, lightly sanded between each coat. Also, paint the back with gesso, as this will help prevent the thin board from warping. For sturdier panels, choose a 5mm board. Anything thicker than this will probably create a painting that is too heavy, especially if painting outside on a larger scale.

When priming your own painting surface with gesso, you might like the slight ridges that are left by the brush marks, but if you don't they can be removed by sanding them down by hand or by using an electric sander. If you like a slightly even-textured surface you can apply the gesso with a fine paint roller.

PALETTES

If you want to look really professional, a traditional, large kidney-shaped palette of varnished wood will do the trick. They are shaped to rest in the crook of your arm, with a hole for your thumb. There are many variations available in design, shape and size, and some of them are a joy to hold and use. The larger variety is probably more suited to studio use, but a smaller version could be used outside. These are for oil paints only, as acrylics may dry whilst in use and will be fairly immovable.

When working in the studio, you may have the luxury of a reasonable amount of space, in which case you may not need to hold your palette at all. It could be rested on a table or a taboret, a kind of workstation on castors that can be moved about accordingly. You don't even need a traditional palette, and an alternative could be a sheet of Perspex or glass, which for safety reasons should have rounded-off edges. A sheet of paper can be placed underneath, which can be in a neutral colour similar to the colour that you will be using to tone down your canvas or board. By doing this you will find it easier to match colours, as you will be starting from a base similar in tone to that of your painting. This can be used for both oils and acrylics, as scraping off any unused paint won't really damage the surface. Even if acrylic paint has dried, it can be removed with a razor scraper. Glass is perhaps a better choice and will be longer lasting, whereas Perspex will be scratched more easily, but cheaper to replace.

When painting outside, a good choice of palette for oils is one that is hinged in the centre, so that the top half can rest on your easel at the same angle as your painting. The advantage of this, particularly in bright daylight is that the colours mixed on your palette will look exactly the same when applied to your painting. A colour mixed on a horizontal surface won't appear the same when placed on a vertical surface because of the overhead light source.

A practical alternative to a wooden or glass palette is a tear-off and throw away one. These are pads of non-absorbent coated paper, the individual sheets of which can be disposed of when no longer needed. Once only produced in white, there is now a more useful neutral grey version, available in a rectangular shape, or in the form of a traditional palette with a thumb-hole.

Acrylic paint dries a lot quicker than oil paint, so it helps to keep the paint moist. The Stay-Wet Palette by Daler Rowney is a plastic tray containing sheets of reservoir paper and semi-permeable membrane paper. The paint stays wet by the process of osmosis. The semi-permeable membrane paper that forms the working surface of the palette is kept moist by the dampened paper beneath. When not in use, the tray is covered in a transparent plastic lid so that the paint remains in a workable condition. Using one of these would be beneficial if you intend spending a reasonable amount of time working outside in any one session. Adding a little gel retarder to the paint can also extend the workable life of acrylic even further.

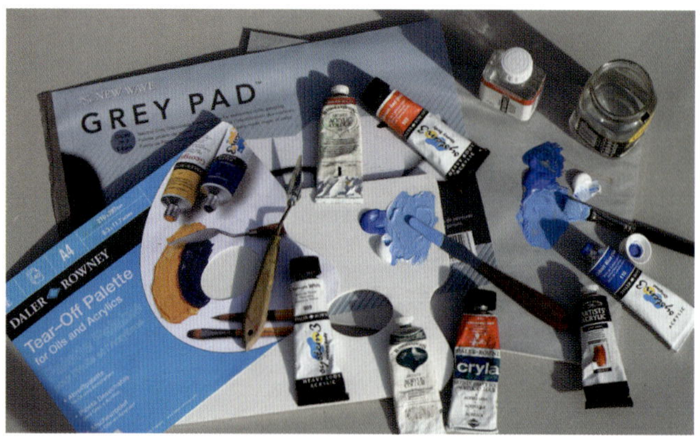

Tear-off palettes are one of the most convenient products for mixing acrylic paints. They are now available in a neutral grey as well as white, which make it easier for colour matching. The image shows a palette knife for mixing paints, together with a painting knife for applying it. The brushes used for oils can also be used for acrylics, although there are special synthetic brushes produced specifically for this medium. You can also use watercolour brushes but it's advisable to use the cheaper, synthetic ones, as sable brushes won't generally last too long when used with acrylics. The image shows a bottle of liquid retarder, which when added to the paint, slows down the drying process.

If you are only going to be working on a painting for a couple of hours, you can use a tear-off paper palette and just squeeze out the amount of paint that you will need. The problem with the tear-off palette is that it tends to wrinkle a bit and this can make mixing paint difficult. So if all of this is a bit too tedious when using acrylics, you can use off-cuts of plastic, or in fact any other non-absorbent, disposable material and just scrape off any paint that you don't use at the end of your painting session. The palette can then be used again or disposed of accordingly.

EASELS

Studio Easels

If you have the space and like to paint fairly large pictures, a studio easel is ideal, and preferably one on castors with a mechanism for altering the height of your painting. If your budget can't stretch to one of these, a radial easel is one alternative if you don't mind tripping over the legs occasionally. If you like to paint sitting down, radial easels with three short, sloping legs at the front are rather problematical, as you have to sit with your legs between the two front legs, or with your legs splayed out either side of them. Tripod easels are better, but rather flimsy in construction. There are many other designs, and some of them are very elaborate and very expensive.

A tabletop easel that can be adjusted to various angles is a good substitute, but you won't be able to paint very large pictures. A sturdy French easel will double as one that can be used for working both inside and outside. It can be set up in your studio with legs extended, and is capable of holding a fairly large canvas or board. If you are short of space, it can be placed on a table with the legs folded up so that you are only using the top half.

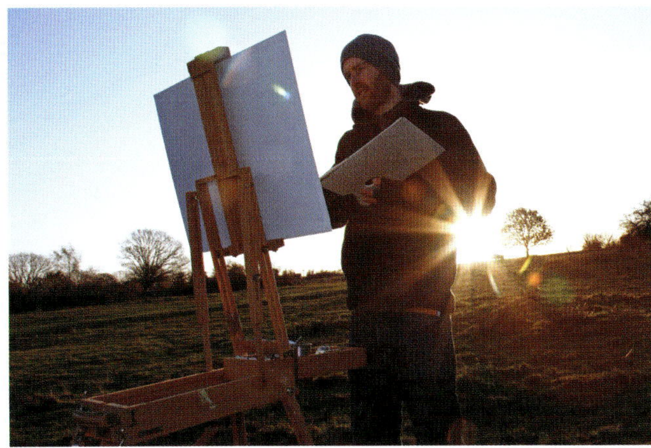

A French easel, set up on Castlemorton Common at the foot of the Malvern Hills. Antony Bridge painting on a 20" × 24" canvas board at dusk, where the low sun is creating a combination of both warm tones and contrasting cool shadows. It seems almost a crime to get any paint on such a practical and beautifully made beechwood easel.

Easels for Painting Outside

If you want to venture outside to paint you will need an easel that folds up into a manageable, portable size that doesn't weigh a ton, and there is a vast selection from which to choose. 'Field easels' in either wood or metal are rather lightweight, and a full-size French easel is rather heavy. A good choice would be a half-size French easel, which folds up pretty neatly into a box with a carrying handle and a pull-out drawer for storing your painting materials.

French Easels

The traditional French easel is essentially an easel and paint box combined, where all the constituent parts fold neatly into the box itself, and its popularity lies in its ability to combine nearly all of your equipment into one single unit. The Mabef product is particularly well made, and will stand up to some pretty rough treatment.

There are two sizes, the half-easel and the full easel, the main difference being the size of the box. The larger version is especially commodious and robust, but if weight is to be a consideration, the half-easel is the best one to buy, being considerably lighter. The larger version will be quite heavy by the time you have filled it with your paints and other bits and pieces. Both sizes will hold fairly large boards or canvases up to about 34" in height, and can accommodate a palette, brushes, paints and all your other painting materials. There is a metal-lined drawer that pulls out to hold paints; this can be used to rest your palette on, and your other equipment can be stored in the box underneath. Initially, the easel can be more than a bit tricky to erect, but once you have mastered the procedure, it can be up and ready for action in just a few minutes. The tripod legs and easel are fully adjustable and can be tilted to any position for painting. This is particularly important if you are painting on a slope as the weight of the unit keeps your easel horizontal when the legs are extended to different lengths.

The 'Jullian' brand comes with provision for attaching a wet board or canvas to the box once it has been folded up, and includes a wooden palette and carrying case. Once highly regarded as a quality French product, the easel is now made elsewhere under a different company name.

POCHADE BOXES AND PANEL HOLDERS

You don't necessarily need an easel to paint in oils or acrylics on location, and instead you can use a pochade box or panel holder.

Pochade Boxes

A pochade box is a self-contained, miniature, portable studio in which it's possible to carry all of the materials you will need to produce small paintings outdoors, and that also allows you to carry your wet paintings back home in safety. A small version can be held in one hand, whilst painting with the other. It can also sit on your lap, or any other convenient surface.

These clever little boxes have evolved into a more sophisticated version of the pochades that artists used in the nineteenth century. Essentially, it's a wooden box with a lid that folds back on hinges. Inside the box there are two or three compartments for storing painting boards. A

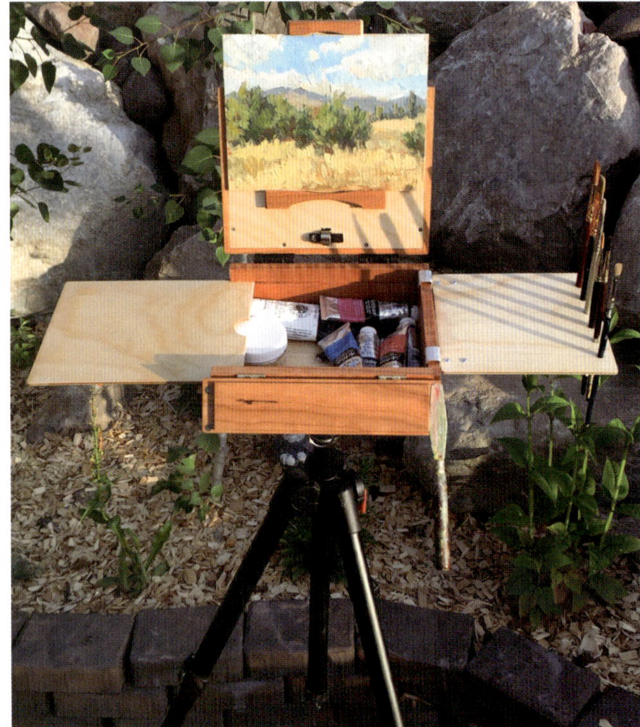

This clever little 'Belly River' pochade box by Alla Prima can hold four 6" × 8" panels in its lid. There is enough storage space to hold your paint and cut-down brushes, and it comes with a mixing area with holes drilled to hold brushes of different sizes, and an extra palette that clips to one side. The spring-loaded panel holder adjusts entirely from the front and the lid is simply pushed to the required angle, where it is held firm. There is a fitting on its base that allows you to fit the box to a standard camera tripod. The painting is by Ben Haggett, who makes the boxes.

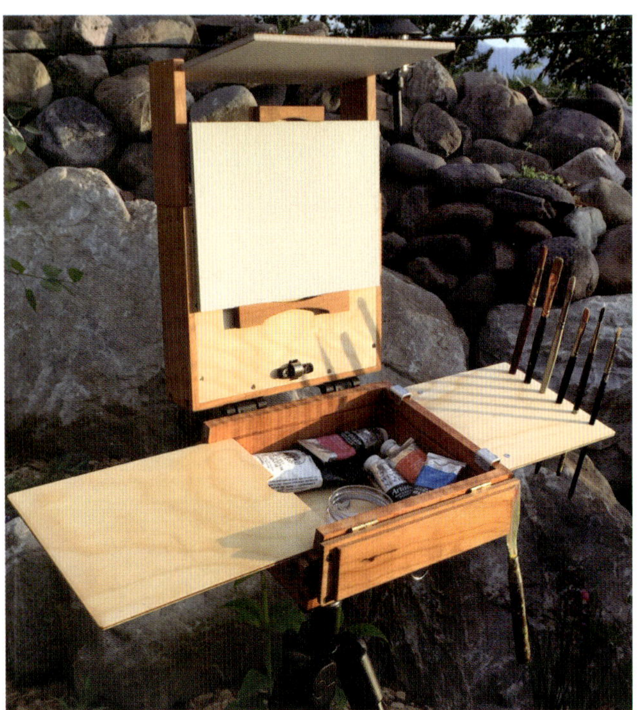

With this clever accessory a panel can be attached to the top of the lid that will keep the sun off your painting surface.

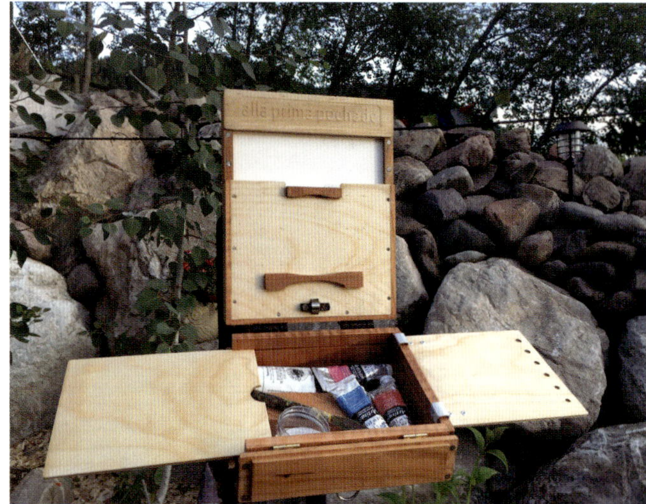

Alla Prima supply an attachment for their 'Belly River' pochade box called a 'Piggy Back', which allows you to carry 8" × 10" panels.

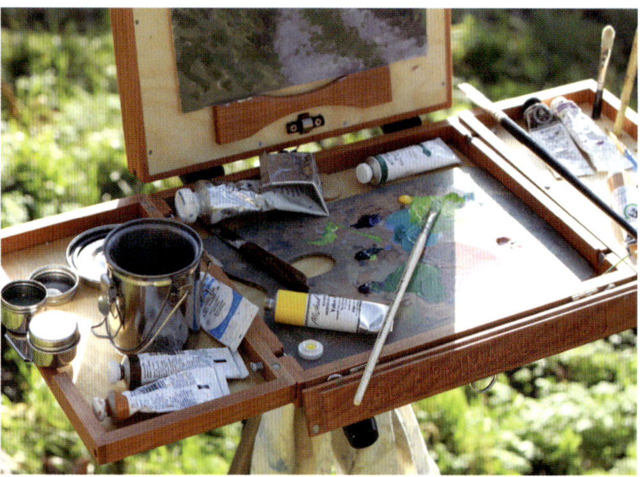

This Bitterrot Lite box by Alla Prima will hold everything you need for painting *en plein air*, and can be attached to a sturdy but lightweight camera tripod. When not in use, it closes up into a neat little box with a carrying handle. Its great beauty is its ability to store wet panels in the safety of its lid.

board can be inserted into the inside of the lid by sliding it into runners where it will be held in place. There is a palette that slides out, and in some boxes this can either slide to the left or the right, and underneath this is a compartment for paints and brushes and so on. Some of these boxes are tiny and no more than 5" × 7", so the handles of brushes will have to be cut down to size. These boxes are perfect if you want to remain inconspicuous when out painting, and even the larger boxes up to 10" × 12" in size will rest comfortably on your lap. The main drawback of these smaller versions is the necessity to carry another bag containing your other materials and equipment, which won't fit into the box.

If you want to be really furtive, you can even sit in your car to paint.

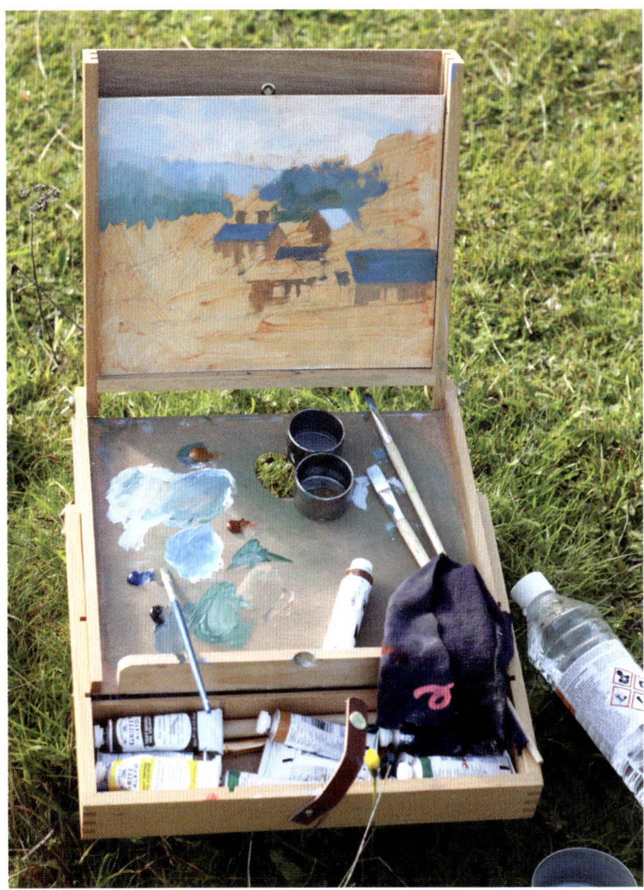

This pochade box is available in two sizes, and has a compartment for storing paints, brushes and so on, below the slide-out palette, which has a thumbhole allowing you to hold the fixed-size panel and palette in one hand whilst painting with the other.

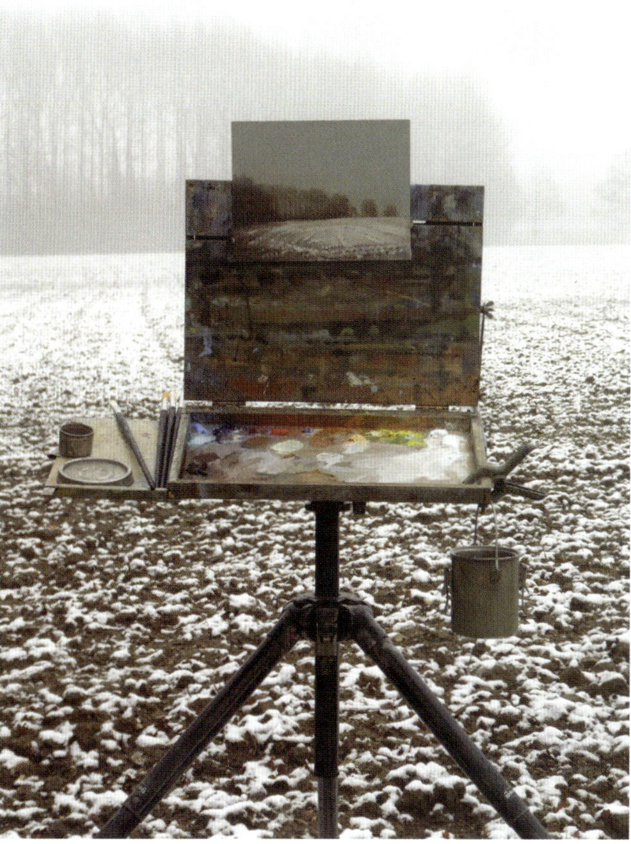

Snow Scene, Roy Connelly. (6" × 8", oil on board)
This was painted after a light snowfall and as a soft mist drifted across the landscape. A small board was chosen for this almost monochromatic painting because the artist knew that the scene would change rapidly, and he wouldn't have time to paint anything on a larger scale. The soft mist gives the scene a very evocative and atmospheric feeling. Every time he sees this image, it reminds him of the melting snow dripping on to him from the branches above. When working outside and immersing yourself in your surroundings, and experiencing everything the elements have to offer, a painting will always offer so much more than merely stopping briefly to take a photograph.

There is one box widely available whereby the lid holding your painting and the palette are hinged together, and can be removed from the box and held in one hand by means of a thumb-hole, leaving your other hand free to paint.

If you like to stand back from your work to paint at arm's length, you can still use a pochade box by attaching it to a robust camera tripod. Most of these boxes have a female threaded screw on the underside, so that it can be connected to a quick-release head on the tripod. Some have extra trays that attach to the side of the box for holding painting mediums, rags and other bits and pieces, and some have pre-drilled holes for slotting your brushes into.

Panel Holders

Panel holders offer an alternative to easels and pochade boxes. This product isn't a box, so there is no storage capacity for paints or brushes, and is merely a very lightweight, neat piece of equipment combining a palette with the means of supporting your painting. It combines a palette, and panel or small canvas holder into one unit, which also can be attached to a camera tripod. They are made in the USA by Open Box M, and come in a range of sizes, the largest of which will accommodate painting boards up to 24" horizontally with no limitation on the height. The panel holder comes with a side palette extension that can be fitted to either the left or right side. The company offers a range of accessories including extra extensions and a panel storage unit, as the panel holder itself doesn't have a built-in compartment for carrying boards.

This product isn't a box, so there is no storage capacity for paints or brushes, it is merely a very lightweight, neat piece of equipment combining a palette with the means of supporting your painting.

GENERAL EQUIPMENT

Drawing Equipment

Before you begin painting the landscape, it would be wise to produce some compositional drawings in a sketchbook to establish areas of different tones and shapes. For this you will only need some basic drawing equipment. Because you should be thinking tonally, you need to be using materials that will produce immediate tonal variations. This could mean a selection of soft pencils ranging from 2B to 8B, and you might even want to include a broad black marker.

For drawing on your canvas or board a simple HB graphite pencil is all you will need, as this can be erased where necessary and eventually covered over with paint. Alternatively you can use a non-soluble coloured pencil.

Containers for Solvents and Mediums

You will need a container for washing out your brushes, so a large tin or glass jar will be adequate, unless you want to invest in a purpose-made metal brush washer, which has a screw-top lid held firmly in place with spring clips. It has a removable, perforated insert through which the sediment filters into the bottom of the vessel, thus keeping the white spirit cleaner for longer. The sediment can be cleaned out and disposed of by pouring off the relatively clean white spirit and removing the insert. When painting outside, this container can be suspended from your easel or tripod for easy access.

'Double-dippers' are a pair of small metal containers, either open or with screw-top lids, for holding your painting medium or solvent, and can be clipped to the side of your palette. Over time the screw tops can become unusable due to a build-up of medium in the thread, and will need to be cleaned, but they are useful for painting outside when you are more likely to suffer from spillages.

For acrylics you will need screw-top jars and a generous supply of water to hand, especially when painting outside.

Rags and Paper Towels

You will need an abundant supply of rags for cleaning oil paint from not only your palette and brushes, but also from yourself. Paper towels are not as useful for oil painting as rags, but they do have their place in the acrylic painter's kit. When on location, a roll of kitchen towel can be suspended on a line of string below your tripod or easel if you are using one.

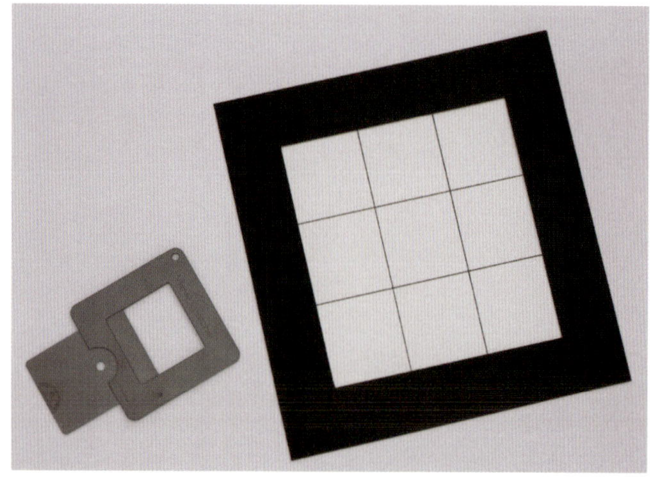

This Viewcatcher is a handy addition to your equipment. It has a slider that changes your viewing format from a square to any proportion of landscape or portrait. Held at arm's length, it can be used to compose a picture by moving it up or down, from side to side, or backwards and forwards, until a satisfactory image has been established. The homemade piece of card with a transparent acetate window divided into thirds is also an excellent item to assist you in arriving at a good composition. It would be useful to have one in landscape/portrait format too.

Viewfinder

A product called a 'Viewcatcher' is a useful gadget for establishing your composition as well as helping you decide upon a format for your painting when on location. It has a slider that allows you to alter the proportions of your format. A few pieces of card in various formats, including a square, with a transparent acetate window divided into thirds, are useful compositional aides for locating focal points in your painting.

Ruler

A fast and accurate way of making sure your horizon line is actually horizontal and the water in your lake or river isn't travelling uphill is to use a ruler, set square or T-square.

Pliers or All-in-One Tool Kit

The screw tops of paint tubes can become impossible to open when the paint has solidified in the thread, so keep a pair of pliers handy, particularly when painting on location. There is nothing more frustrating than being unable to open a tube of paint that you desperately need for your painting. A mini tool kit is handy for many things, including tightening screws on wobbly easels, and a pocket-knife will also have a variety of uses.

Mirror

Viewing your painting in a mirror will help you in determining any compositional imbalances that may have crept in. Keep a larger one in the studio and a small one for working on location.

Camera

A camera is invaluable for accumulating reference material and inspiration when looking for subject matter. Although the camera rarely captures the atmosphere and sensation of the three-dimensional landscape, it does record detail that can be useful back in the studio.

Umbrella

One extra piece of equipment worth considering for painting on location is an umbrella that will keep both rain and sun off your painting and equipment. Choose a white one so that no colour is cast onto your painting, which would otherwise make colour mixing confusing. The umbrella could be clamped to your easel or tripod. There are companies that produce an umbrella specifically for this purpose, and one such company is 'Best Brella'. They sell a semi-translucent white umbrella that clamps to any surface and rotates to any angle. It is also vented, and that means it won't take off, and take your easel and painting with it!

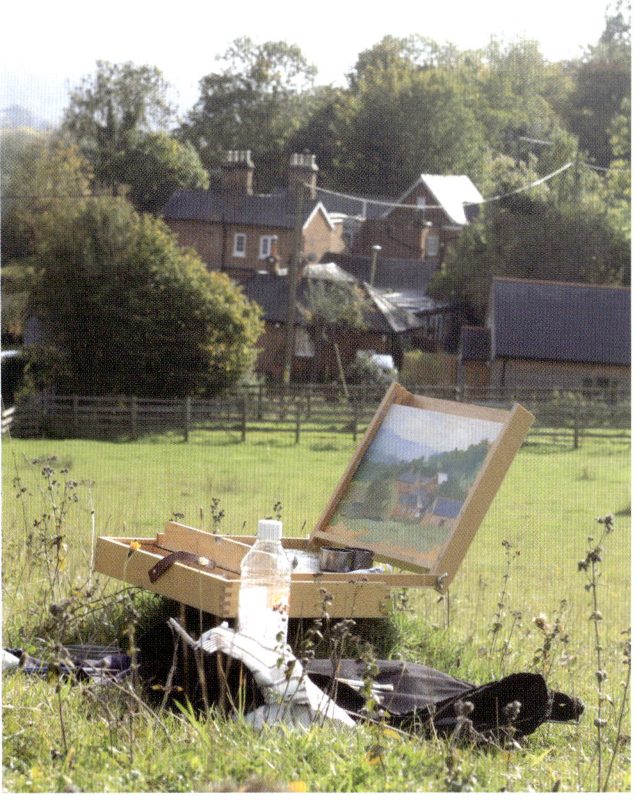

This pochade box has no camera tripod attachment, but is lightweight enough to be used balanced on your knee or on a convenient wall.

Other Items for Painting Outside

When painting outside, take a plastic bag with you for any discarded rags, used paper towels, empty paint tubes or any other unwanted items, which can then be disposed of in a convenient litterbin or back at home. You will need to wear some old clothes for painting in oils or acrylic, because it can be a messy business! You may want to take a seat with you, and a fold-up fisherman's stool is one that will take up the least room in your bag. If you have chosen to paint at a basic easel or panel holder, you will need a box or bag in which to keep your other equipment. A box is probably the best option for storing paints and brushes, as it will prevent them from being damaged. Providing it's not too big, it can be carried in a bag or backpack along with your other materials.

A good choice is a cantilevered box. These are usually made from lightweight plastic and can be left open to give access to individual trays divided into compartments, in which you can keep your bits and pieces. Tubes of paint, brushes and larger items can be stored in the bottom of the box, as placing heavier items in the top section will cause the box to tip over. You can buy these boxes in most art shops, and a similar item can be found in shops selling fishing equipment where they are used for storing hooks, fishing flies and so on.

If you are planning on painting larger pictures than those that fit into the lid of a pochade box, you will need to be able to transport them safely, especially if they are wet. There are various cunning devices on the market including a pair of carrying clips that allow you to carry two paintings face-to-face without damage. A product from the Guerrilla Painter Company is the 'Handy Porter', a cardboard box with foam inserts that allows you to carry two canvases or four panels. A much cheaper way of doing this is to insert double-ended pushpins into each corner of the painted side of your canvas or board, and then gently push your other painting, face-to-face onto the pins. You can then tuck them under your arm and carry them home.

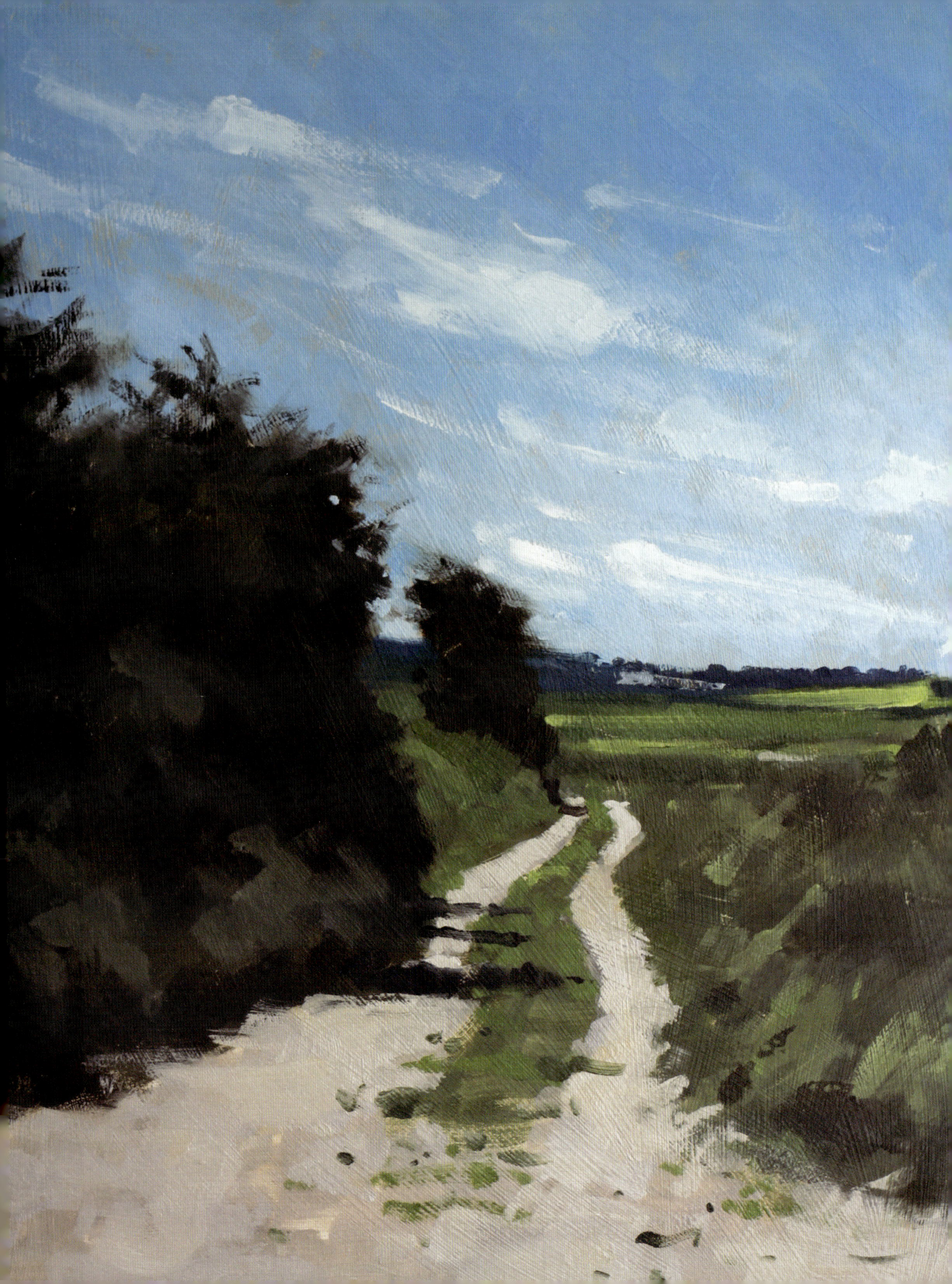

CHAPTER 3

Working on Location

Painting requires the bravery of solitude. Painting requires disciplined labour. To be a painter is to search the world with a benevolent eye for every subtle beauty that the infinite world offers.

CHARLES PHILIP BROOKS

It isn't always necessary to know what you're looking for when you venture out seeking inspiration, but it can certainly help. There is of course a kind of subject matter that will appeal more than others, and some subjects will be dismissed out of hand. You will almost certainly have considered some scenes that you have encountered in your everyday travels as potential material for a landscape painting, even if you haven't travelled very far. Seeking inspiration requires patience and careful consideration, and even though you may have a deep passion for nature and its ability to draw on your artistic and perhaps spiritual sensibilities, translating it into paint is another matter.

It helps to have an organized approach, especially if you are an inexperienced painter, because translating what you see into an expression of how you feel, and then translating your response into a painting can be tricky. It's of little virtue painting a scene that doesn't really fire you with inspiration and anticipation, and it will almost certainly end in failure and disappointment. Many experienced painters will admit to producing paintings not only *en plein air*, but also in the studio that fall some way short of expectation. There is nothing quite so bad as beginning a painting with excited enthusiasm, only to experience it slowly deteriorating into one that has become irretrievable. Conversely, there is nothing to beat the exhilaration felt when a painting that you thought was all but lost is miraculously transformed into a success with the addition of a few brushstrokes here and there.

We all experience failures from time to time, but these should all be looked upon as part of the learning process. This doesn't necessarily mean we won't make the same mistakes again, but at least we will know why the painting has failed.

Unless you are an experienced painter, it pays not to be too ambitious when painting outside, so size is something to be considered at the outset. A size of perhaps 10" × 12", or 10" × 14", would be quite manageable. It takes a great deal of experience to create a successful painting *en plein air*, so attempting one on a larger scale is asking for trouble, unless you intend on returning to the scene at the same time of day, and during similar lighting conditions over an extended period. Doing this, though, can mean diminishing the effect of *plein-air*'s immediacy. Painting *alla prima* (all at once) fires a painting with the vigour and energy often absent from one that has been laboured over.

A few compositional sketches will be invaluable in helping you decide on what you intend including and what you decide to leave out. If you have concerns about being able to complete your painting before the light changes, you can

The Ridgeway Near Compton, Kevin Scully. (12" × 10", oil on board)
This was painted wet-in-wet over a pale Raw Umber ground in about forty minutes. In truth there is very little content in this painting, but an attempt has been made to make something of what is a very plain composition. The track running through the centre of the composition leads the eye into the landscape and around a bend. The directional brushstrokes either side of this strengthen the sense of travel, with each going in opposite directions to describe the grassy banks. The treatment of the clouds alludes to a bright and breezy day.

Blackthorn Blossom (early stage, detail), Roy Connelly. (16" × 20", oil on stretched canvas)
This shows a section of the artist's painting at an early stage of its development, and at this point he has been working for about twenty-five minutes. The canvas has been toned with a fairly neutral earth colour, which has provided the ground for the initial blocking-in. The shapes of the larger masses representing the sky, foliage and grass have been painted simply with their general local colours, and these will later be painted into, adding further detail as the painting progresses. The tonal value of the sky has been set as the key for the rest of the painting, and as he is pleased with the way it is developing, he is intent on disturbing it as little as possible.

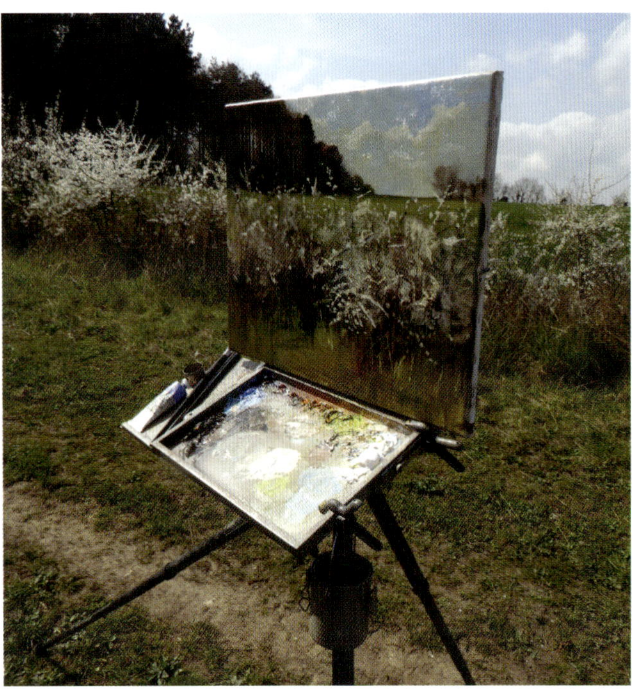

Blackthorn Blossom (work in progress), Roy Connelly. (16" × 20", oil on stretched canvas)
A photo taken approximately ninety minutes after the previous one, so roughly two hours after the painting was started. It is nearing completion at this stage, with just a few final details to be added. Apart from some areas in the sky, the darker passages in the picture were painted in fairly thin washes, and as these started to dry, Roy Connelly was able to place the lighter colours on top in thicker paint towards the end of the session. It is evident from this photo that he has matched the mood of the scene perfectly, with careful and accurate colour matching.

always spend some time drawing out your composition one day, and returning on another day at that time which you feel provides the most interesting lighting and atmospheric conditions, to complete the painting. Having your scene already drawn out shouldn't in any way detract from the vitality you inject into the painting. With experience you will find that you spend less and less time on the initial drawing out on your canvas, particularly if you're not including any buildings that might require some carefully studied perspective.

Travelling Light

As a novice *plein-air* painter, one of the difficulties you may experience is having everything you need about you in an organized manner, so that you can expend your mental and artistic energy on the actual painting rather than wondering where you've put the white spirit, or your rag, or how to stop the easel wobbling about. Most of these potential distractions and irritants can be minimized by forward planning. Painting outside requires a certain amount of efficiency, which means that if you have brought along the entire contents of your home studio with you, you'll be spending an inordinate amount of time looking for things. There's no point bringing twenty brushes with you when three or four will suffice, and you probably won't need five tubes of different red paints when the scene you're painting is predominantly blue, green and yellow.

Two of the heaviest items in your kit are likely to be your easel and your paints, so take a lightweight easel, and partly used tubes of paint, which will cut down on the load you have to carry. As with your home studio, there are items that you cannot do without, but their size and quantity can be minimized. If you plan on painting on a fairly small scale, you may opt for a pochade box, in which you can store all of your paints, brushes, palette, painting boards and most of your other equipment. Some items will need to be carried separately though, and for these you will need a bag of some sorts. You may be able to paint with a pochade box balanced on your lap, but if you like to stand whilst painting, this can be attached to a lightweight but sturdy camera tripod with a quick-release attachment. If you are using a panel holder, you will need to carry your painting boards, paints and brushes in a bag.

Full-size French easels, although sturdy and commodious, can be heavy to carry, so a half-size version is probably a better bet if you have to walk any distance. In this, you will be able to carry most of the equipment you're going to need.

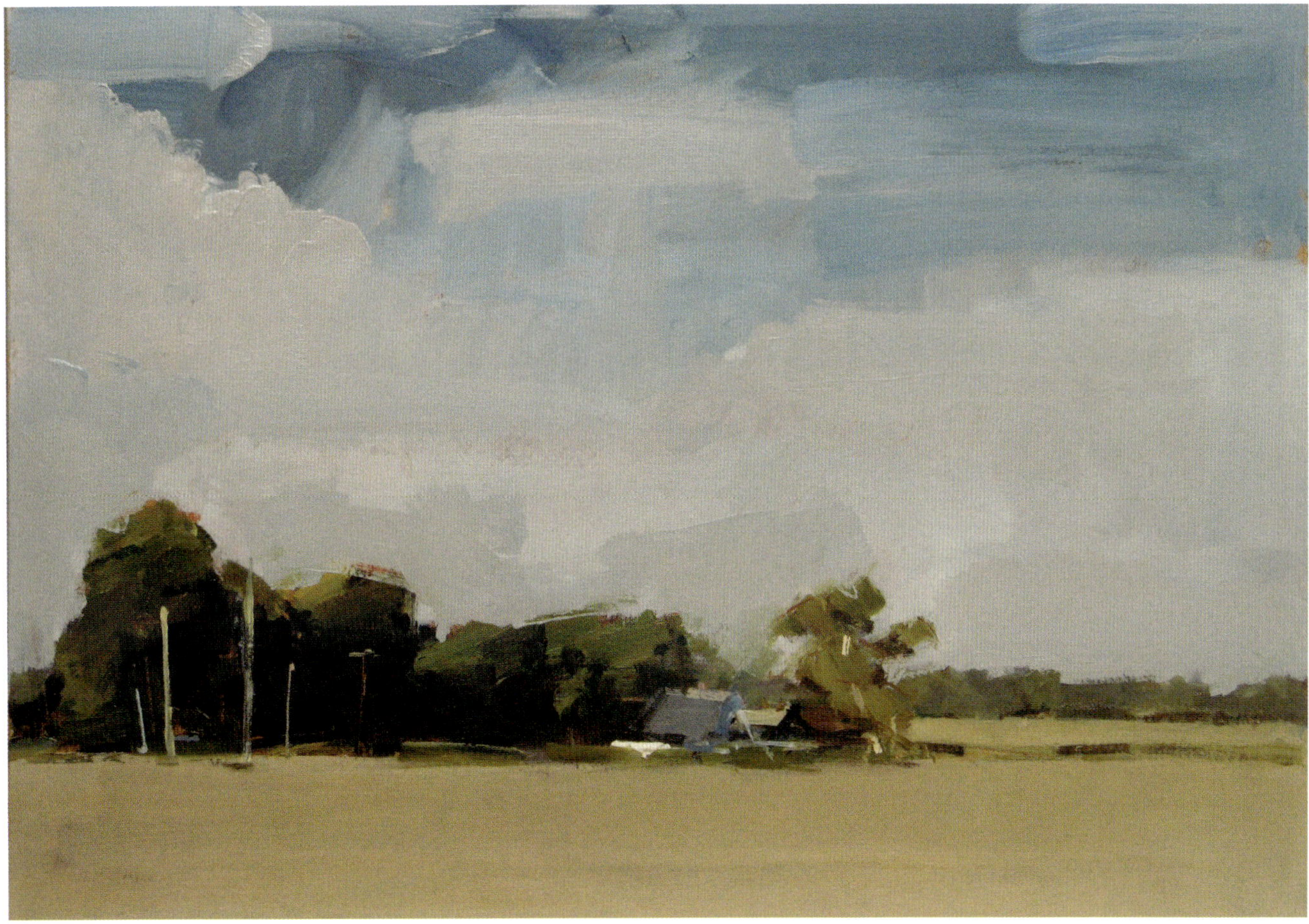

Salters Heath Road, Hampshire, Stephen Palmer. (17" × 24", oil on canvas) A major part of the challenge with this composition was pitching the weight and colour of the field in the foreground against the lower half of the sky, so that the line of trees and buildings sat in a convincing manner 'spatially' between the two. Large brushes and flat colours helped Stephen to quickly work and rework the painting, and prevented him from getting caught up in too much detail. Finer brushes were used to indicate the telegraph poles and farm buildings, the latter borrowing some of the blue from the sky in order to connect the two chromatically. This has also created a focal point in the painting. The canvas had first been prepared with a dark Sienna ground, adding depth and unifying the whole image.

Other essentials are thinners for washing out your brushes, or water if you're using acrylics, rags or kitchen towel, painting medium and container, and a plastic bag for keeping all of your rubbish in. These are the essentials that you will need to operate effectively, but you may want to include some of the other items listed in more detail in the previous chapter.

You should also be prepared for both cold and hot weather, and dress accordingly. Although you don't want to be burdened down with the contents of your wardrobe, you have to be sensible about protection from the elements, which will mean choosing appropriate clothing. If necessary, include insect repellent, sun cream, a sun hat, and certainly a basic first-aid kit, some drinking water and your mobile phone.

It's not compulsory to paint at 100 miles an hour, even if you have been painting for years, so work at your own pace, and if your painting remains unfinished for whatever reason, you will have begun to experience painting *en plein air* in a considered and useful way. Speed and quantity are

PAINTING IN THE SUN

Limit yourself to no more than a couple of hours' painting. It's unlikely that you will be working under a constant light source for any longer than this, particularly if the sun is shining. There is always a danger that you'll be forever chasing shadows and highlights. It's better to leave a painting unresolved rather than forever altering it as the light changes. Nothing looks worse than inconsistently placed shadows, where in one part of the painting, the shadows are to the right of an object, and in another part, they are on the left.

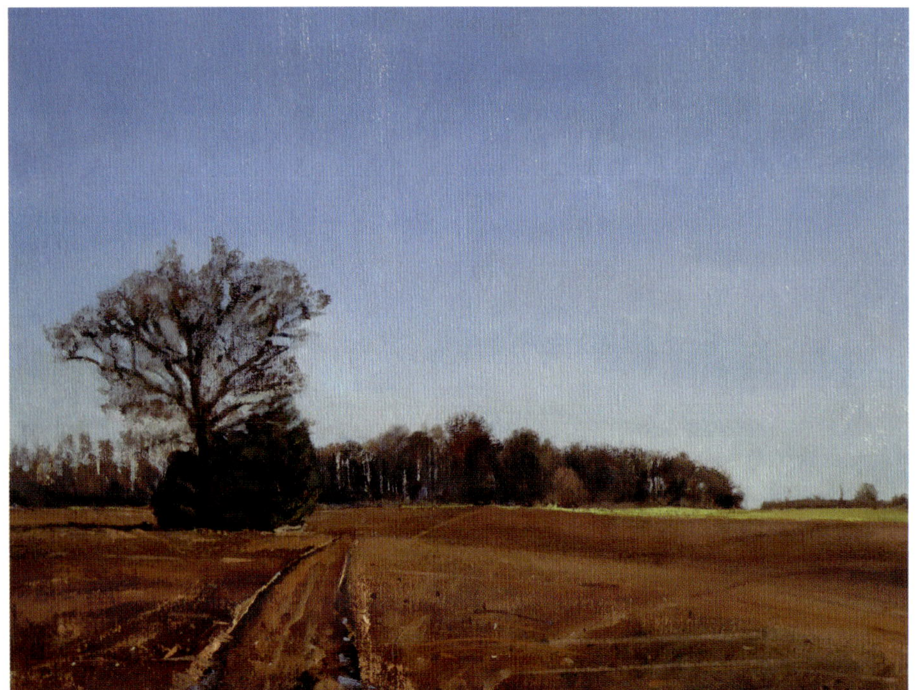

Sussex Farmland in Winter, Roy Connelly. (20" × 24", oil on stretched linen canvas) There was a gap of three years between starting and finishing this painting. When the artist is working on larger paintings he likes to have a few days for the paint to dry between sessions, but sometimes the weather conditions and landscape change so dramatically that he'll put a painting aside and come back to it a year later. In this case it was actually three years before he returned to it, by which time there was a crop growing in the field that had previously been bare. He decided not to change the foreground, and just worked on the sky and trees. The entire sky was repainted in one go in order to capture the subtle gradation of colour and tone.

not important, but spending too much time on a painting can lead to problems and frustrations.

Your *plein-air* paintings may be finished works in their own right, or they may be intended merely as reference material for a larger studio picture, but successful or otherwise, producing them will have been a vital tool in your armoury, to be used in helping you understand the complexities and subtleties of nature. Without ever having painted outside, landscape paintings will never possess the same integrity as those where the artist has confronted nature, and taken it on at first hand.

In a couple of hours you are not going to be able to include every leaf on the tree, or every blade of grass, and nor should you be trying to. What you should be striving for is capturing the essence of the scene before you. This may mean painting shapes rather than precise detail, and blocks of colour rather than many individual colours. Directional brushstrokes can imply movement in clouds or trees, and soft blending can suggest mood and atmosphere. It's a learning process of devising ways in which sensations and emotions can be expressed in a kind of shorthand, which often tells a story in a far more convincing way than merely just copying what you see.

If you are new to painting landscapes in the raw, dramatic sunrises and sunsets might have you dashing out with your paints and brushes, but you will find that it's a lot more difficult to capture the spirit of dawn and dusk than you think, and fraught with potential disaster. The speed at which the light and colours change at these times of the day can be quite daunting for the novice painter, so it would be better to choose an alternative time of the day. The light is fairly constant for a reasonable length of time when the sun is at its highest, and although the scene may not be that exciting, it will give you a chance to paint without having to worry too much about moving shadows. Even better still would be to choose a day when there is no sun at all, and although the day may be without any drama, it doesn't mean that you can't paint an interesting picture.

PACK A *PLEIN-AIR* KIT

To take full advantage of the moments when inspiration strikes, it's a good idea to have a *plein-air* kit ready and waiting in quiet anticipation. Have some small painting boards or canvases readily prepared and toned. Your kit may consist of half-full or small tubes of paint, some special cut-down brushes, some small, screw-top containers for liquids, and all of the previously mentioned essentials.

FORAYS INTO THE LANDSCAPE

If you haven't already decided on your choice of subject matter, you will have to seek it out. Nature isn't perfect, and she doesn't always present herself in naturally

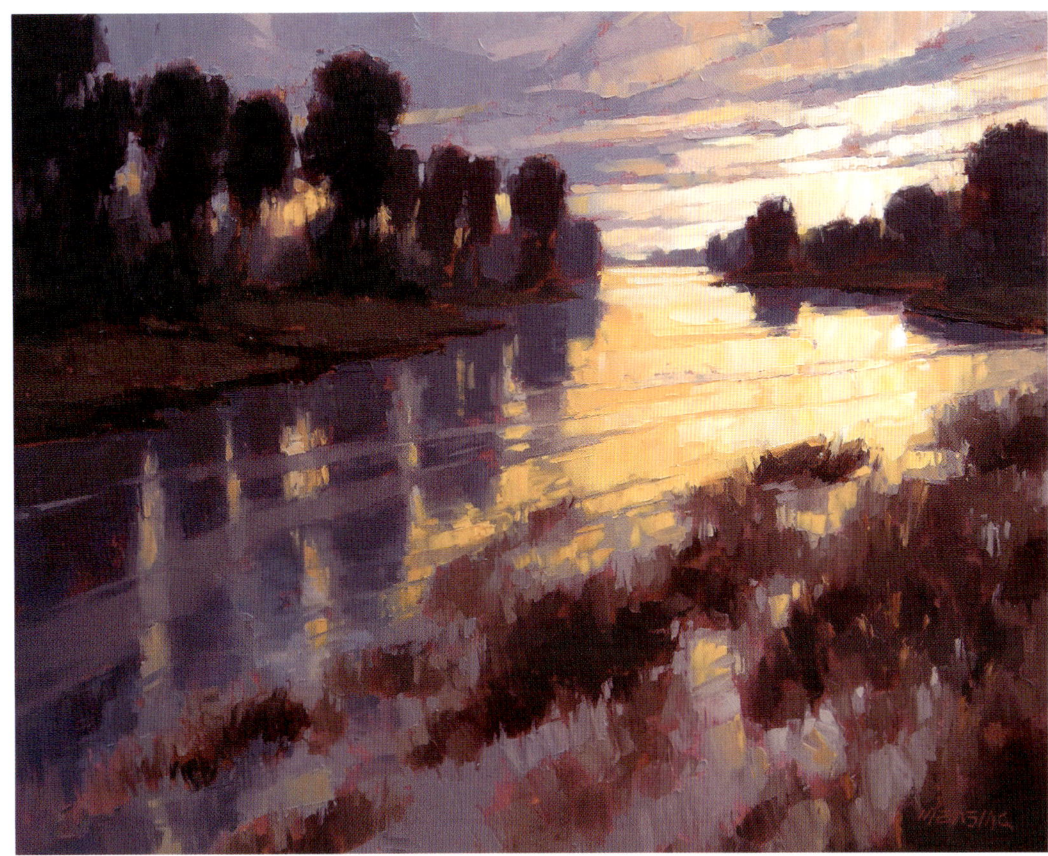

Longing, David Mensing. (24" × 30", oil on canvas) The artist was inspired by the richness and warmth of the evening light reflected on the water. The distant trees and the reeds in the foreground were kept in dark and fairly neutral tones to emphasize the strength of the setting sun. The intense red underpainting is allowed to show through in places, where it hints at reflected highlights in the reeds and at the edges of the trees. This also helps to create a halo of light, which serves as a transition between the dark silhouettes and the bright sky. The combination of the complementaries violet and yellow has been used to generate an image of spectacular intensity.

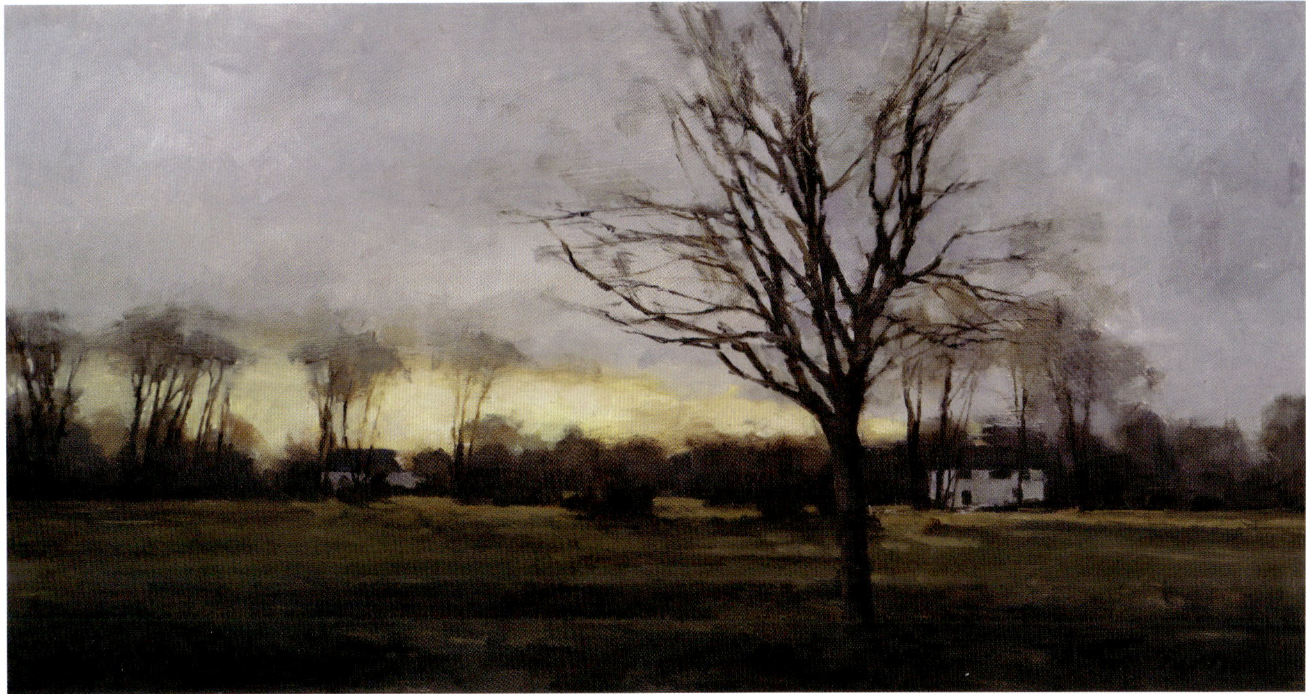

Dusk on the Common, Deborah Tilby. (12" × 24", oil on board) Deborah Tilby produced a watercolour of this subject some time ago when she lived in England, and felt it would make a good subject for an oil painting. The challenge was to get the greens and browns dark enough whilst still keeping the colour mixes clean and fresh. As common land is usually unmanicured, and left in a natural state, she wanted to create this impression by not overworking the painting, or getting into too much detail. The complementary colours of violet and yellow in the sky have been mixed together to produce a lovely, neutral tone, which contrasts perfectly with the orange of the setting sun along the horizon. The strong verticals of the trees break up the elongated double square format of the composition.

painting-friendly ways, and whilst there are wonderful scenes to be stumbled upon and just itching to be painted, there are others that pose pitfalls and problems. You have to train yourself to see with new eyes and look for certain criteria that are likely to delight those viewing your paintings without them fully understanding why they are so appealing.

The perfect scene will contain many specific and essential ingredients that together delight the eye, both consciously and subconsciously.

Colour

The way in which we perceive colour is probably one of our most fundamental visual instincts. It may be the arrangement of subtle, harmonious colours that instil in us a sense of tranquillity and inner peace, or it may be the visual tension created by the juxtaposition of contrasting colours that engage our eye in a totally different way. We can categorize colour in terms of being either warm or cool in temperature, and a combination of both warm and cool passages, and how they relate to each other can imply volume and space. Colour can be exaggerated or subdued for visual effect, and the choice of a dominant colour in a painting can hint at various sensations. Green suggests harmony and calmness, whilst red suggests excitement and strength. Yellow indicates sunshine and light, and white clarity and cleanliness, whereas black, together with almost any of the darker colours introduces an element of mystery and the unknown.

Tone

The variation in the tonal value of objects, regardless of colour, describes their form, and assists us in determining both space and distance. It informs us as to whether or not something is flat or curved, textured or smooth. When reduced down to their most basic form, tones create both patterns and shape, and help us in distinguishing one object from another. Tonal contrast is essential in creating a balanced composition, regardless of whether this contrast is dramatic or subtle. A painting can contain a myriad of exciting colours, but unless there is a balance of tone, it will generally fall flat in terms of visual interest.

Light is a thing that cannot be reproduced, but must be represented by something else – by colour.

PAUL CEZANNE

Light

Lighting conditions will affect the mood of your paintings in many different ways. Deep shadows will suggest a bright sunny day, and this sensation can be suggested by intensifying the contrast between the warm, bright highlights and the cool, deep shadows. Consider also the light source, for if the sun is low and the shadows are long, this could indicate either dawn or dusk, as the lighting conditions can sometimes produce similar impressions. If you wish to convey a tranquil scene, you may decide upon a softer, diffused light, which means that there will be less contrast between the highlights and shadows, and indeed there may be no shadows at all. A scene that is backlit will appear more dramatic than one lit from the front, as the light will create a combination of diffused and hard edges, and possibly strong directional shadows. Some objects will be devoid of detail and be seen simply in silhouette. A scene lit from the front will have less variation in tone, and there will be little to suggest the form of individual elements.

Scale

Elements of varying sizes within the landscape will greatly enhance visual appeal, and where they overlap their relative sizes to each other will also give a clue as to their positions in space.

Shape

Shapes themselves, and particularly the outline they form, regardless of any variation in tone, should be sought out and used as strong compositional elements. They perform many functions, and the way in which they interact with and overlap each other determines the spaces that objects inhabit, and indicates the distances between different elements. Added interest is created by the interaction between positive and negative shapes, where a light shape is silhouetted against a dark shape and vice versa.

Line

Our eyes can't take in everything we look at all at once, so by seeking out directional lines in a scene, either in the form of a path, the course of a river, a line of trees or fence posts that coax the eye into a particular direction, we are able to dictate where we want the focal point to be in our paintings. Contrasting vertical lines with horizontal ones can create interesting semi-abstract or negative shapes by dividing the image up into zones.

Thistle Creek, Douglas Fryer. (28" × 28", oil on panel)
This painting describes perfectly not only the beauty of the land, but also the harsh and difficult conditions of farming and ranching in the Rocky Mountains of Central Utah. The location is Birdseye, a few miles south of the ghost town of Thistle, which was destroyed in a landslide in 1983. There is a strong, graphic harshness to the composition, where low diagonals give way to softer horizontals and curves higher up in the painting. At first glance the composition is almost black and white, and it is only on closer inspection that the viewer realizes the more inviting play of the primaries of red and blue, and a soft warm white. With all of his paintings, the artist uses a combination of tools: painting knives, 4" putty knife, and a variety of bristle and nylon brushes. A final glaze then unifies the colour and enriches the surface texture.

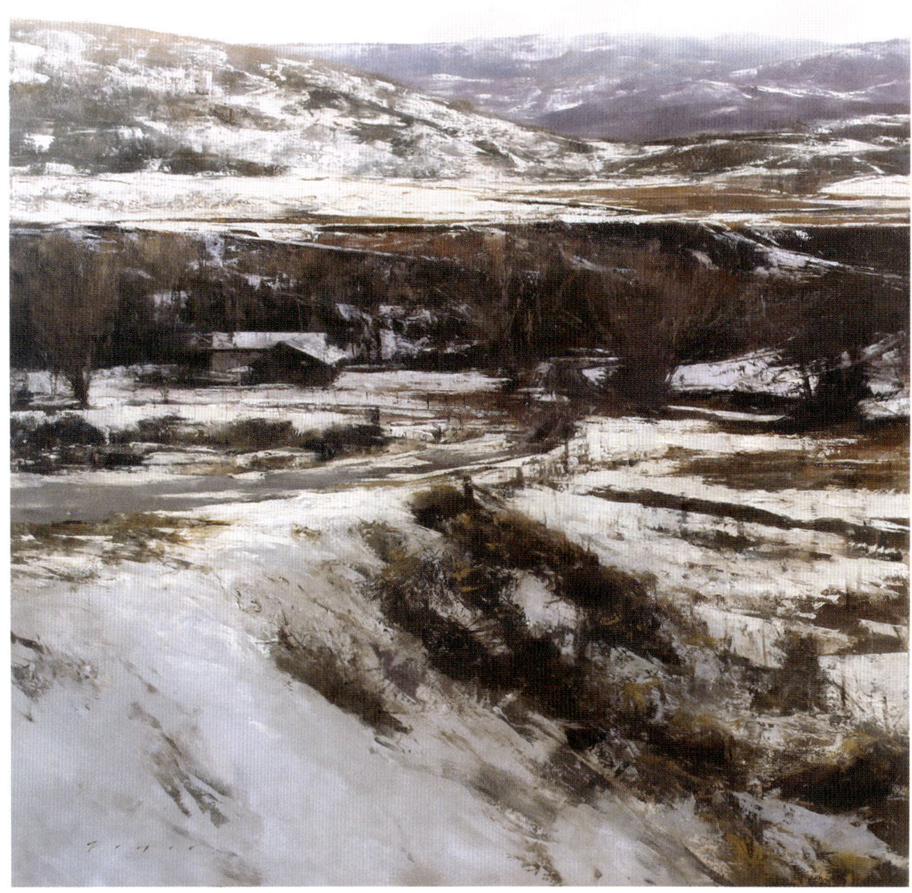

The Thames at Streatley, Kevin Scully. (20" × 22", oil on board)
Combining water and fog guarantees a winning recipe for an evocative and atmospheric painting. In this autumnal river scene, the decorative boat provides the perfect foil to the soft and blurred surroundings created by the fog.

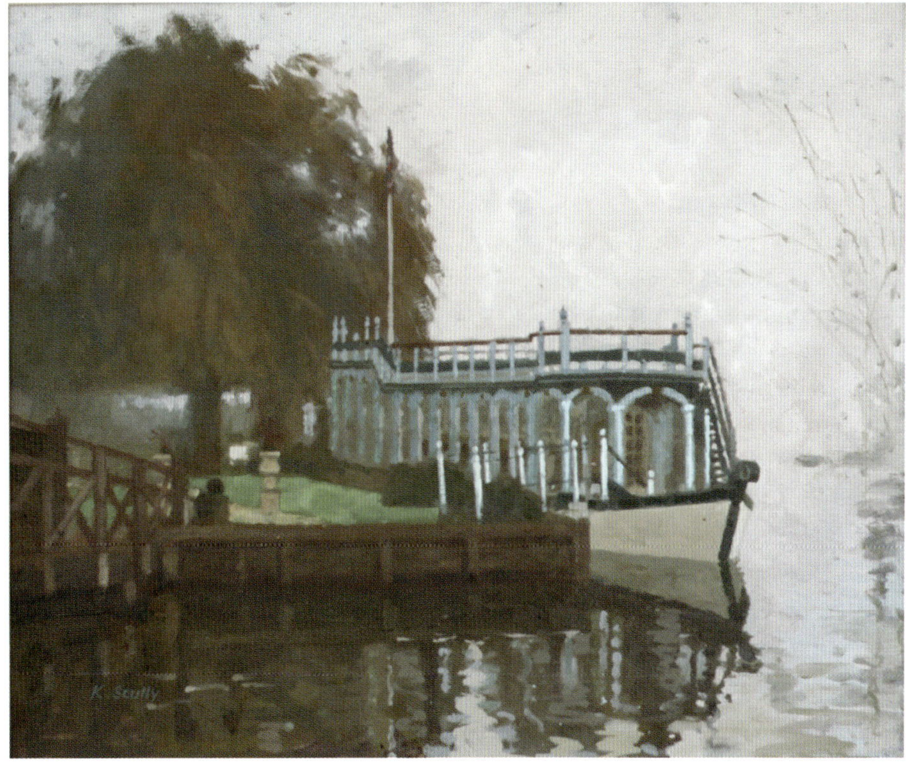

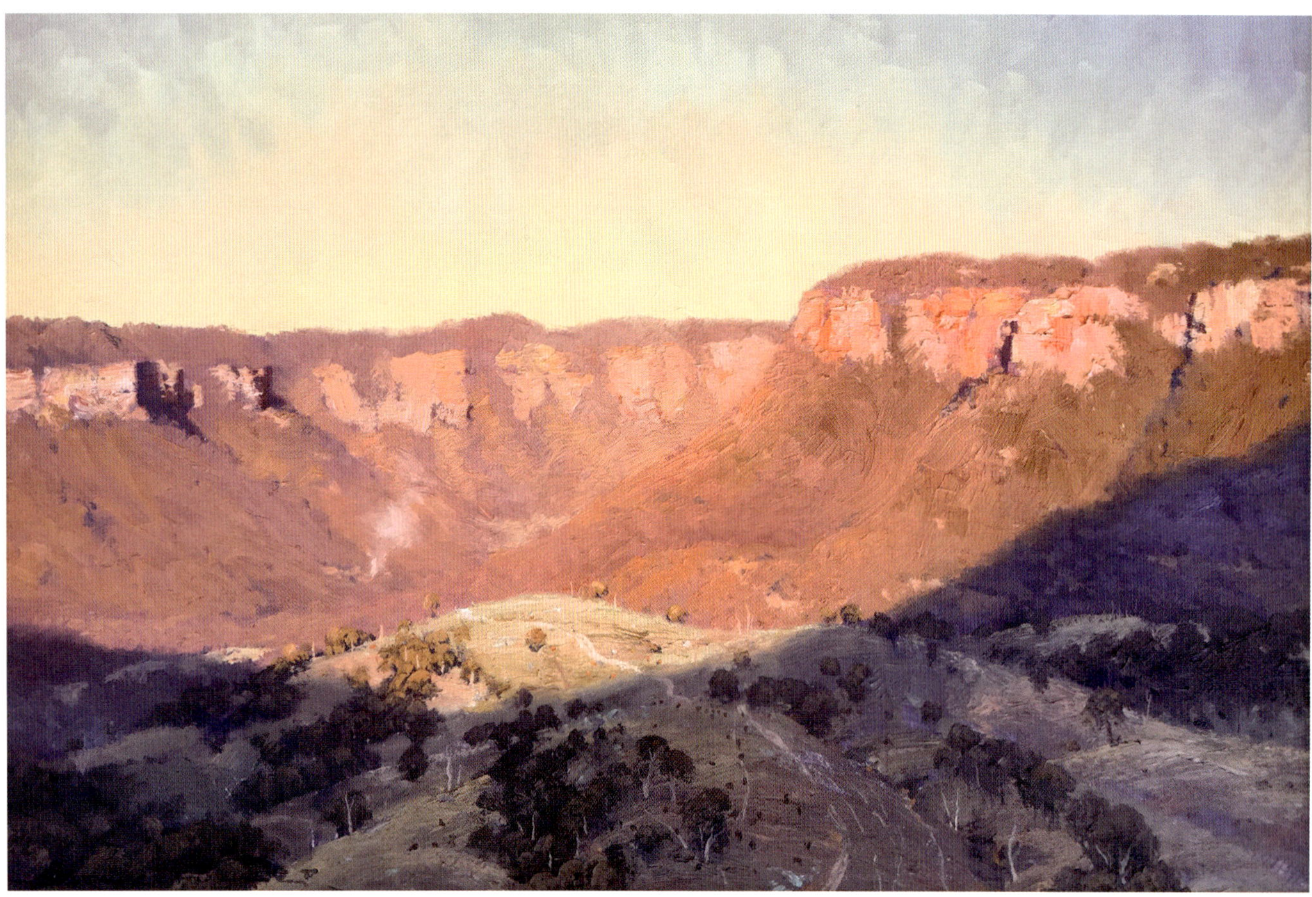

Cliffs Ablaze, Blackheath, Warwick Fuller. (24" × 36", oil on canvas, stretched onto board)
It can be argued that two of the best times of day for painting are at dawn and sunset, although the rapidly changing lighting conditions mean that it's very difficult to produce a painting quickly enough before all of the drama disappears. The artist has produced this studio painting that captures the blazing, last few minutes before sunset, from a sketch made on the spot, which contained all of the relevant information needed to create an accurate rendition of that sensation which first inspired him. The cool, violet shadow creeping across the landscape contrasts beautifully with the rich, warm colours of the rock, still bathed in intense sunlight.

Repetition

Look for repetition in a landscape, which can present itself in a variety of ways including patches of similar or the same colour in a few places throughout the composition. A repetition of shapes or angles can be used to visually connect different elements, such as the shape of a cloud and silhouette of a tree.

Pattern

Often overlooked are the interesting patterns created by shadows on the ground or on buildings. These can sometimes be used in forming the main focus of a painting, leaving other more obvious elements as subordinate. This also applies to reflections in water, where the patterns created by gentle ripples result in broken fragments of colour often far more exciting than the objects being reflected.

Patterns can also be detected in buildings when they are included in a natural landscape. Consider also the symmetrical or asymmetrical arrangement of windows and doors and the way that a building's façade is sometimes bisected by downpipes, both vertical and horizontal. A line of individual or terraced buildings where each has been painted in a different shade of pastel colours will form a pleasing pattern and variety of shape. Also hunt for the patterns created by the negative shapes made by gaps in the foliage of trees (sky holes).

Variety

Look also for variation in a scene. Combine different shapes, sizes and textures by overlapping different elements to generate variety and interest. Mix manmade components with natural ones, roads and hills, barns and crops, bridges

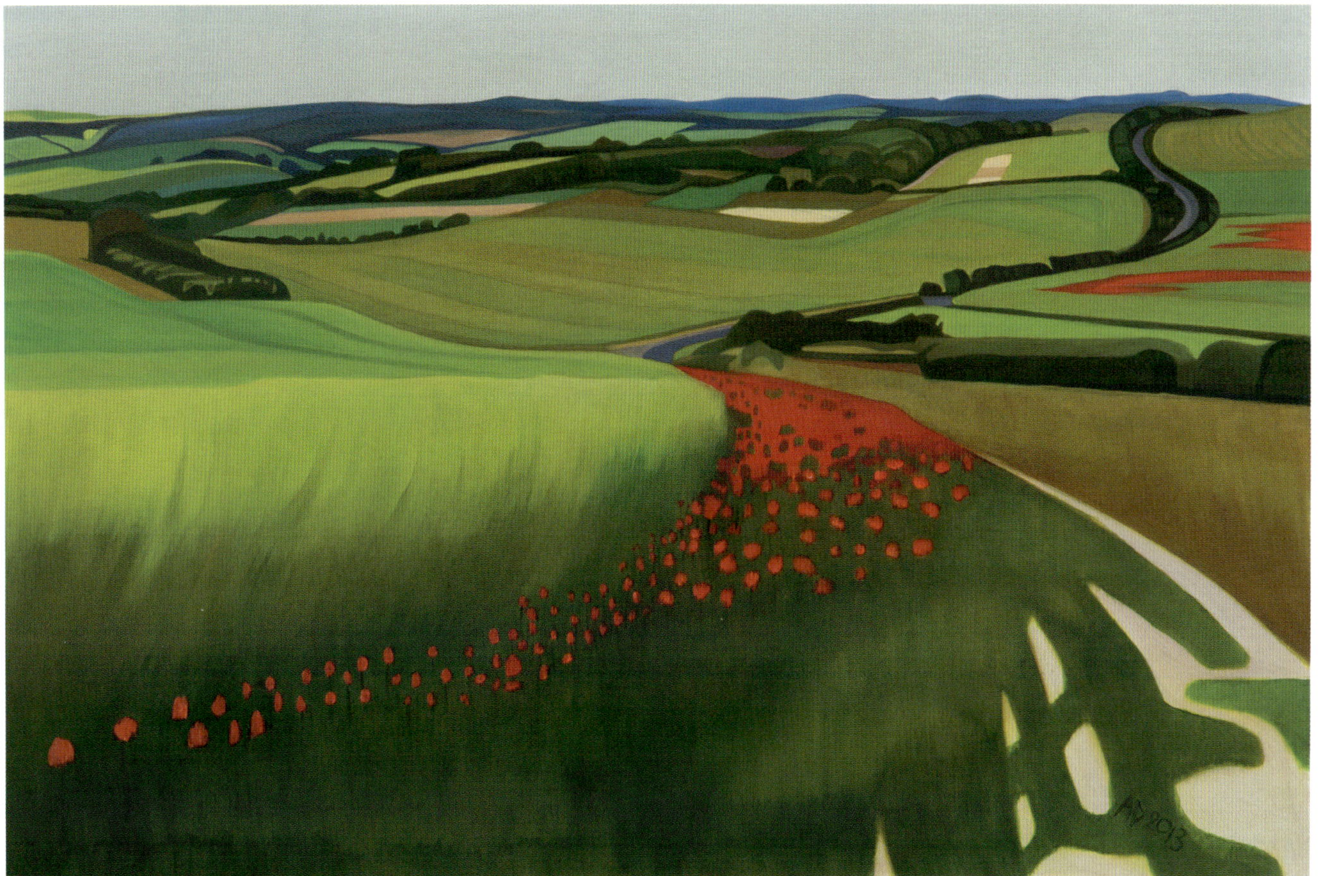

Kingstanding Hill, Anna Dillon. (27" × 32", oil on board)
A field of poppies follows the edge of this busy road in South Oxfordshire. Kingstanding Hill, near the artist's home, lies at the intersection of the Roman Road, a spur of the ancient Ridgeway, a chalk escarpment that runs along the Berkshire Downs, and Britain's oldest road. The artist has a deep awareness of the history of this location, and its association with King Aethelred and his brother Alfred in their campaign against the invading Vikings in the ninth century. In the treatment of this landscape there is a sense of this connection with its history, and the ancestors who once walked these roads. The vivid, red poppies among the gently rolling hills hint at the events that would have taken place many centuries ago.

and rivers, and windmills and clouds. Also think about a change in direction, so instead of a river meandering from the bottom of your composition straight up to the horizon line, let it swerve when it gets there, and run along the horizon for a while before disappearing into the distance. Place a vertical pole in front of the curved contours of a line of trees, and in front of the pole plant a low shrub or hedge.

Contrast

A certain dynamic occurs when a very strong colour is placed next to a subdued one, or a very dark tone in front of a light one. Rough, textured paint to indicate an old corrugated iron roof will contrast well with a smooth, flatly painted sky. Think about the way that certain brushstrokes can be used to render a field of barley, whilst alternative marks may be required to indicate the timber material of a barn.

Focal Point

Although it can be noted from several of the successful paintings featured in this book that it isn't necessarily a hanging offence if you neglect to include a focal point in your painting, it certainly helps to have one. The inclusion of a human figure or figures in a landscape is a matter of personal preference, but it is one way of introducing a focal point to the composition. Other alternatives are probably the more obvious choices, such as a track, a farm building, or perhaps a church spire in the distance.

Subject Matter

When considering the term 'landscape', what automatically comes to mind is the countryside with its fields, hills, rivers and trees, but this is only half of the story. Excluding the more remote parts of our world, man has left his imprint

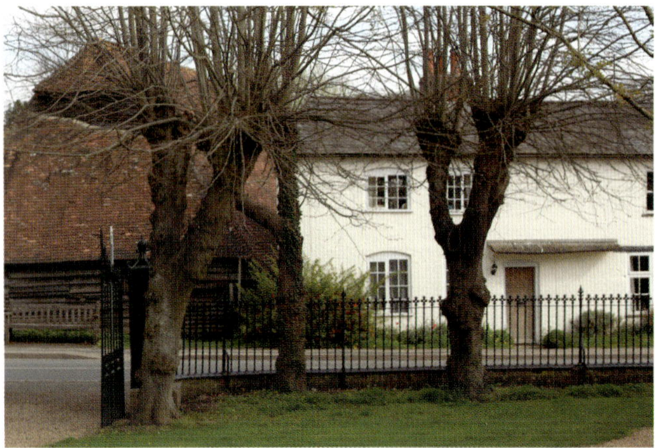

In this photograph taken as reference for a possible future painting, a few things exist that would cause problems were it to be used as it is in a painting. These weren't noticed when the photograph was taken, and were only spotted when reviewed later on. The central tree sits uncomfortably at the point where the rendered house meets the barn with the clay-tiled roof, and the limb extending to the left of this same tree stops too abruptly at the tree next to it. The tree to the right frames one of the upstairs windows, drawing far too much attention to it. Another problem area is the path in the bottom right-hand corner taking your eye away from the image. Some branches in the top right-hand corner are distracting and would add nothing to the painting.

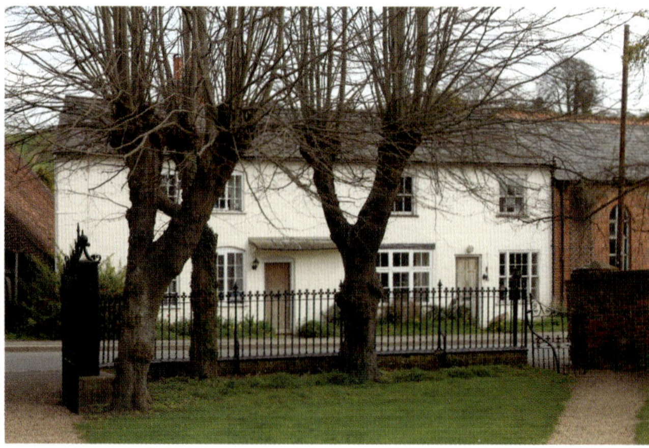

A photograph taken from a slightly different angle reveals a more acceptable viewpoint, but there are still areas for concern, particularly the two paths travelling in different directions. The limb on the central tree still looks uncomfortable, and the wrought iron pillar and position of the gate creates a distracting dark shape in the corner of the image. The photograph shows the house at a more oblique angle, which is preferable to showing it straight on.

on the land that most of us occupy, work in and visit. He has cultivated fields, planted woods and hedgerows, and constructed residential, industrial and agricultural buildings. In the natural landscape there are telephone posts and cables, electricity pylons, fences and roads. He has also built manmade lakes, canals, bridges, dams and reservoirs. It's perfectly possible to totally ignore these constructions, but often they provide an acceptable contrast to fields, trees, water and sky.

Take a sketchbook with you, and when you come across something that you sense has possibilities, settle down and give yourself some time for careful consideration by doing a few quick compositional sketches. It would be useful to have a viewfinder with you so that you can investigate the alternative viewpoints and formats. Just because you're going to be painting a landscape, it doesn't necessarily mean that your chosen subject has to be landscape in format. It might be more successful in a portrait arrangement, or even a square. Look also for the ingredients mentioned previously; colour, tone, form, shape and line, and think about how you can use one or more of these as the basis of your composition. The stronger these elements appear, and once you have incorporated them into your composition, the more likely you are to produce a winning painting. Don't just settle on the first thing that takes your fancy. Quite often, just by taking a few steps in one direction or the other, you will come across an even better viewpoint. And don't forget to turn around occasionally, as a scene you may have disregarded on passing may have possibilities when viewed from the opposite direction.

The drawings in your sketchbook can be as simple or as intricate as you like. In their simplest form they can assist you in dismissing certain compositions and formats, whereas a more complex study may help you get to grips with the finer details of your subject matter. With experience, this stage can be simplified further and even omitted altogether, as you become more confident in knowing exactly what you want to paint. Some artists, with years of practice and knowledge under their belts who will know what works, and what doesn't, will simply draw out their chosen composition directly onto the canvas, and dive headlong into the painting stage.

You can also use a camera to not only take a few photographs, but if it has a zoom lens, it can also be used in helping you compose your picture.

Although there is no reason why an empty field on the edge of a wood can't provide a good subject for a painting, you may feel distinctly uninspired by this, and prefer to look for something with more going on. It would probably benefit from the addition of some strong shadows and highlights, or a dramatic cloud formation to give the image more substance.

Unless you are especially skilled there are certain scenes that are fraught with possible pitfalls. A garden crammed with flowers in a kaleidoscope of colours and patterns is something most people would advise avoiding, because although you may find it beautiful to look at, it's very tricky to pull it off in a painting. This type of scene is often devoid of any depth and layers of perspective that give a painting a sense of three dimensions. Too many different colours in a painting, especially when they are scattered in small patches throughout, tend to confuse the eye, the result being that it doesn't know where to settle and consequently flits about all over the place looking for direction and a point of focus. This may be acceptable in a more stylized or decorative image, but in a landscape painting, less so. Lines of trees identical in size, colour and form, in particular when viewed from straight on tend to look boring, and cry out to be broken up and reorganized into a more random arrangement.

The Sketchbook

Regular use of a sketchbook undoubtedly improves your powers of observation and will certainly help you develop your drawing skills. It's as well to remember that a composition that has been well-drawn means you are halfway along the road to producing a successful painting. If you have created a picture displaying all of your painting skills and techniques, but you have failed to provide a sound underlying, structured drawing, where the composition and perspective are a little suspect, the painting is doomed to failure. Conversely, if you have spent some time in producing a sound, well-composed drawing, you have won half of the battle already.

With inexperienced painters there is sometimes a reluctance to execute some quick thumbnail sketches, but it is well worth the effort to do so. A few well-considered, small drawings will help you explore other compositional possibilities, and will also expose any potential problems. There's no need to be too precious about these thumbnails, as they are meant simply to be a way of expressing your thought process regarding composition. If you want to take things a stage further, you might want to produce a more detailed drawing, which will allow you to become fully absorbed in your chosen subject matter. This drawing can then be used as reference for the finished painting, should you decide to produce it in the studio rather than on the spot. You might want to add some colour to your drawing, which will be a more reliable aid than that recorded by a camera. Providing you have matched colours accurately, it makes an interesting exercise back at the studio to compare your colours with those of the image produced by the camera.

Some people like to make colour notes in the margin of their drawings, but I don't find this particularly helpful, especially if some time has elapsed between making the drawing and painting the final picture. I find that it takes about the same amount of time to mix the colours and add them in their relevant places to a drawing, than it does to describe them in written form. Perhaps it's more important to make written colour notes if you don't have any actual colour with you at the time.

There are a countless number of sketchbooks available, so choose one in a size that you are comfortable with. A good general size is A4 (297 × 210mm), or thereabouts. Anything larger may be a little unmanageable. If you just intend to use pencil, one made from good quality cartridge paper will be adequate, but if you want to use colour, one in a heavier weight of paper will prevent your drawings from buckling too much. You could go a step further and treat yourself to a watercolour sketchbook containing paper available in a variety of weights and textures from smooth to rough. If your drawings are going to be predominantly in pencil, with just a little colour added, you might go for a smoother, hot pressed (HP) paper, but if your drawings are full-blooded watercolours, then a Not or Rough paper will probably suit you better. It probably makes sense to buy a sketchbook that is landscape in format, as you will be working mainly to this shape.

Preparing for Changeable Weather

As we all know, the weather forecast isn't always infallible, so you have to be prepared for some variation. Wear suitable clothing and footwear, and ensure that it's as lightweight as possible and not too cumbersome.

Make sure you are comfortable, because if you're not you won't be able to concentrate sufficiently on your work. An inflatable cushion is a useful item to carry with you, for use not only with a seat or stool, but also if you need to park yourself on some uncomfortable rocks.

If it's going to be hot, be sure to take some suntan lotion and a hat, as it's all too easy to forget about the strength of the sun when you're engrossed in your work. There is nothing worse than the sudden realization that you are sunburnt. Sunglasses are a must if you are using white paper and particularly if you are stationed near water where the reflected light can be blinding, but they can also be a hindrance when trying to match colours.

If the weather becomes cooler, you'll need a warm jacket or top, and don't forget to take some food and drink with you if you're going to be out for some time.

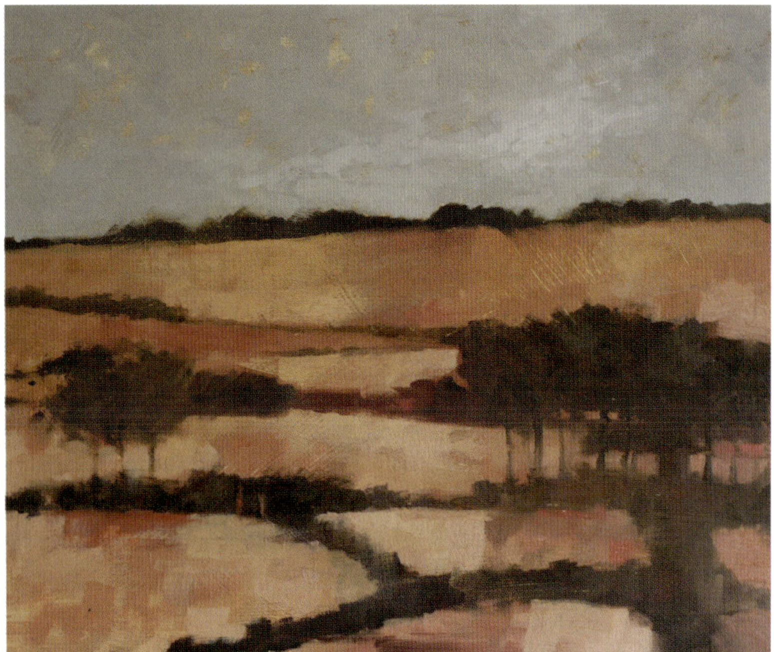

Ochre Fields, Kevin Scully. (10" × 12", oil on board)
A small study made in Spain, where fading daylight has cast a veil over the burnt landscape, diffusing both colours and detail. The neutral colour of the sky emphasizes the richness in the colour of the earth, which has acquired an almost abstract quality in the patchwork-patterned fields. Painted with just a few colours; Titanium White, Burnt Sienna, Raw Sienna, Perylene Green and Payne's Grey.

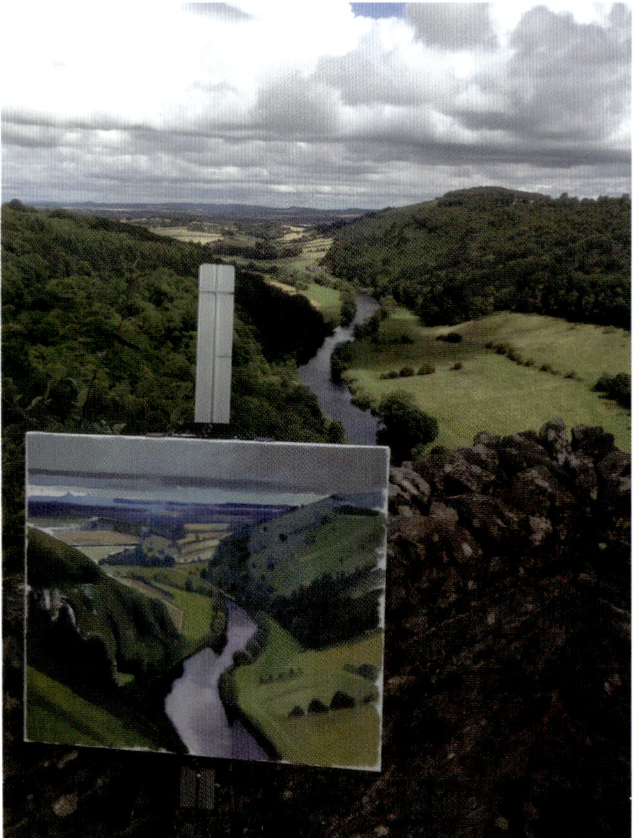

Painting at Symonds Yat Rock, Antony Bridge. (20" × 24", oil on canvas)
Painting from a vantage point high above the River Wye in a location designated as an 'Area of Outstanding Natural Beauty'. The view from this position more or less dictates the painting's composition, the focal point being the river winding through the valley into the distance. The only real decision to be made is whether to use a portrait or landscape format, as either would be effective. Positioning the river anywhere other than in the centre of the painting would create an unnecessary imbalance.

Choosing your Medium

Give careful consideration to your medium, not only if you intend completing finished paintings *en plein air*, but also if you are just venturing out seeking inspiration with a sketchbook. It makes sense to choose a medium you are at home with, rather than one that you have never used before. This book concentrates mainly on oils and acrylics but you may choose to do some colour sketching in watercolours or another medium, so go forth armed with whatever you feel happy with. Experimentation is best carried out in the studio, as painting outdoors throws up enough challenges without having to grapple with a medium with which you are unfamiliar.

Time Limitations

Time isn't really an issue if you are merely sketching, but if you are painting in oils or acrylics, it would be wise to set yourself a time limit, particularly if it's a sunny day with intermittent cloud cover. Shadows will appear and disappear with frustrating regularity, and you will be chasing them all day as they change position. Allow yourself perhaps one-and-a-half to two hours maximum on a painting no larger than 12" × 16". This should be sufficient time to allow you to put down the essence of the scene without getting into too much detail. A couple of hours around the middle of the day when the sun is at its highest will allow for a minimum amount of change in the position and shape of shadows, whilst either side of this time slot they can alter at an alarming rate.

If your plan is to complete a fairly detailed painting outdoors, you can always return on another day at the same time when the weather conditions are similar.

Transporting Finished Paintings

Especially if you're working in oils, there will be times when you need to transport wet paintings back home. Many people have come up with ingenious homemade ways of doing this, but there are products available on the market that will do the job perfectly. If you favour the cheaper, do-it-yourself approach, and you like to work on canvas, double-ended pushpins can be inserted into each corner of two canvases of the same size, which will keep them separate from each other without damaging either. You can then tuck them under your arm and carry them home. Another method is to place cut-down corks on each corner, and either tape or strap the two canvases together, or for a modest outlay you can buy special 'canvas carrier clips' which will hold them together without piercing or smudging the canvas.

If you prefer to work on painting boards, pochade boxes have special compartments for holding standard-size boards of modest proportions. For larger paintings, there are companies that make 'wet canvas boxes', some of which are able to carry items of different sizes by incorporating adjustable slots into the design.

THE OUTDOOR STUDIO

Palettes, easels, pochade boxes, and panel holders are described in detail in Chapter 2.

STUDIO PAINTING

Lighting

When it isn't convenient to paint on location, it is important to have a studio space of some sort where you can

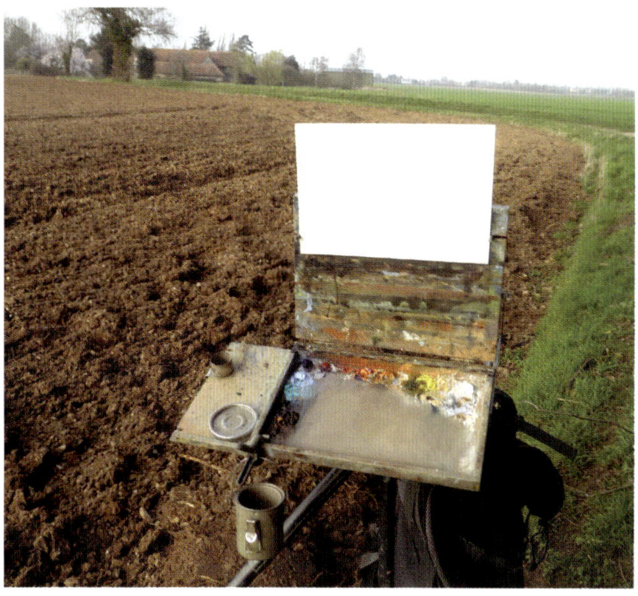

Moors Farm, Suffolk, Roy Connelly. (8" × 12", oil on board)
The artist's easel has been set up close to a hedge in an effort to keep out of the cold wind that was blowing across the field. The rucksack hanging from the tripod helps to keep it steady in the wind. The board has been attached to a panel holder, ready for painting. The first stage of this painting was to cover the white board with a wash of oil colour diluted with white spirit/painting medium. When wiped off with a rag, this dries almost immediately allowing him to get on with the business of painting as soon as possible.

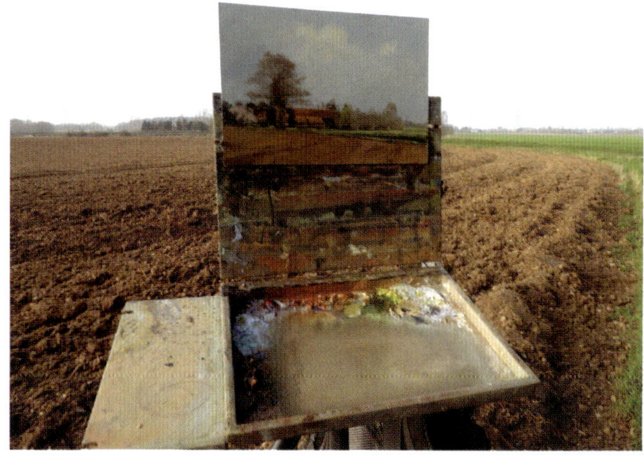

Moors Farm, Suffolk (later stage), Roy Connelly. (8" × 12", oil on board)
A photograph taken approximately forty five minutes after having started the painting. Despite the bright sky, it was a cold day with a brisk wind, so the artist was working fast. Although he felt that the shape of the tree in front of the farm buildings needed some attention, he was happy at this point with the way that he had captured the essence of a Suffolk farm on a bright afternoon in March.

WHAT TO PACK

As discussed in Chapter 2, there are some essential materials and pieces of equipment that you will need for painting outdoors, but for the sake of lightness and transportability these should be kept to a minimum. The items listed below can form your basic '*plein-air* painting kit'.

- Paint: Small, or half-used tubes, together with a larger tube of white
- Brushes: A small selection of hog and synthetic brushes in a variety of sizes
- Easel: Or pochade box and lightweight but sturdy tripod
- Palette: Wooden palette for oils or tear-off palette for acrylics
- Painting surfaces: Canvas, or painting boards
- Painting medium: Your chosen medium for mixing with either oils or acrylics
- Solvent: White spirit for oils, or water for acrylics, in a screw-top plastic container
- Clip-on palette cup: For oil painting medium
- Brush Washer: For oils, or jar for acrylics
- Palette knife: For mixing and removing colours on palette
- Rags: Or kitchen towel
- Straight edge
- Sketchbook and pencil
- Plastic bags: For discarded rags or kitchen towels
- Mini tool-kit or combination knife: Containing knife, screwdriver and pliers
- Camera: For taking reference photos
- Viewfinder: To help with composition and format
- Food and drink
- Mobile phone: For emergency use
- First-aid kit
- Carrying bag

This may seem to be a lot of equipment, but when packed up sensibly, it should be quite manageable. Depending upon weather conditions there are a few other items that you should also consider taking:

- Umbrella: For protection from sun or rain
- Plastic sheet: To keep your feet dry on wet ground
- Sun lotion
- Insect repellent
- Sunglasses
- Fold-up stool or chair
- Hat

work in comfort. Whether or not you already have a studio set up at home, there are a few things to consider when planning to make your space as user-friendly as possible.

It's always more pleasurable to paint in daylight, but very few rooms have ideally positioned windows for painting, and if it's sunny outside sunlight may streak across your painting at different times of the day creating unwanted shadows. Venetian blinds help to keep out unwanted light, and even curtains may help.

Adequate and balanced lighting is essential, and in most instances this means artificial lighting at certain times of the day. In an ideal world we would all have large, north-facing windows on one side of the room, and restrict our painting to daylight hours, but in reality this is usually an unattainable ideal.

What you don't want is any lighting that is going to cast shadows on your painting, so if possible use diffused 'daylight' bulbs to illuminate your workspace, as these are about the nearest thing you'll get to natural lighting.

Customizing Your Space

Paint the walls of your studio in white, or a pale neutral colour, as any stronger colour will be reflected onto your painting. It really is surprising what a difference this makes. You'll notice that you will rarely see an art gallery with pea green, mauve or orange walls.

Buy or construct some sort of racking that will allow you to store your paintings and unused canvases and boards safely.

Create a pleasant atmosphere in your studio, and surround yourself with personal belongings and those things that will inspire you, such as art books, magazines, cards, other artists' work, photographs, and your favourite music.

Have some of your *plein-air* paintings and sketches on display, perhaps on a shelf around the walls. They may remain untouched and gather dust for some time, but there will come a day when you will be fired up with enough inspiration to develop one of them into a studio painting

Having said all this, there are some brilliant artists who produce fantastic work from their kitchen table, or garden shed that they share with a lawnmower, hedge trimmer and bags of compost.

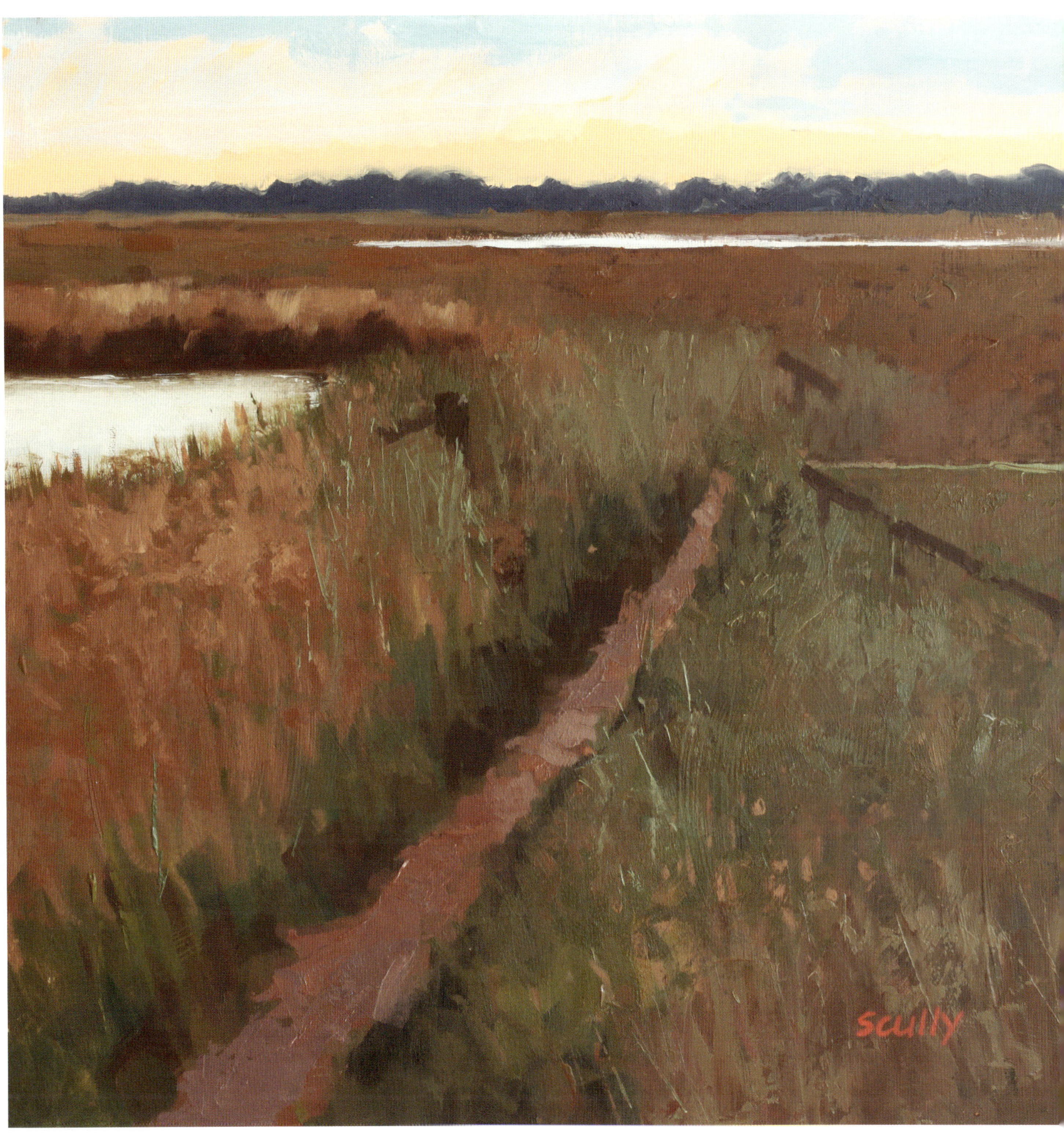

Reeds at Snape, Kevin Scully. (12" × 12", oil on board)
A slightly unusual composition in that there is no real focal point in evidence. The interest lies in the diagonal and horizontal directional lines, which break up the reed beds and grasses. The scene is bathed in the light of a sunset, with the Burnt Sienna base providing a rich, warm glow to the peaceful landscape. The colour scheme is analogous, knitted together with a range of neutrals, which ensures that no two colours are jarring, or seem out of place.

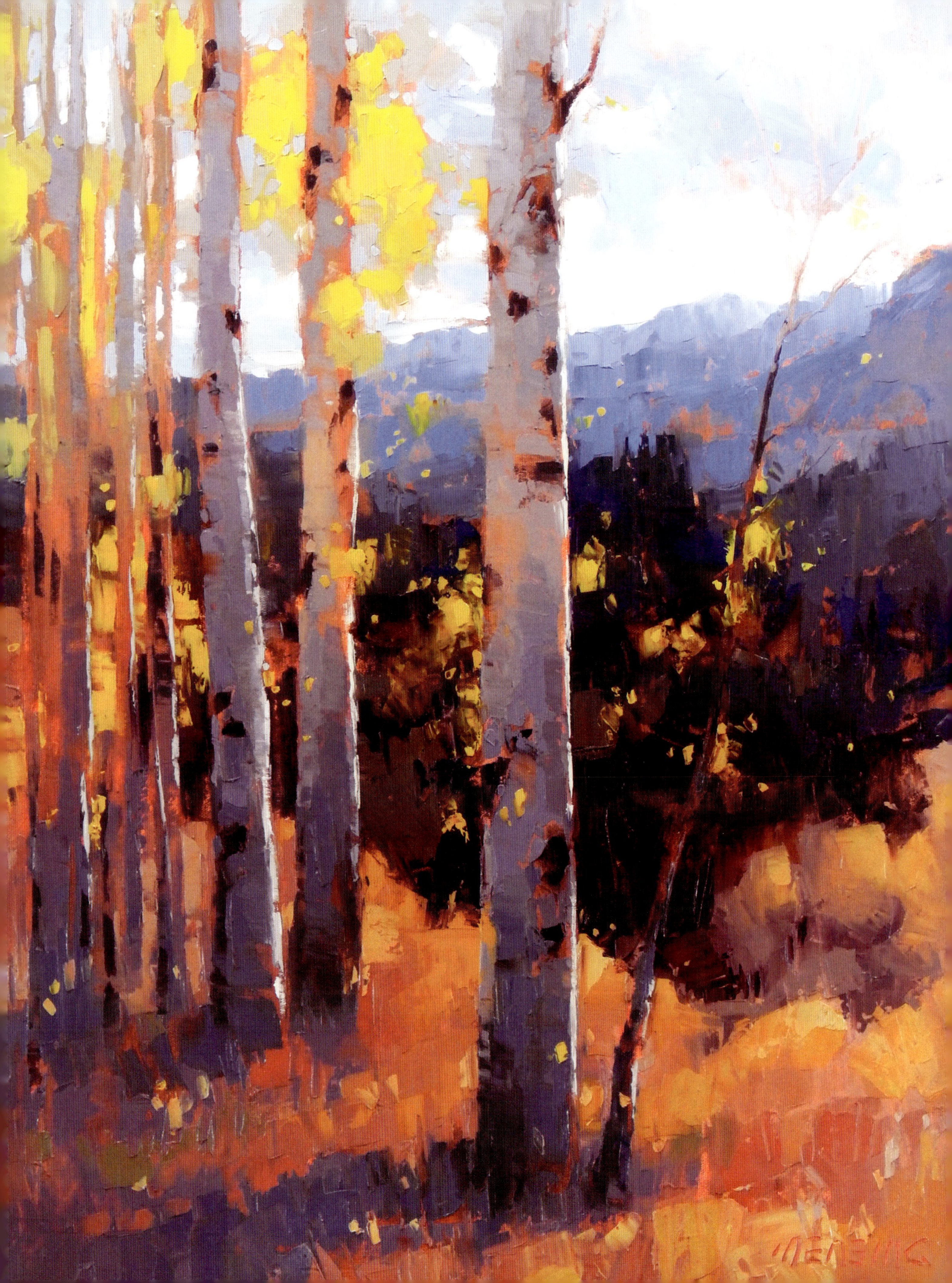

CHAPTER 4

Choosing your Subject Matter

All works, no matter what or by whom painted, are nothing but bagatelles and childish trifles... unless they are made and painted from life, and there can be nothing... better than to follow nature.

CARAVAGGIO

If you are fairly new to landscape painting you probably won't have yet trained your eye to determine what will and what will not make a successful painting. The landscape is vast and often daunting, and the more closely you observe it, the more you begin to realize that although it can be inspirational, it can also be flawed and imbalanced. A certain amount of rearranging, editing and deleting needs to be carried out.

Look for less complex subject matter, devoid of any complicated perspective issues and excessive detail. Even though a scene may look interesting at first glance, translating it into a three-dimensional representation can be fraught with complications and frustrations.

You will be naturally attracted to certain subject matter that other painters will shy away from, but if it appeals to you on a personal level, then this is a good starting point. If you elect to dismiss all forms of manmade structures and decide to focus solely on the natural landscape, you may have to work a little harder on producing a painting that encapsulates much of the criteria discussed in the previous chapter covering colour, tone, light, scale and so on. But that doesn't mean it can't be done. If you choose to go down this route, you should be looking out for overlapping layers of the landscape that will assist you in creating a sense of perspective, light and shade that describe the form of objects, and some kind of focal point that entices you into the painting. Alternatively, you might concentrate on evocative, atmospheric conditions, such as an early morning heat haze, an autumnal mist or a sunlit winter snow scene.

If you are lucky enough to have access to the countryside, a river, a lake or the sea, this is where you will be headed. Water, with its reflections, ripples, and glare will provide great contrast with the land, and a waterfall will add movement and energy. If you live in a town or city and don't have easy access to the great outside world, you will either have to travel, or turn your attention to whatever nature can be found locally in the form of parks, or other green spaces.

By including a certain amount of manmade elements into your compositions you will give yourself more scope for variation in shape, scale and strong directional edges. This could involve the inclusion of something as simple as a path or road that leads your eye into and around the picture. If you include buildings, make sure that your drawing skills are sufficiently adequate to establish realistic and convincing perspective otherwise any errors in that department will always be detected. If you are keen on painting buildings and are competent at perspective, there's no reason why you can't focus on urban landscapes, or even industrial ones.

Of the Thousands, David Mensing. (30" × 24", oil on canvas)
The aspen trees in the Wasatch Mountains in northern Utah have provided the inspirational material for this colourful painting. The air was crisp and cold on the day of David Mensing's trip there in late October. The scene is quintessentially autumnal, and the complementary axis of violet and yellow in this piece brings a calm excitement to the scene. The mountains in the background have been painted in a series of diminishing tonal values to create a sense of distance, and their blue colour is complemented by the strong orange in the foreground.

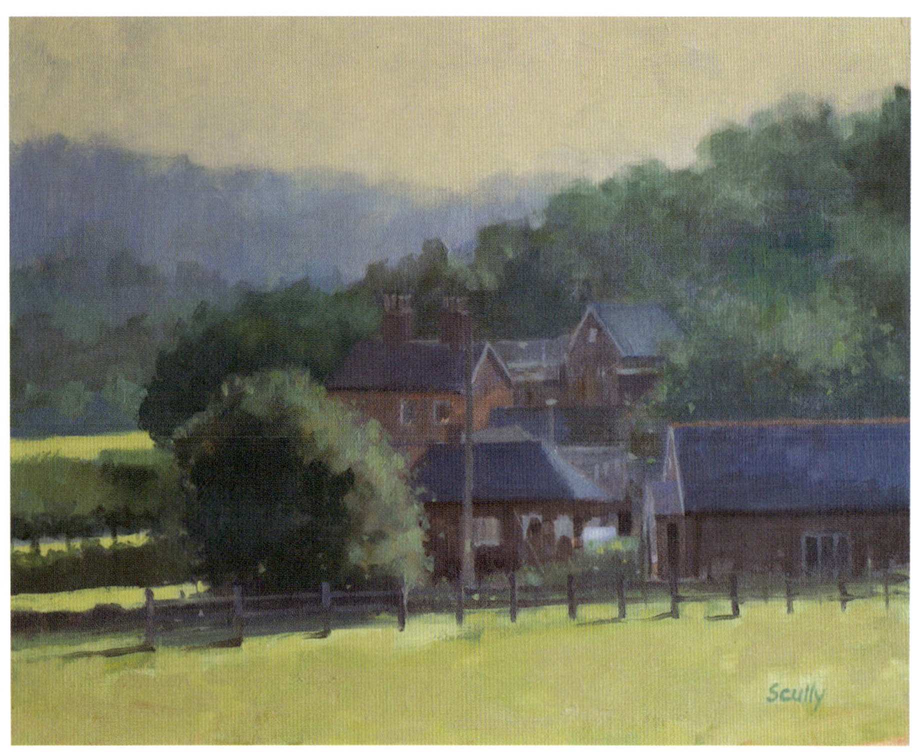

Streatley Hills House, Kevin Scully. (10" × 12", oil on board)
This early morning summer scene needed three visits at the same time, on equally sunny days. It's surprising how quickly the light changes at this early hour, and because the painting included several buildings, it was impossible to capture the whole scene in one session, even in such a small painting. The first trip was spent making a careful drawing, which was then transferred onto a board back at the studio. This was then followed by two painting sessions *en plein air*. The shiny slate roofs actually appeared to be almost white where the sun struck them, but because this looked wrong in the painting, the colour was toned down considerably.

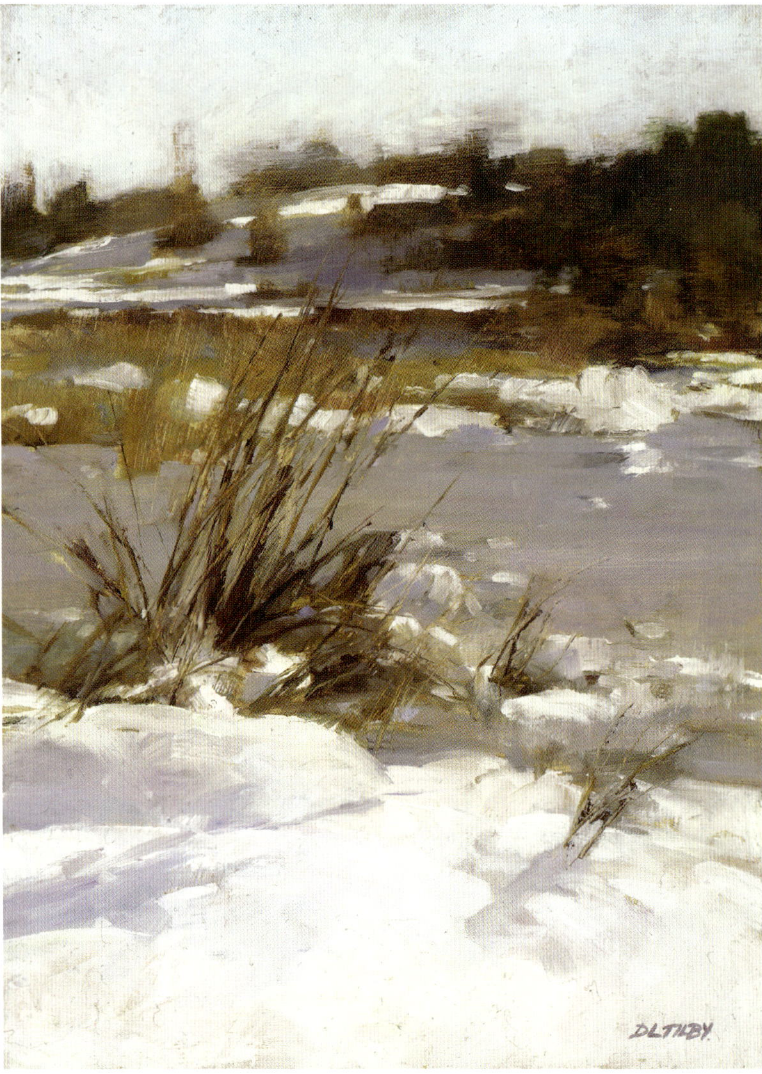

Winter Grasses, Deborah Tilby. (12" × 9", oil on board)
This painting makes use of the complementary pairings of blue/greys and oranges, together with violets and yellows, and combines passages of both warm and cool tones. The background trees and grasses have been scumbled-in, before the shadows have been added to give weight and a sense of three dimensions to the foliage. The bright sunlit patches were then placed around the darker colours to provide contrast. Finally, the foreground grasses were painted using a painting knife, with just a few definitive touches being added with a brush.

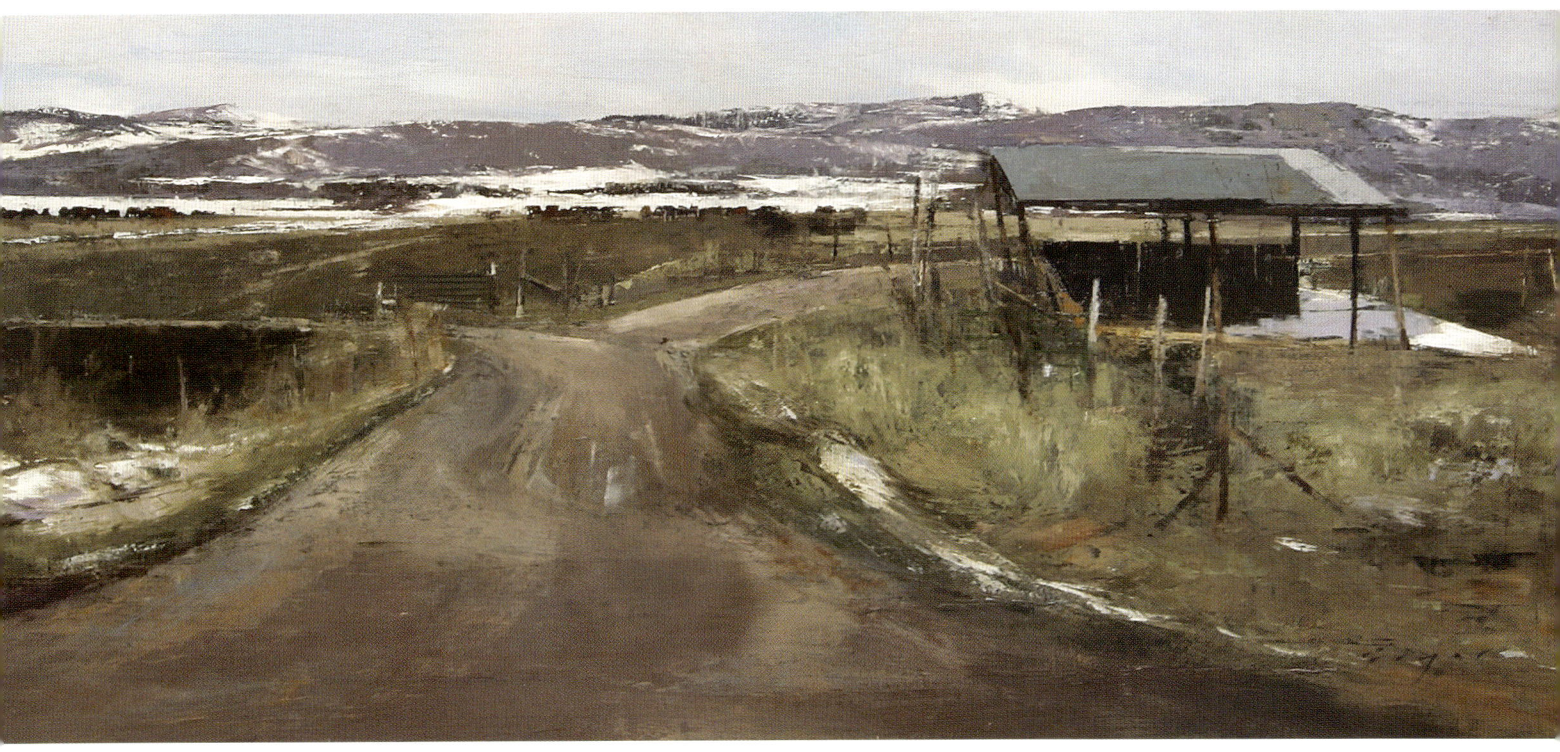

Farm near Hilltop, Douglas Fryer. (12" × 28", oil on panel)
The strength of this composition relies on its big shapes, together with the subtle colour and tonal transitions within those shapes. The colour scheme is purple and green, with the purple in the mountains also echoed in the road. There is a repetition of tonal value in the field on the left, and the shed on the right, which helps to move you through the painting, a sensation reinforced by the directional lines of the road. The angular patch of snow by the shed almost leads your eye off the right-hand side of the painting, but is picked up again to go back, by the curve of the road. The exaggerated, elongated format emphasizes the scale and expanse of the landscape. The shed unfortunately collapsed the following winter, and was hauled away, but the cattle seen grazing in the distance are there every season.

Where there is water, there are infinite possibilities for the painter. You may be inspired by crashing seas, tumbling waterfalls or tranquil streams and rivers, but there will always be a great deal of subject matter to inspire you. Boats are often difficult for the novice to paint successfully, so this is an area where drawing skills are important, as a boat that doesn't actually look as though it's sitting in the water can spoil an otherwise good painting. Even if you are painting in a very loose, impressionist style, the underlying drawing should be sound. There are other aspects of water that generate interest for the painter, including boatyards, docks, canal bridges and harbours. Reflections provide wonderful and sometimes complex patterns that can form the basis of abstract or semi-abstract interpretation. The translucency of shallow water contrasts strongly with the deeply opaque water of the sea.

For the purpose of this book, the sea has been included as another aspect of landscape painting. Its beauty and ever-changing nature, and the way in which it is affected by the elements, will provide endless subject matter. As with all forms of landscape painting, you should include a degree of both linear and aerial perspective when painting the sea, in keeping with the elements of landscape that may be present. As the tones in the landscape diminish in value the further away they are, so should those in the sea. Studying the anatomy of waves will allow you – with practice – to paint them from memory. Look for warm and cool areas within the shadows beneath the foaming wave caps. To add drama to seascapes, place the horizon either low down in your painting, or high up, depending on where you want the emphasis to be. If you want the sea to be the main focus, paint the tops of the waves in a higher key than the clouds, and conversely, if the sky is to be the main draw, give it the greater dominance.

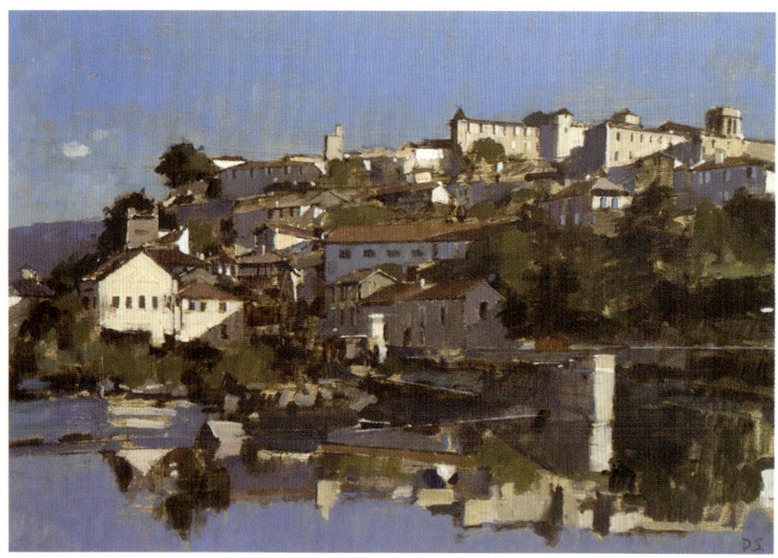

St Lizier, Reflections on the Salat, David Sawyer. (18" × 24", oil on canvas)
Painted very close to the artist's studio in the village of St Lizier, this has become a favourite painting subject. In this picture he has tried to keep the focus directed towards the Bishop's Palace at the top of the painting by using the dramatic contrasts between the highlights and the dark shadows. The central area has been treated in a more simplified manner, and has even become 'lost' in some parts. At the bottom of the picture a little more clarity has been achieved in the reflections where the brushstrokes have taken on a harder edge, as seen at the top. The emphasis afforded to the different areas of the painting encourages the eye to initially focus on the building at the top of the picture, then to the sunlit building at the centre left, and finally to settle on the reflections in the water at the bottom.

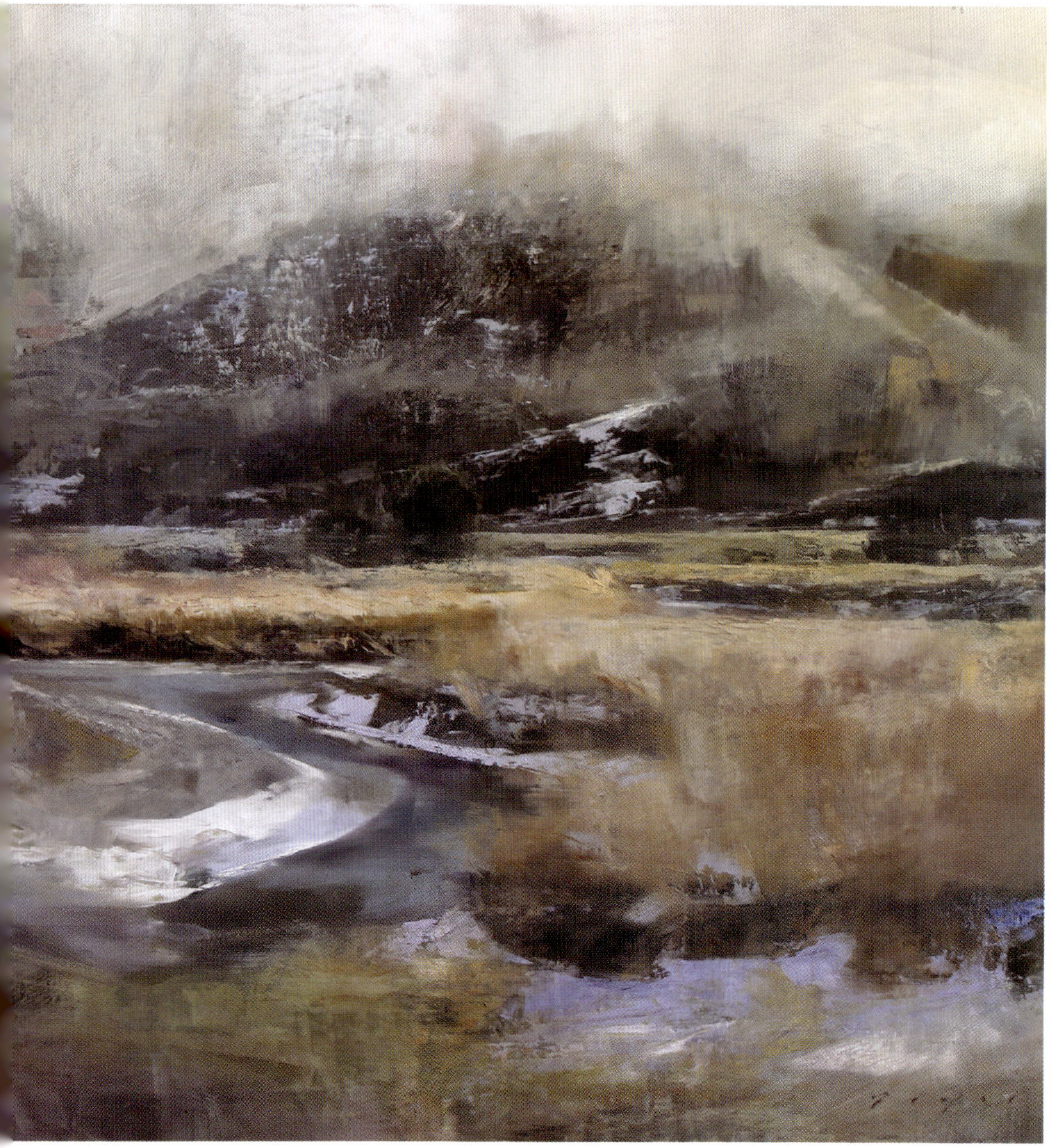

Sevier River, Douglas Fryer. (24" × 24", oil on panel)
The area taken up by the focus of the painting here is minimal, whilst the majority of the image is a merging together of shapes where they meet, become blurred, and interpenetrate each other where the melting snow breaks them up, creating pattern and texture, camouflaging the structure of the land. In some sections of the painting, there is a juxtaposition of brittle edges and feathery softness. The colour palette is quite limited, but still retains a sense of warm and cool, which helps to suggest a fuller range of colour. Most of this painting was created with a broad, 4" putty, or filling knife, including those parts that appear most detailed. By using a tool that is seemingly far too large and inaccurate to create detail, the artist can make shapes, patterns and textures, as the paint skips and plays across the surface of the painting in a way that is reminiscent of the random nature of the elements that make up the landscape.

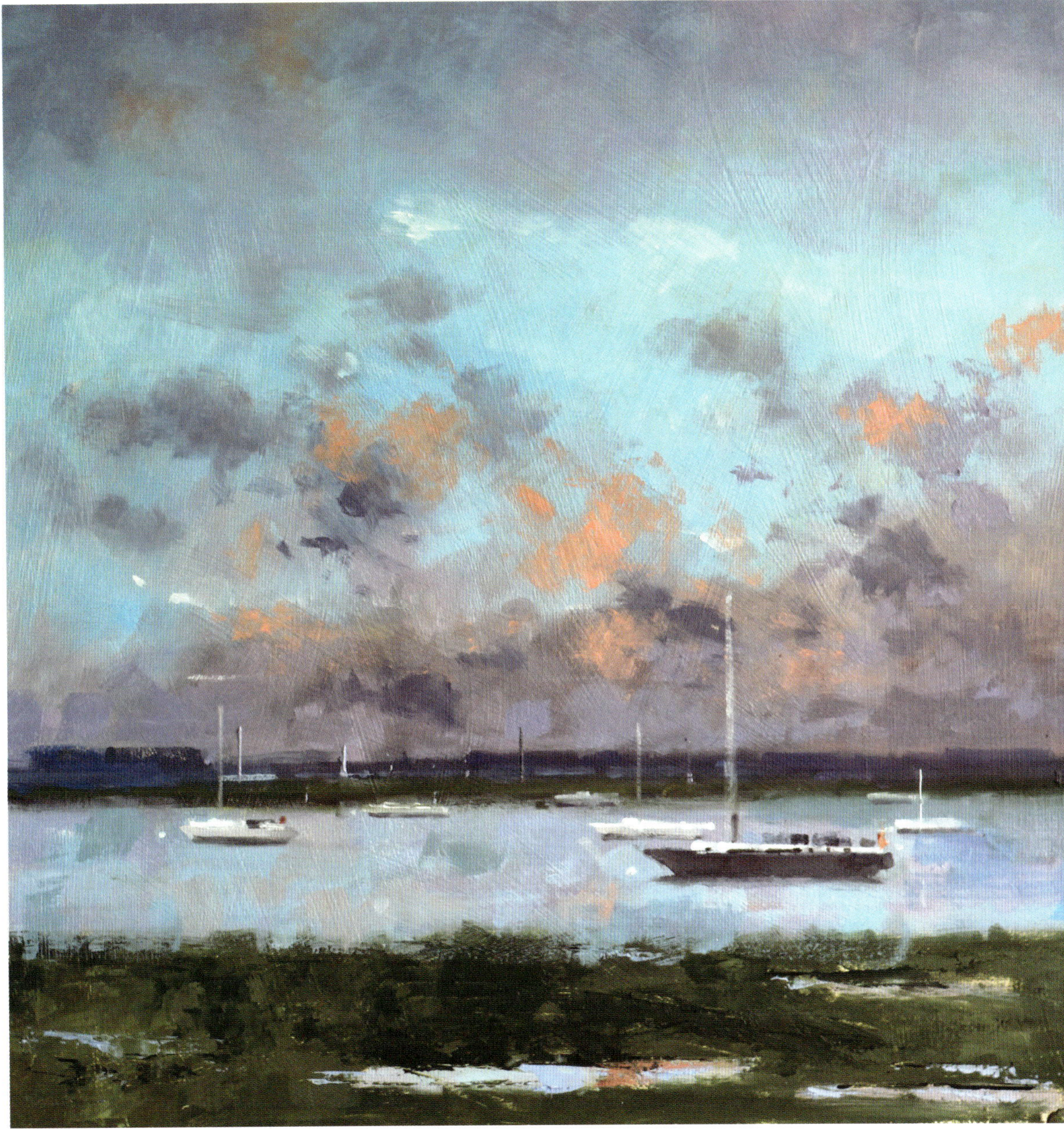

Boats at Aldburgh, Suffolk, Kevin Scully. (12" × 12", oil on board)
Although the boats in this painting would normally have taken centre stage, it's the sky that is actually the dominant feature. It occupies about three-quarters of the total image area, and has been afforded more attention than all of the other elements. The low-lying countryside along the horizon line has been rendered in a dark violet tone creating a silhouette, which suggests an unseen setting sun behind the clouds. To integrate the water and foreground into the overall composition, touches of colour seen in the sky were dragged across them with a dry brush. The vertical masts add directional emphasis to the sky as well as providing a contrast to the overall horizontal composition. The painting was created partly from memory, but largely from imagination after a short trip to the Suffolk coast.

Looking Further Afield

Painting similar scenes over and over again will of course mean that you will get to know your subject well, but it may also lead to repetition and a certain kind of inertia. If you love to paint and are seeking inspiration that can't be satisfied by your immediate surroundings, you will need to consider a trip away from home. This may involve going off on your own, or signing up to a *plein-air* workshop or weekend course in a different location. A change of scenery, environment and climate can work wonders for you, and may revitalize your general wellbeing and creative yearnings. If you inhabit a flat, agricultural landscape with wide, open skies, spend some time painting in a wooded valley surrounded by rolling hills dotted with small farms and villages. If you live in the mountains, a thousand miles from the sea, spend some time painting in a fishing harbour surrounded by all of the paraphernalia that goes with this kind of location. If you live in a cold northern climate, take a trip south where the sun will be bright and the shadows will be strong. By merely stepping out of your comfort zone and into a different setting, you will be giving yourself new challenges. Even if you decide that you are happier in your own familiar surroundings, you will return refreshed, and more open to new challenges.

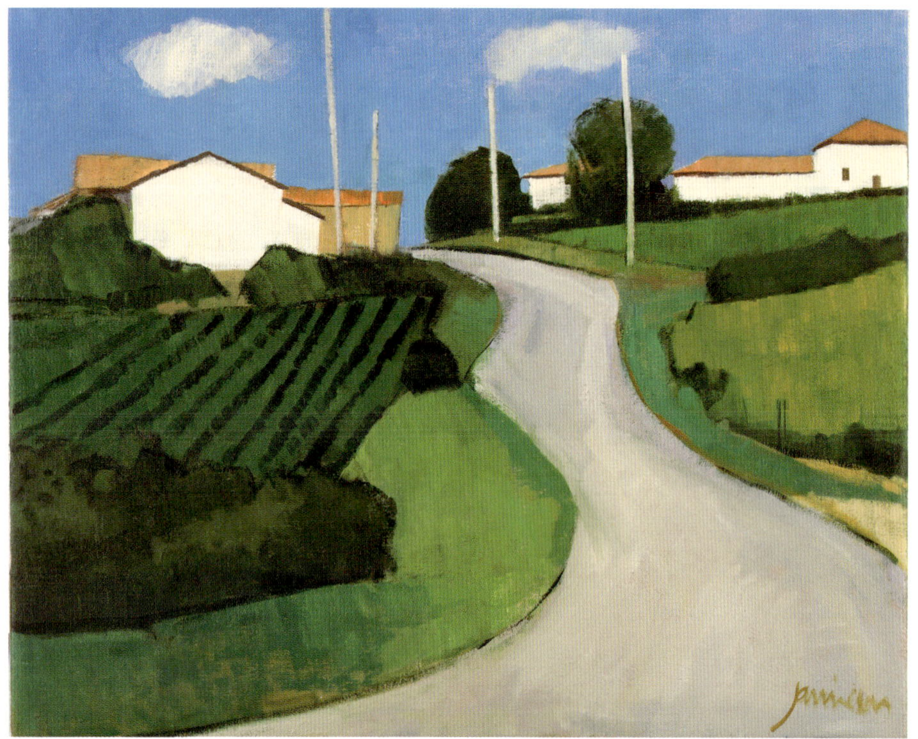

Landscape, Moiré, Beaujolais, Charles Jamieson. (28" × 30", oil on linen)
Painted from sketches and photographs in the artist's studio. This painting leads the eye through the landscape and up to the buildings on the horizon. The winding road transports the eye to the upper central part of the painting, where the buildings are simplified so as not to divert the eye too much, but interest is retained by adding a splash of warm colour amidst the greens of the land, and the blue of the sky. The denseness of the greens on the left of the painting leads the eye towards the centre, and then upwards and to the right, whilst the simplified lines indicating vines emphasize that direction of movement. The eye is then captured between the clouds and the telegraph poles and finally roams across the buildings.

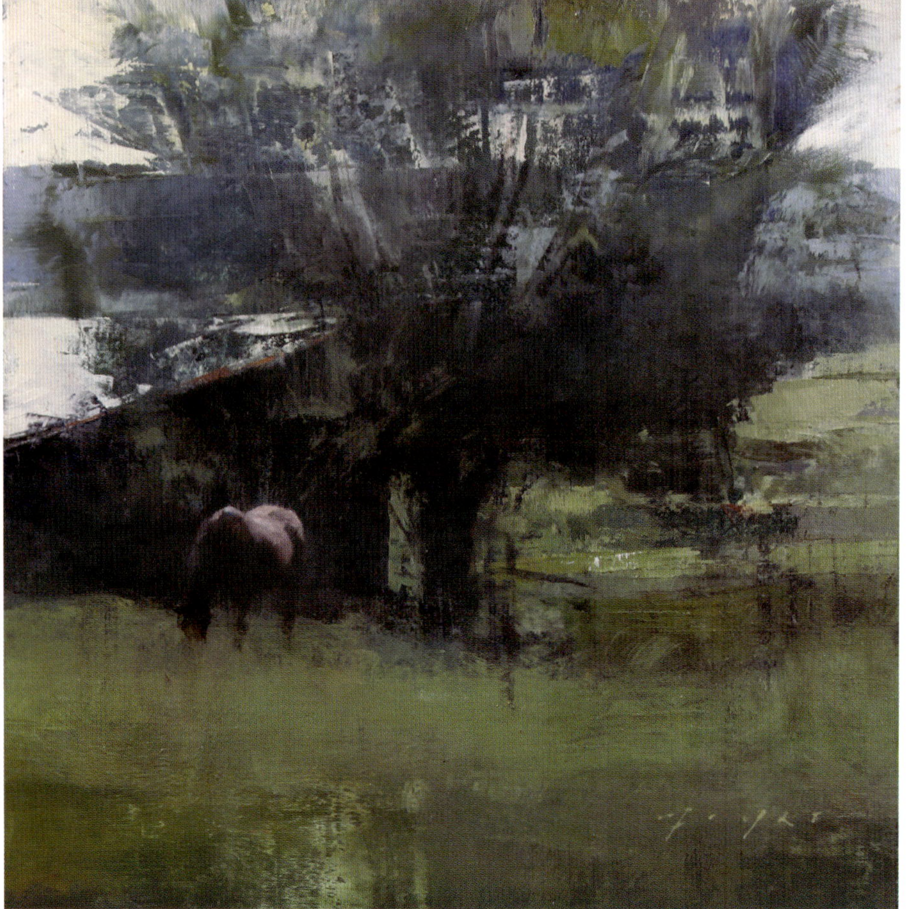

Silver Light, Hillside, Douglas Fryer. (10" × 10", oil on panel)
In this small painting the artist has endeavoured to simplify the image as far as possible, whilst still retaining the essence of the scene. The tree has been rendered in a way that not only establishes a strong structural element, but also evokes a sense of air, light, wind and movement. The simple, straight lines of the shed indicate that this is a man-made construction, without resorting to any unnecessary detail. The light hits its roof with a tonal value that is lighter than the sky, which tells us that it is metal. The angle of the roof is echoed in the subtle repetition of shape seen in the lower branches of the tree on the right. The grass has been rendered as simple shapes and passages of warm and cool colours, without any attempt to suggest detail, and the fence posts appear as they would in the peripheral vision of the viewer. The horse has been painted in subdued tones in harmony with the overall colour scheme. The painting is held together by strong tonal contrasts, but the various marks and transitions that break up the edges of those large shapes add variety and interest to an otherwise symmetrical and stable composition.

Initial Impressions

If you have taken the plunge and wake up one morning in a different country with a different climate, unusual sounds and smells, give yourself a little time to acclimatize to your surroundings. Don't make the mistake of being too ambitious too soon. You will probably find that you will be using a different palette of colours than those you are used to, so don't immediately reach for the well-trusted selection that serve you so well in your own familiar environment. It is all too easy to opt for the clichéd images that have become so familiar to us in paintings of famous landmarks around the world. Because they have been painted so many times before doesn't mean that they can't be painted again, but it would be far better to choose a scene that is less well known, and seldom painted.

Having come from a mild and temperate climate, if you find yourself in a hot, sunny country, the highlights will be brighter, the shadows will be stronger, and the contrasts will be greater. You may have to amend your approach to this new subject matter, or you may even have to adopt a slightly different style of painting. You may find this easier to cope with, or you may find it more difficult, but you will be tested nonetheless, so be prepared to adapt and experiment, as these are some of the challenges of landscape painting.

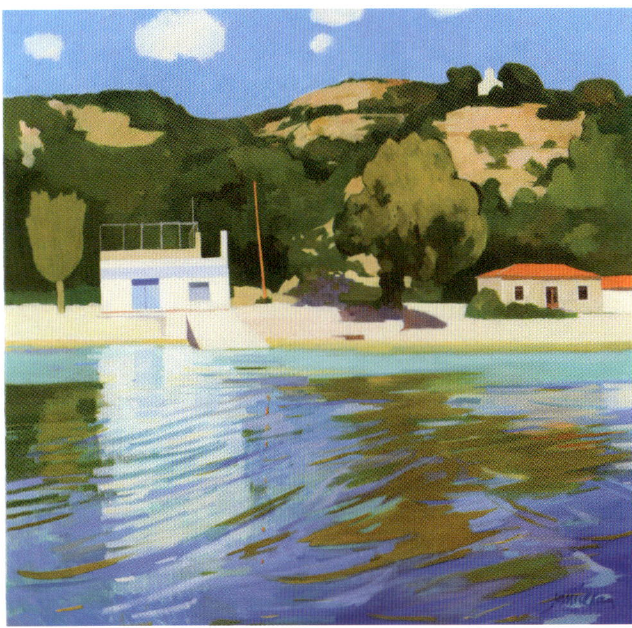

Coastline, Limni, Evvia, Greece, Charles Jamieson. (37" × 38", oil on linen)
The emphasis in this painting lies in the reflections on the surface of the water. The landscape and buildings act as an anchor, pulling the eye downwards, whilst also giving somewhere for it to travel, and at the same time providing visual justification for the reflections themselves. The objective behind the painting was to portray the beauty and stillness present in the water, producing a calm and contemplative sensation in the eye of the viewer. The two distinct areas of reflection, the white of the building and the ochre green of the tree, give the eye plenty of opportunity to roam across the canvas without it getting overtired. The colours capture the brightness of the day, and the artist deliberately kept the colours fresh to enhance the overall feeling of thoughtful and tranquil peace.

PAINTING THE ELEMENTS

Skies

As with painting waves, it is possible with a little practice to develop a systematic approach to painting skies and clouds. There are basically two kinds of skies, one being merely a backdrop to the landscape, and the other being a major component that is part of it. Even if you are painting a cloudless sky, there will usually be a graduation of colour and tone within it. Where the sky meets the horizon it will be paler in tone than that part of the sky immediately above. On a sunny day, it will also be slightly warmer in colour the closer it is to the horizon, and generally speaking the further away an area is, the cooler the colour, and the closer to us it is, the colour will be warmer. These shifts in colour and tone can help us to infer space, distance, and to a lesser extent the curvature of the Earth and the atmosphere that surrounds it.

As with all things that we perceive, the sky and clouds follow the same rules of perspective, so scale and proportion are of paramount importance. The most important

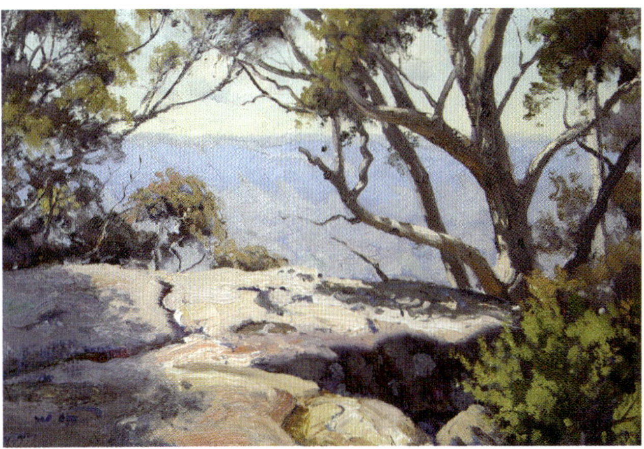

Sketch for *Cliff Top, Sublime Point*, Warwick Fuller. (18" × 24", oil on canvas, stretched onto board)
This is not a finished painting, but rather a sketch for a larger work to be undertaken in the studio. The view is from the weatherworn, sandstone ramparts at the top of the Blue Mountains National Park in Australia, where the artist has indicated the mountains and valley in the distance by painting them in an azure blue haze. This has created a sense of distance using aerial perspective, further reinforced by the stark fretwork of branches and foliage in the foreground.

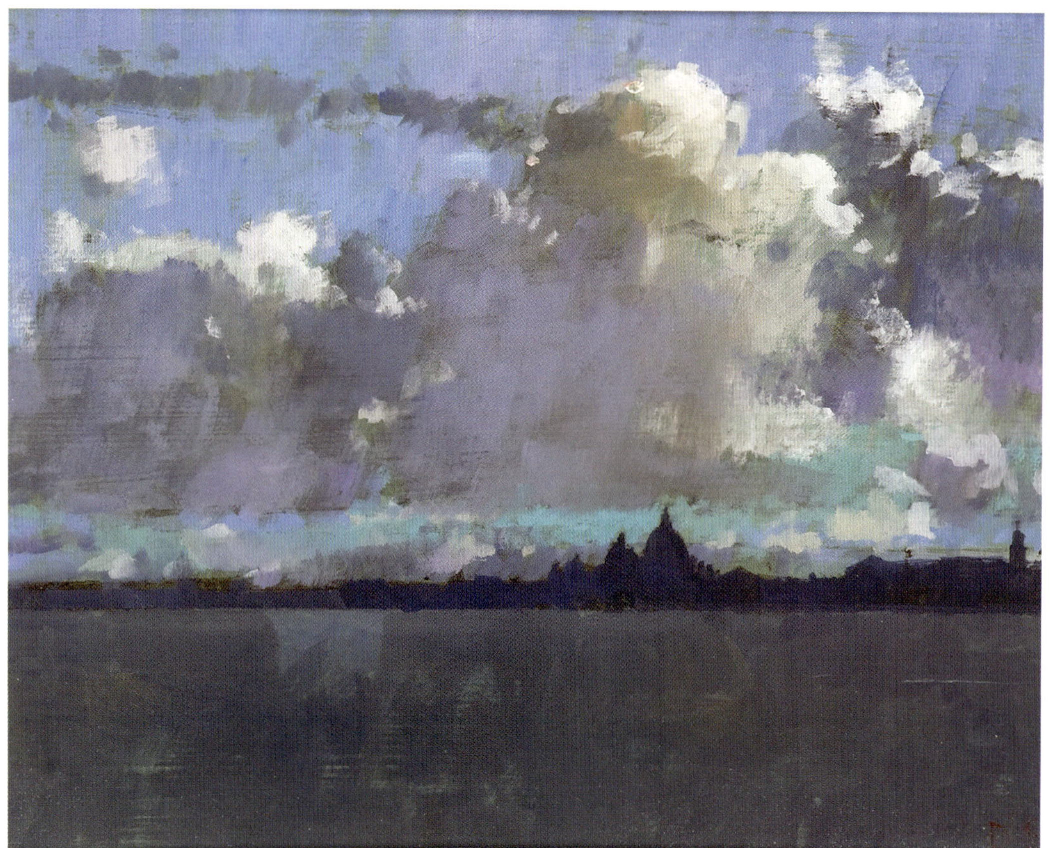

Big Skies over Venice, David Sawyer. (10" × 12", oil on board)
A small and quick study painted at a time when David Sawyer was interested in the work of the artist Samuel Palmer, and in particular his 'Big Cloud' series of paintings and drawings. The board was prepared with a turquoise/green ground, which the artist had been experimenting with, and this has worked beautifully with the purples, greys and blues used in this direct, fresh and simple painting, which has given the subject matter a great sense of drama.

HOW TO PAINT SKY

There is often a tendency for the novice painter to paint a sky in the same way that they would paint a wall in their home, and that is to start in one corner and continue the brushstrokes in horizontal bands across the surface. This results in bands of colour giving the sky a stripy appearance. This is especially true of watercolour painters where the overlapping bands produce a hard edge, exaggerating the stripes even further. When you look at a cloudless sky, you would be hard pressed to detect stripes in evidence. It's far better therefore to use a variety of brushstrokes, softly blending them together if necessary, and so avoiding the horizontal look. Even if the clouds in the sky are in horizontal bands, the sky behind them won't be.

thing to remember is that clouds become proportionately smaller the closer they are to the horizon line. Obviously some clouds are larger than others, but generally speaking, those immediately above us when we look up into the sky are far larger than those in the far distance. This effect can be exaggerated in our paintings to intensify the illusion of distance in the atmosphere.

The appearance of clouds furthest away from us also differs from those closest. If we are viewing them on a fairly bright, sunny day, we are doing so at a distance through the fine particles of dust in the Earth's atmosphere, so they appear more diffused and usually paler in tonal value. Their colour will also be more subdued. When we look directly above us, the clouds are closer to us and so not affected as much by atmospheric interference. At sunrise and sunset things are different, and we quite often see clouds as dark silhouettes because the sun is low in the sky and perhaps immediately behind them.

Although they consist of mere vapour and may be transparent or semi-transparent, they have a three-dimensional quality, which means they often appear to have a side that is in shadow and a side that has a highlight. If you bear this in mind when painting them, you will be able to suggest their volume rather than rendering them as flat shapes. Depending on the time of day and the position of the sun, the clouds may have highlights on their tops and shadows underneath, or vice versa. Sometimes you can just suggest where the light source in the sky is, simply by the positioning of highlights or shadows.

When painting outside on a still day, you may be lucky enough to be able to spend some time studying clouds,

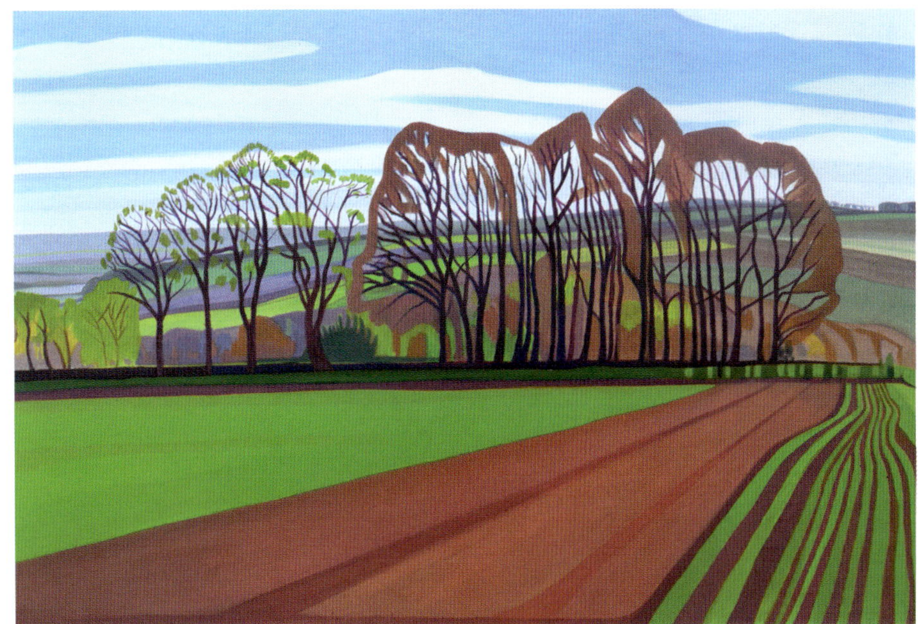

Trees on Long Hill, Anna Dillon. (11" × 16", oil on board)
This line of skeletal trees bordering a freshly ploughed field of red and green caught the artist's eye whilst she was seeking out subject material for a new painting. The strong, directional lines create a certain dynamism to the composition, which is further emphasized by the streamlined, horizontal clouds. The colours in the foreground are echoed in the leaves that still cling to the filigree branches of the trees, and beyond them the artist has used atmospheric perspective to create distance in the landscape beyond, by using paler tones, and gradually introducing tints of mauve towards the horizon. This painting is an example of the artist arranging all of the elements before her in a satisfactory way to achieve a perfectly balanced composition based on a sound underlying structure.

and they may remain stationary for long enough for you to paint them. More often than not though, they will be there one minute and gone the next. They will also change shape as you look at them, which makes it very difficult to paint them as you see them. It is therefore important to conduct a study of clouds and their formation, so that you can build a visual memory of their behaviour, and render a reasonable likeness of their appearance even away from the subject.

There are subtle differences regarding how the sky will appear during the various seasons. In winter the sun is lower in the sky and often creates less light, and winds from colder climates can carry more widespread cloud, reducing much of the colour that we see in summer skies.

Sunsets

Glorious sunsets will always attract painters, but rendering them successfully is not always that easy. They can often fall victim to over dramatization brought about by introducing too many bright and gaudy colours into the equation. Even in the most brilliant of sunsets there are subtle shifts in colour temperature. Generally speaking, the colour of the sky and clouds closest to the light source will be warmer in colour than those elements furthest from it. So as you move from the immediate vicinity of the light source, the colours will become cooler. This applies to the colour shift in individual clouds as well as those further away.

If you don't include any neutral colours in the sky, or perhaps the surrounding landscape, the dramatic effect of your sunset may be minimized, as too many contrasting bright colours can cancel each other out.

Sunrises

Even as an artist, you may sometimes find it difficult to tell whether or not a painting is supposed to represent a sunrise or sunset, as the two events can appear very similar. It could be suggested that a sunrise can be characterized by using warmer, softer colours in a dreamy haze, and that sunsets are rendered in more vibrant and fiery colour combinations, but this isn't always the case. If you were to paint a sunrise *en plein air* that faithfully corresponded to the scene you witnessed at the time, and showed it to a fellow painter, would it be instantly recognized as a sunrise? I think often not.

As a suggestion, perhaps you can bend the truth a little and show the sun lower in the sky when painting a sunset, and higher in the sky for a sunrise. As a basis for your sunrise colour range choose yellow and pale blue as the predominant hues, and for your sunset a richer, darker palette containing red, orange, and purple. For the sunrise, and if you are showing the sun, you could perhaps paint it in the palest of yellows or even white, whereas for the sunset you could choose a stronger yellow or even orange or red.

If all else fails, you can always hang it on your wall with a label below saying *Sunrise over San Marco*, and then there can be no doubt about which it is.

The Land

All of the criteria mentioned previously are also relevant to painting the land itself, and for the purposes of the title of this section we can concentrate in general on fields, hills, mountains, valleys, grass and so on. In the landscape, we

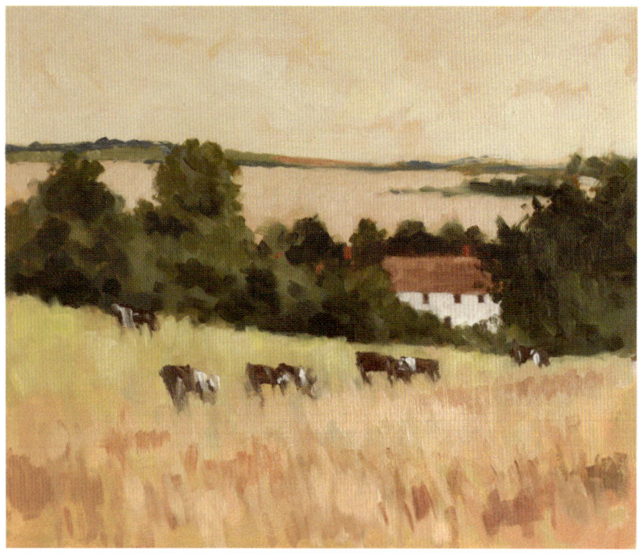

Lough Down, Kevin Scully. (10" × 12", oil on board)
A thirty-minute colour study for a possible future picture. The image was painted over a toned ground of Raw Sienna to establish the warm colour range of this mid-summer landscape scene. Painted wet-in-wet, the directional brushstrokes of the grass and cattle suggest a gentle breeze. Although the day was bright, the sky was colourless as it so often can be when the day is hot, so some artistic licence was used to include a little of the colour seen in the foreground, which added unity and retained an all-over sensation of warmth.

are unlikely to want to paint any of these things in isolation, so even if we elect to simply paint some mountains with sky as a background, they are inexorably linked, with each reflecting the way that we see the other. When we look at a mountain range, there will be colours in its make-up that are influenced by everything else around it, even if this is only sky. Depending on atmospheric conditions, the furthest range may appear to be purple or blue even though there is undoubtedly vegetation on their slopes, whereas on the slopes of the foothills we may be able to distinguish trees and shrubs. Even on a sunny day there may be drifting clouds that creep across the sky, throwing areas on the land into shadow and giving the clouds even more emphasis and purpose.

If you are painting a landscape with a full range of features, you will first have to decide upon what is to be the focus of attention. If it is to be the middle distance, and this is the most common area of concentration, then the sky and immediate foreground must be made subordinate, otherwise the centre of interest will be diminished. If however, you are keen to make the sky dominate, then everything else must be painted in a lower key. If you intend to paint a moody and evocative scene, then the contrasts between the various elements will be reduced and possibly merged into each other with a blending and softening of edges.

The way in which the foreground is treated in paintings is of great importance and often overlooked by the inexperienced. Because things such as grass and flowers are closest to us, there is always a temptation to paint them in greater detail than those elements of the landscape further away. This only works if we specifically want the viewer to look at the bottom of the picture, but generally when we look at a landscape we instinctively view it at eye level, which directs us to the middle distance. So by trying to paint every flower and blade of grass in the foreground, we are distracting the eye from the focus of attention. A certain amount of detail can be added, but it should be inferred rather than stated by using larger brushstrokes and playing down the strength of colour. Any detail within these larger gestural passages should be subordinate to the whole.

Trees

When painting trees, particularly when they are grouped together en masse, it is far more important to suggest their form and volume than it is to try and paint every leaf. They have to be simplified into their basic shapes and tonal values. The degree to which this is done is a matter of personal choice, as it's perfectly possible to suggest detail with a variety of brushstrokes without actually painting it. These techniques will be dealt with in a later chapter in the book. Trees can also be simplified to little more than two tones and shapes, one in local colour and one in shade.

Painting the trunks and branches in a way that follows the rules of nature in general terms means that the trunk diminishes in girth as it grows upwards, and the branches taper as they grow outwards. There are of course exceptions to this rule, but more often than not, they can look unnatural and uncomfortable if painted as such. Some trees have an open structure, which means that there will be areas where the sky, or distant landscape is visible between clumps of foliage, and this can sometimes be tricky to paint, as it often appears to be too light when surrounded by the darker shapes created by the leaves. One trick is to make these 'sky holes' slightly darker in tone than the general tone of the sky or landscape behind.

Depending on the species of trees, they can add a dynamic element to your landscape, from the tall and majestic Cypress trees of Tuscany to the gnarled and twisted ancient olives of Greece, they can help to typify a landscape. By gentle streams and rivers, willows will droop and sway, whilst on a windswept hillside or moor, others will be bent at an angle by the prevailing winds.

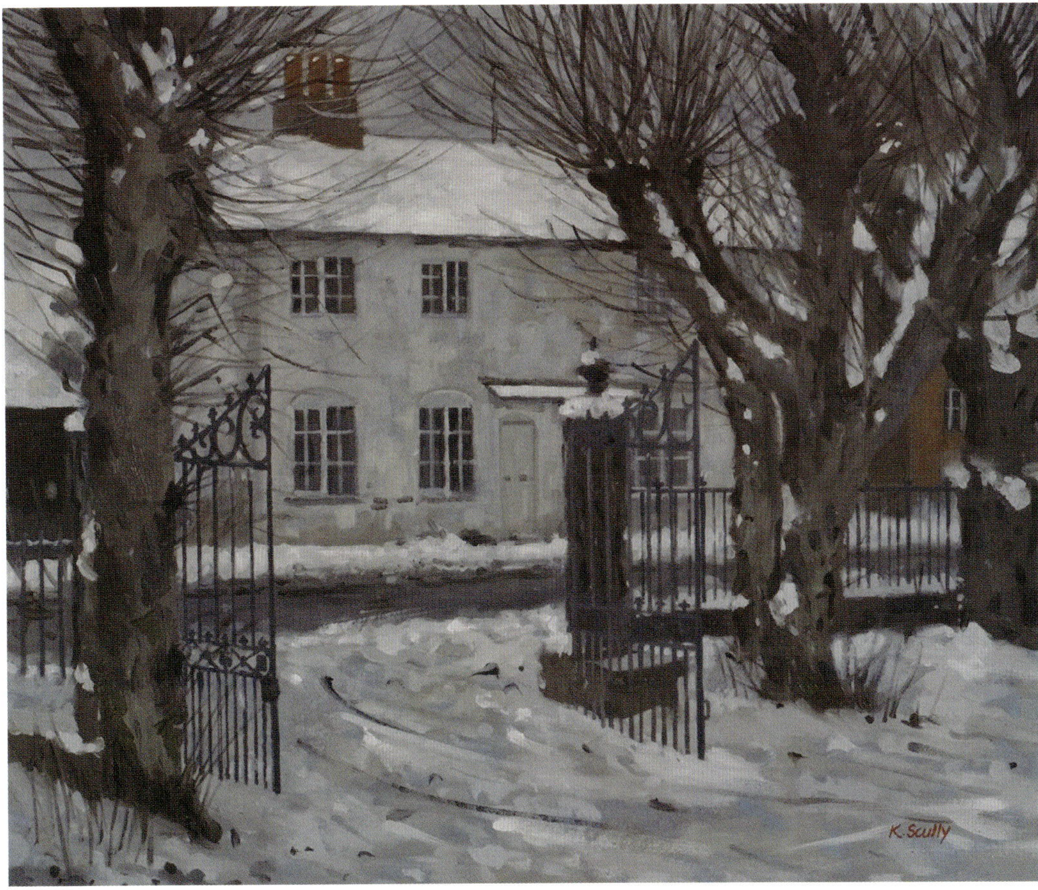

Posey Place, Church Street, Kevin Scully. (18" × 14", oil on board)
A dull and quiet late afternoon scene represented in a rather monochromatic colour, with just a few touches of Burnt Sienna and Raw Umber. To emphasize the quiet mood of winter, everything has been created with relatively small and unhurried patches of paint, each slightly different in colour and tone, positioned side-by-side. The only signs of life are the marks made by a sledge in the snow. These brushstrokes are echoed in the bare branches of the pollarded trees.

The point at which the tree grows from is an area that requires some thought; it is often merely shown as an entirely different element to the ground around it, and appears to have been cut off at its base. Remember that trees grow from the ground up, and particularly with older trees, their roots often form a raised mound around them, and there is sometimes little distinction between the roots and the trunk itself. Although trees possess a definite structure, it's a mistake to make their trunks and branches look too uniform, so they will benefit from a more random arrangement. Be wary also of making them look like telegraph poles, so they will look more natural if their trunks are not too straight or regular. Some species of tree have 'opposite' branches, which means their branches don't grow from the same point either side of the trunk.

As well as foliage creating shadows further back inside the tree, remember that certain parts of the branches and trunks will also be in shade. Be sure also to replicate the general pattern of the tree's foliage in its shadow cast on the ground. So if the tree is a conifer with dense foliage, the shadow on the ground will be correspondingly dense, but if the tree is of an open nature, the shadow will be dappled.

Water

The various forms of water found in the landscape demand a set of different treatments, but water in all its forms provides a fantastic range of material for painting subjects. Whether you are drawn to tranquillity or wild and ferocious seas, the possibilities are infinite.

Still water found in rivers and streams will provide reflections, and these will alter to some degree, depending on your viewpoint. The reason why some things are reflected in water whilst others aren't isn't always immediately obvious, as a great many other things influence their existence.

If you examine the shallow water that exists in streams, you will find that it is generally warmer in tone than deep water, being affected by whatever kind of material is lying on the bed of the stream. The soil, rocks and plants will each have an influence on its colour. When the water is moving, it produces ripples as it travels over rocks, stones and natural organic debris. These ripples contain complex reflections of light echoed from colours present in the surrounding area. The colour tends towards green, with the small particles of sediment and debris reflecting light, creating a pale tonal value in the water. It's almost

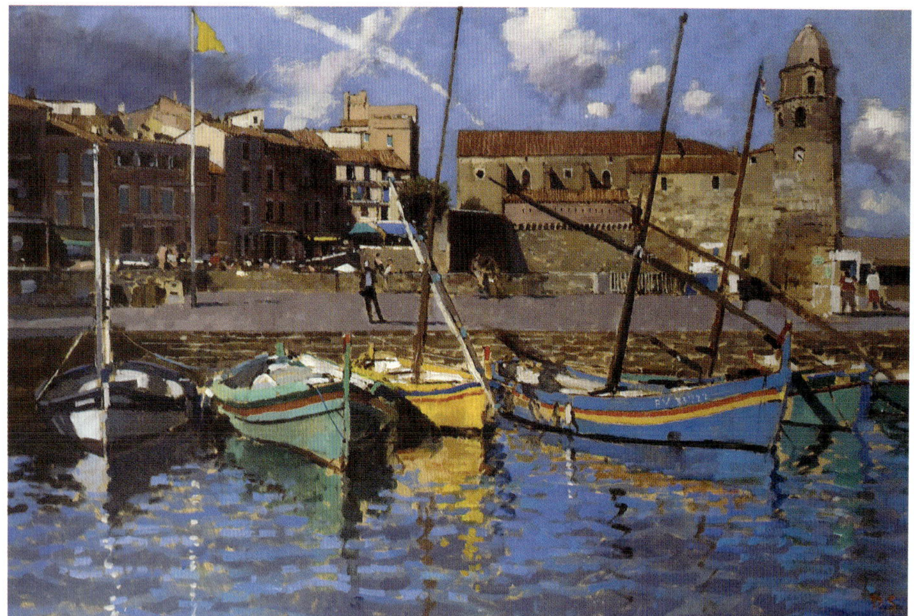

Fishing Boats, Collioure, David Sawyer. (24" × 36", oil on board)
A large studio picture based on three smaller studies made on site. The decision regarding composition was arrived at through the artist's interest in the dynamic forms of the masts and spars of the boats. This sense of movement has then been echoed in the sky with the positioning of the clouds and the vapour trail. However, he wasn't entirely convinced about how well this had worked, which is one of the problems encountered when working in the studio rather than working directly from the subject. Given too much time to think can lead to the picture becoming too composed. Nevertheless, he felt that the bottom half, with the brightly coloured boats and their reflections has retained a greater degree of spontaneity, and has indeed been beautifully painted.

impossible to distinguish the individual colours in these reflections when the water is moving, as they are quickly broken up into indistinct patterns, so trying to paint them is a challenge. In places where the water is deeper, the colour becomes darker in tone.

When the sky is reflected on the surface of water, it is usually a tone darker than the sky itself. One of the generally perceived observations of reflections is that the colour of objects reflected in water appears in a slightly lower tonal key than the objects themselves, and that sometimes the lighter coloured objects that are reflected appear darker, and vice versa. However, having spent a great deal of time studying reflections, this doesn't always seem to be the case. Further scientific investigation could probably explain these complexities more fully, but as artists, all we need to do is rely on observation, and if something looks wrong in nature, it will certainly look wrong in our painting.

It's worth noting that the closer you get to water, the less the sky and surrounding features are reflected. The water closest to you will have rather indistinct reflections, whilst that further away will reflect much sharper images. Also, the water closest to you will appear darker than that in the distance, which will be brighter and lighter. A peculiarity of reflections and something that people often don't notice is that occasionally you will see the reflection of something that isn't visible when looking at the object itself. For example, when looking at a boat sitting in still water, you may notice the reflection of the underside of the buoys hanging from the side of the boat, whilst this cannot be seen when looking at the buoys themselves. This occurs because you are looking at the reflected object from an angle of view as far below the water's surface as your eyes are above the water.

You may also have noticed when walking along the beach at the water's edge that the seagulls wading in an inch or so of water not only create a strong reflection of themselves, but depending on the angle of the light source, often cast a shadow as well. This will also occur occasionally when looking at boats in shallow water.

It isn't really necessary to be able to understand fully why all of these things occur, but it is advisable to take note, and to look out for these peculiarities if you are striving for some kind of realism in your paintings.

Painting fast-flowing rivers demands a completely different approach in execution to that when attempting to capture the myriad of reflections of boats in a calm estuary. The effect of moving, deep water, whether it's the result of a fast-flowing current, waves created by a moving boat, or merely a strong wind blowing across its surface, creates an absence of reflections. When water is in motion, the light around it is concentrated, and there will be few if any reflections visible in a river that is in full flow, unless the water is clear and shallow. Movement can be suggested by the direction of brush marks, and the positioning of highlights reflected by the light from the sky. In some instances there will be a mixture of both moving and calm water, which means there will be some reflections as well as white water.

Because water is fluid and often moving, it is therefore a challenge to paint, because it's difficult to focus on what

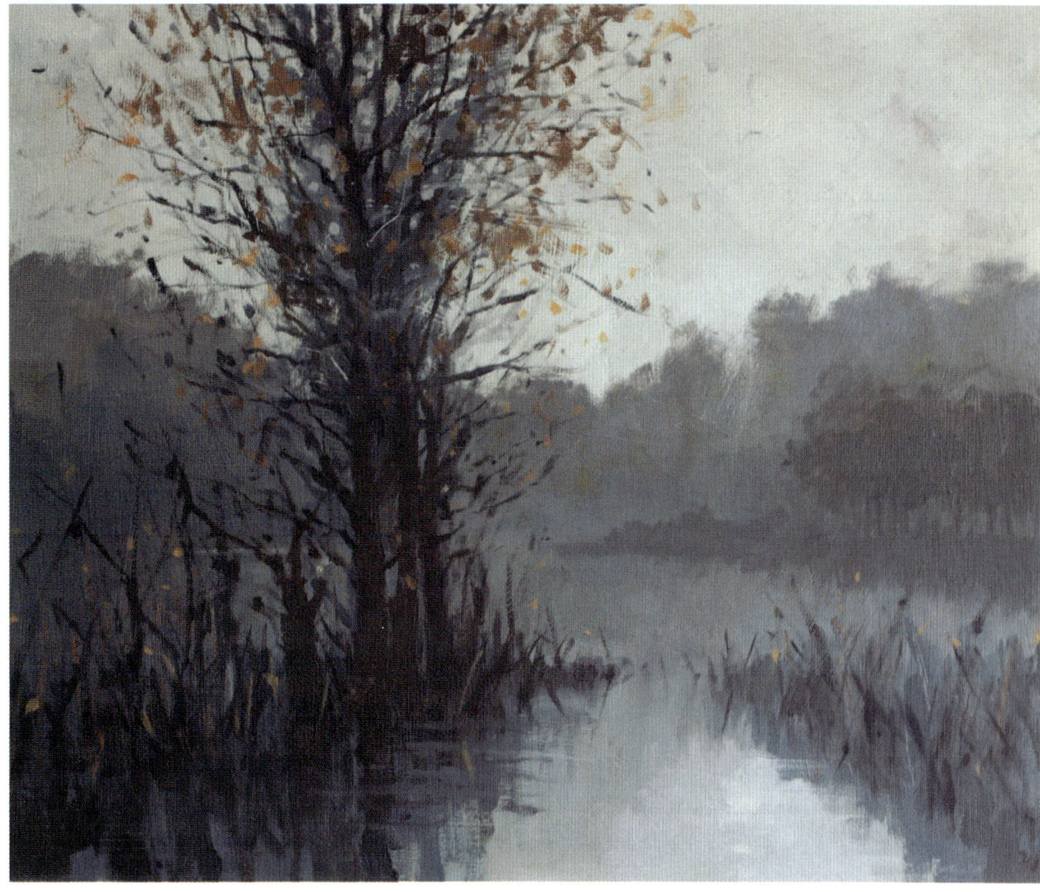

Autumn Flood, Kevin Scully. (12" × 12", oil on board) Painted from imagination with a limited colour palette, the mood is melancholic, with just a few autumn leaves hanging on to the otherwise bare trees, with their feet in the flooded river. Virtually monochromatic, the moody, misty atmosphere is relieved with just a few touches of a pale Burnt Sienna that hint at the beginning of winter. The image is a combination of colours carefully blended together to suggest distance, and a looser treatment of the foreground trees and grasses, where detail has been merely hinted at. Here the colour has been applied with both brush and painting knife. Some of the detail has been added by using the tip of a knife as well as a liberal amount of dry brush treatment, which keeps the marks as random as possible.

is really happening. Painting waves in a seascape is a real test of your observational skills. As the water is constantly moving, it's impossible to paint waves exactly as they are at a particular moment, but by studying their repetitive pattern and observing how they roll over, it is possible to paint them from memory. Photographs of waves will hold a clue to their shape and the way in which they form and then break up, how they arrive in staggered lines and how the water deposited on the beach retreats back into the sea. When painting waves *en plein air*, standing fairly close to the sea, there is a temptation to keep altering them as each one rolls in in a different position. A good strategy is to spend a reasonable amount of time just observing, and then to paint them in just four different tones; the shadow, the mid tone, the highlight, which is usually white, and the tone beneath this highlight. These tones can vary slightly in hue, depending upon what you see. The darker tone may be greener in colour, the mid tone greyer, and the shadow under the foaming highlight a pale turquoise. Once these colours have been pinned down, and the structure of the waves established, a few subtle variations can be added as details. If you are painting the sea from any distance, it's likely that you will see much less variation in tone, so using three colours will probably be sufficient.

The sea of course needn't be painted in isolation, and by including other elements such as shoreline, cliffs, rocks and beaches there will be added interest. Waves crashing onto rocks or over a seawall will make a far more interesting painting than waves crashing over each other. Consider also painting the sea or a lake from an elevated viewpoint, or perhaps just as a distant backdrop to a landscape.

The sky is vitally important and not to be neglected when painting water, as it is often the sky that determines its colour, especially when painting large expanses of water, such as lakes and estuaries. A painting that demonstrates no connection between the two is lacking in unity, as the two elements are interwoven and inseparable.

Boats, naturally enough, are an integral element associated with water. Colourful fishing boats and canal boats will provide you with fantastic reflections, and if your style of painting veers towards the abstract, sometimes just the reflections themselves make wonderful paintings in their own right. Sailing boats with their glistening white hulls and rigging flashing in the sunlight provide an often-needed vertical contrast to the horizontal nature of water. Don't dismiss the more utilitarian vessels even though they

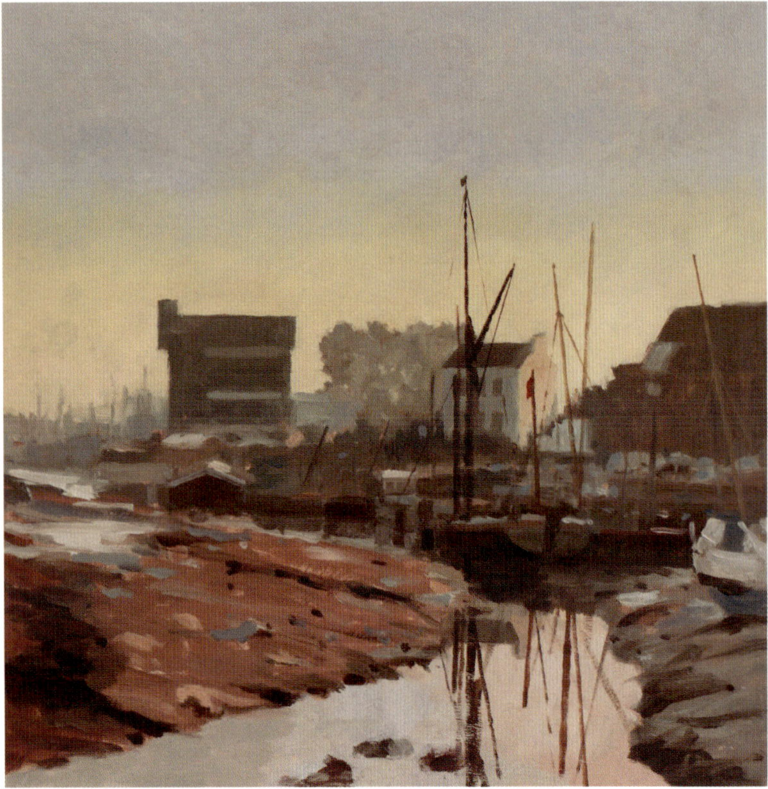

The Quay, Sunday Morning, Kevin Scully. (12" × 12", oil on board)
A warm glow pervades this early-morning river scene, where much detail has been suggested where as little detail as possible has actually been painted. The sky has been painted fairly carefully with softly blended gradations of colour, whilst the reflections in the water have been indicated with loose dry brush marks.

may not afford much colour, their rugged forms and bulk can provide an excellent foil to a softer, watery background. Boat yards contain a treasure-trove of nautical paraphernalia and provide outstanding material for paintings.

These are only general guidelines, and of course the best way to paint water is to get out there and paint what you see, and not what you think should be there.

Including Buildings and Manmade Objects

For our purposes, the concept of painting the landscape encompasses many things, and depending upon your viewpoint, buildings and manmade objects may enhance or detract from your landscape paintings, but they are nevertheless part of our environment. You may also be of the opinion that urban landscapes shouldn't be considered as landscapes at all. If you fall into the former group of painters who are happy to include buildings, roads, bridges and other things manmade you will be seeking out compositions that include some of these components.

Some painters will shy away from including architectural elements in their compositions, and this is often because they are frightened of grappling with perspective. You don't have to be a genius to learn a few of the basic rules to help you overcome your fear, and most of their implementation beyond that is just a matter of using your common sense and observational ability.

Buildings within the landscape have to look right, which entails a bit of careful drawing. Once this has been achieved there are a few other things to consider. Particularly when painting from a photograph, it's too tempting to include all of the straight lines forming the hard edges of buildings, which can be confusing to the eye, so they have to be manipulated in order to make them more visually appealing. A photograph will record everything that the camera has seen, which means that much of the surrounding landscape will also have hard edges, making the overall scene look rather flat. By softening some of the buildings' edges, and most of the distant landscape, we can restore some semblance of how our eye sees things when focusing on one area and viewing the remainder in peripheral vision.

By introducing other manmade objects into our paintings we can create in the mind of the viewer many different emotions. A telephone pole and cables in an otherwise empty and remote landscape can suggest isolated human habitation nearby, or a bicycle leaning against a tree in a cemetery could allude to many things.

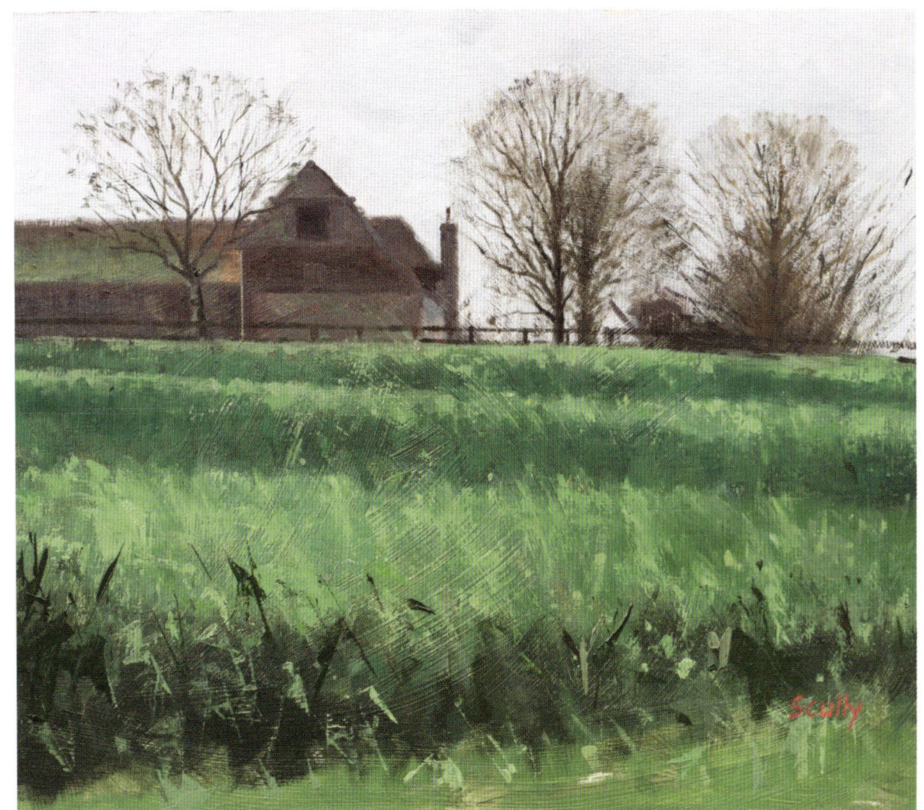

Manstone Farm, Kevin Scully. (10" × 12", oil on board)
To depict the farm's elevated position in the landscape, it has been placed at the top of the image above eye level, which is around the centre mark. The board has been toned with a pale Raw Umber earth colour, which is the same colour that the trees appeared to be from a viewpoint lower down the hill. The board had been primed with acrylic gesso, and the brushmarks from this can be seen in the lower half of the painting where a painting knife has been used and colour deposited on top of the ridges. The farm building has been painted with little detail, and the trees in dry brush to imply distance. The field of crops has been painted loosely using a brush, painting knife and the edge of a credit card.

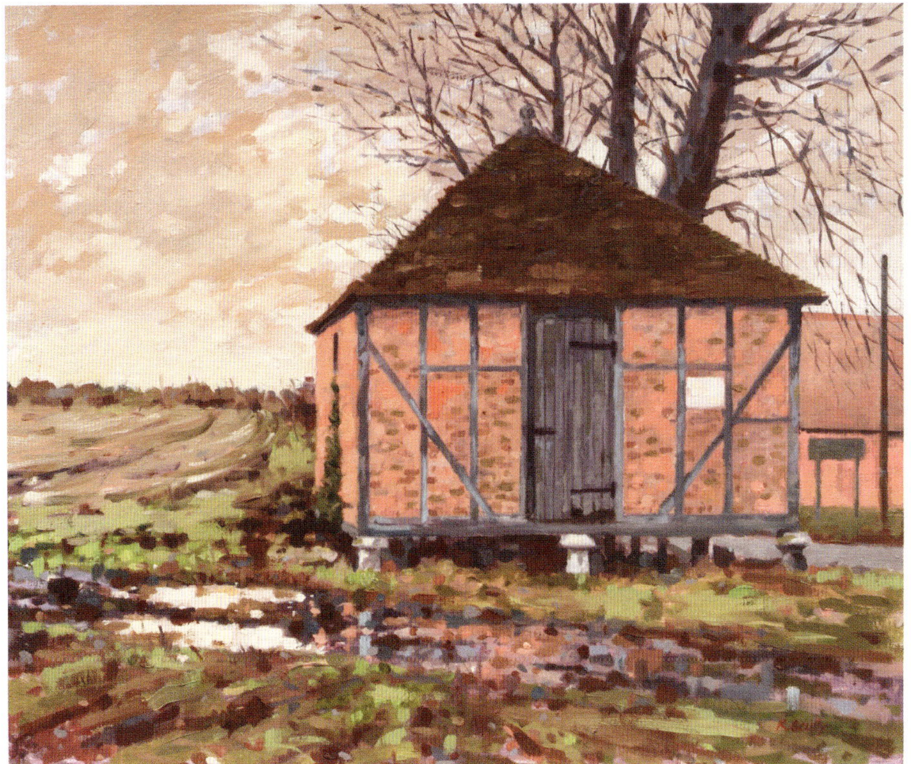

Grain Store, Ipsden, Kevin Scully. (19" × 24", acrylic on board)
This ancient building sits on staddle stones whose mushroom-like shape prevents vermin from entering the store. The colour of the bricks is echoed in the earth, and it would have been from the earth nearby that these bricks were made locally by hand. The dark tree in the background adds a slightly sinister mood to this painting of a muddy field in winter.

EXERCISE

Making Preliminary Sketches

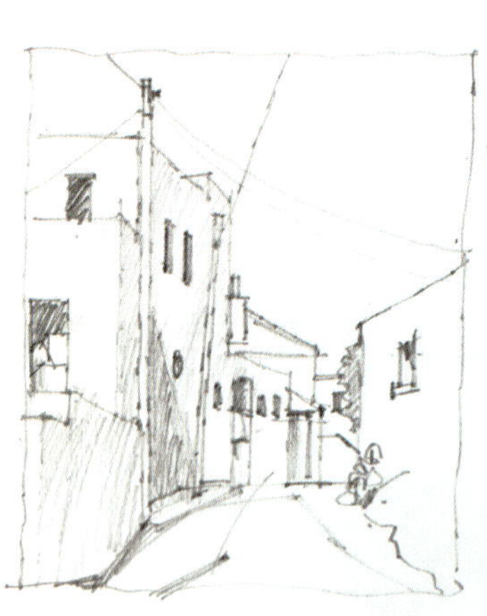

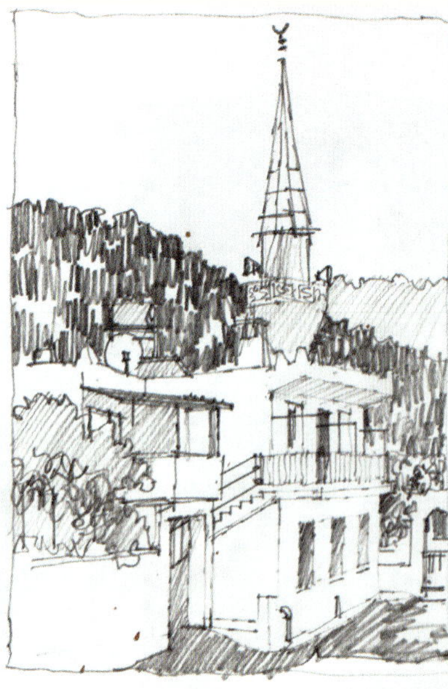

A sketch can include the briefest amount of detail, or it can be a more considered, carefully drawn image for future reference. It may consist of an idea that is taken no further, or it may just be the product of a visual exercise.

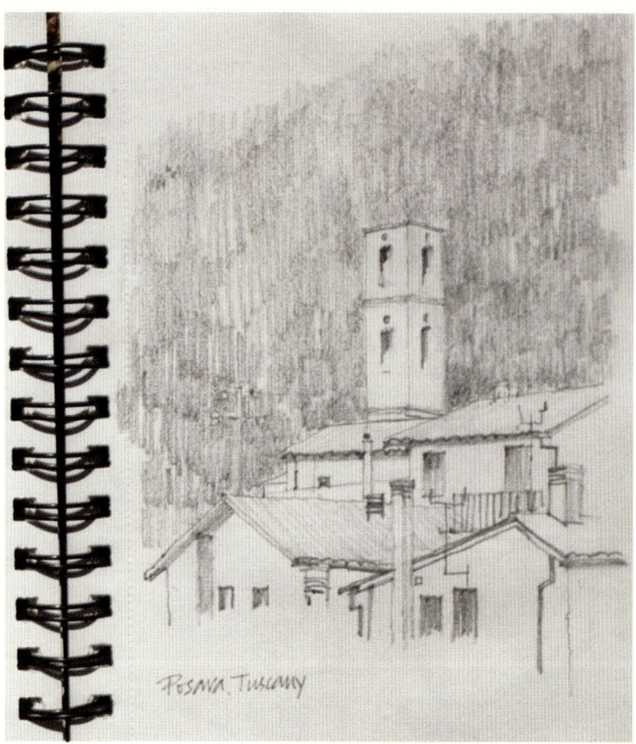

The initial seeds of inspiration can be sown by making preliminary sketches, and this early stage of the process of planning a painting is probably the most crucial. By producing a few small sketches, it will help you establish a broadly accurate image of how your painting will be best composed. Even though you may be short of time when working outside, the importance of this phase cannot be stressed too strongly. By arranging the basic shapes and adding tone to your sketches, you'll be able to establish a pleasingly balanced composition even before you start to think about colour. Be sure to draw a frame around your sketches to establish the picture's edges.

If you are working outside, patrol your chosen subject matter, viewing it from different points and angles before deciding on the most favourable viewpoint. If you have a viewfinder, this will help your decision-making regarding composition and format.

If you are working from a selection of photographs, the process is the same, except that you will have already cropped the images when composing them through the viewfinder of your camera. You can of course crop them again if necessary when making your thumbnail sketches.

Produce as many sketches as you like, remembering that broad decisions made at this stage will be the basis for your finished painting, and that a thumbnail sketch that almost works, but you're not entirely sure about, will probably be doomed to failure before you even start painting it.

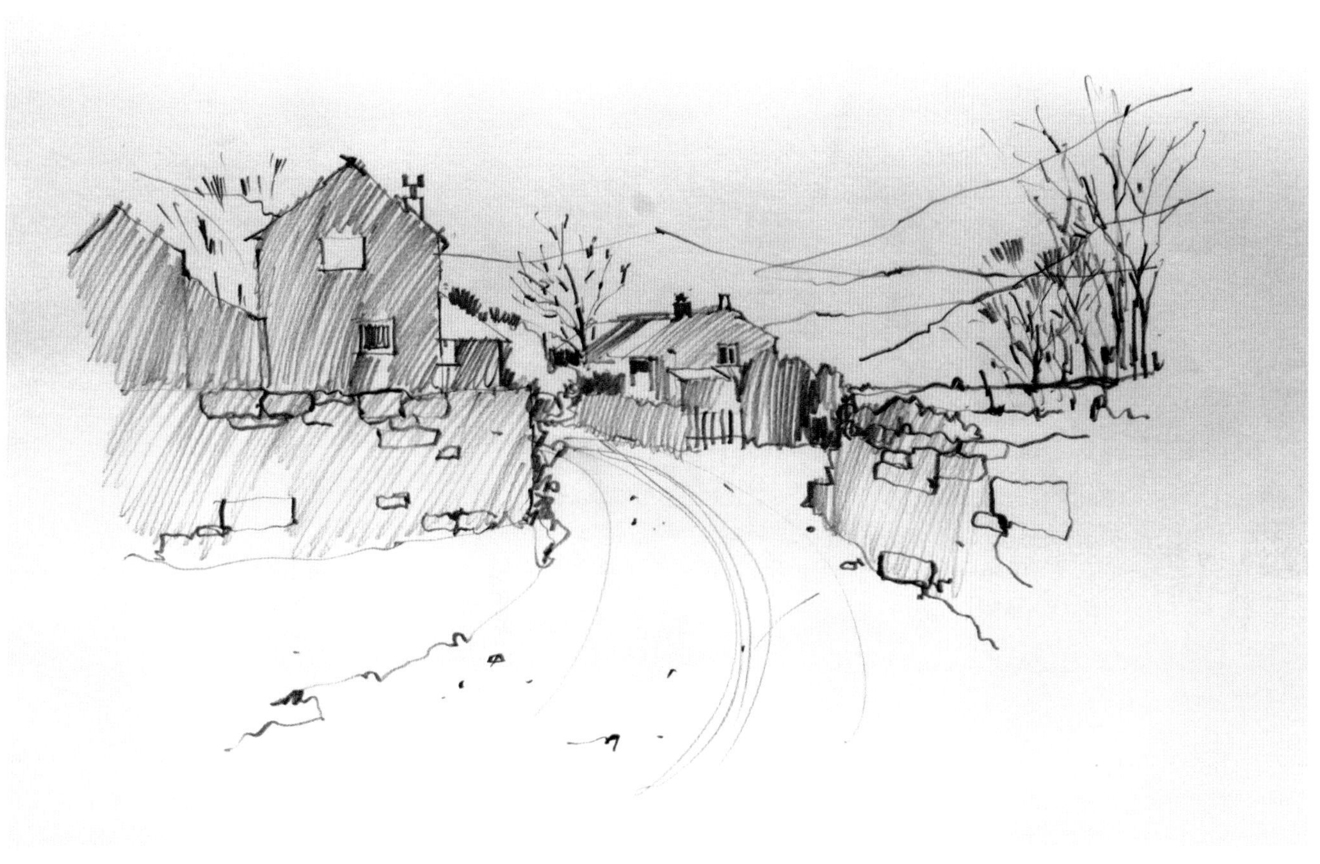

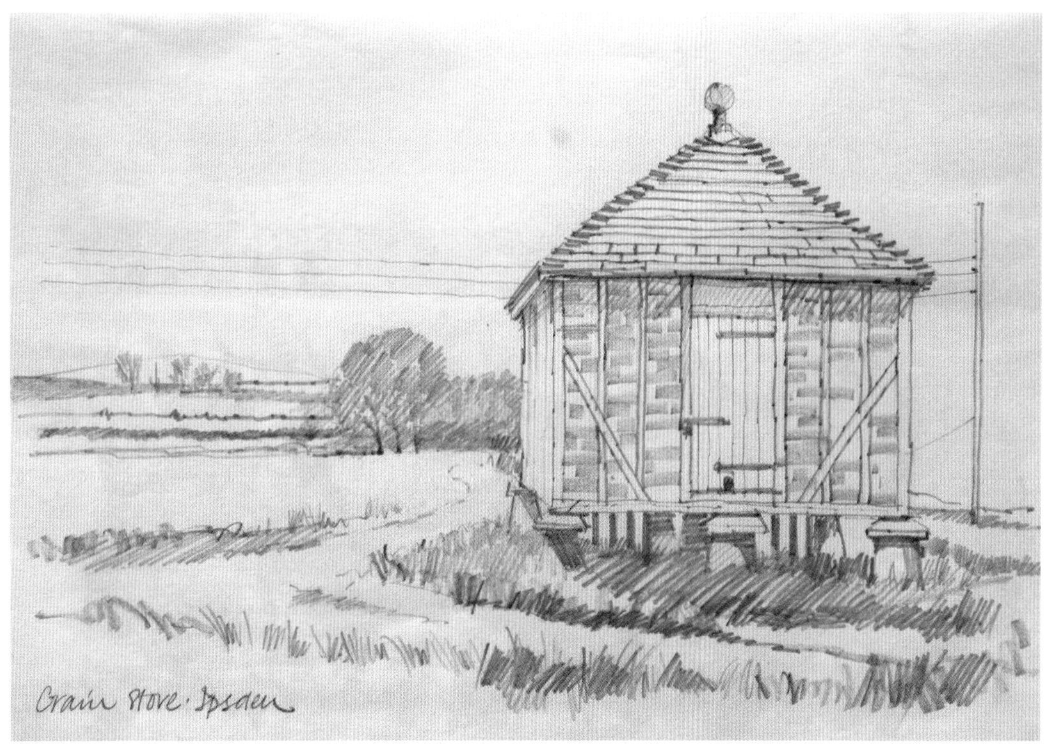
Grain Store · Ipsden

EXERCISE

Creating Good Compositions

Consider this photograph as one that you would like to use as reference for a painting. Devise as many compositions as you can from this one image, and include in your sketches:

- A variety of formats
- Tonal drawings
- Possible deletions
- Possible additions
- Relocation of some elements

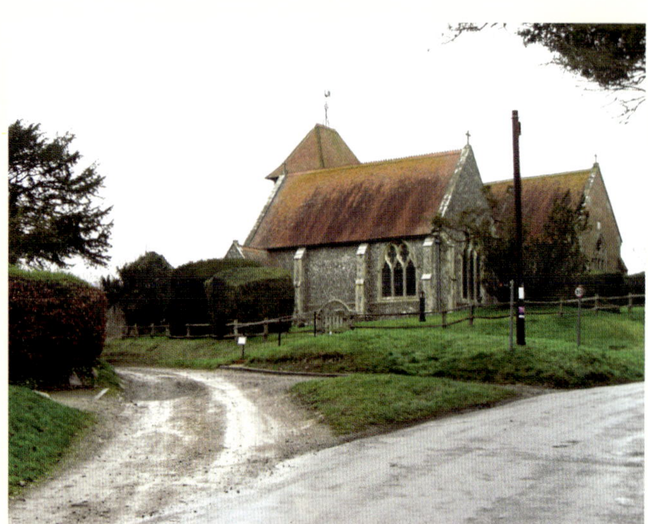

Taking Photographs for Reference

Whether your photographs are to be used to back up sketches made outside, or as direct reference material for paintings to be produced in the studio, they should be taken with as much care and consideration as you would use for your compositional sketches. Unless you are a professional photographer, your photographs will be unable to compete with the three-dimensional world that we see. For use as direct reference, they record indiscriminately, and have to be manipulated and interpreted for use in our paintings, or our paintings can end up looking as flat as our photographs. The camera is a tool that has no aesthetic sensibilities, and is unselective in what it records, for better or worse. Slavishly copying a photograph will suppress our creativity, and will lead to us producing a painting that has little artistic merit or integrity.

You must be careful not to take for granted what you see in a photograph, as some things just won't look quite right, and you don't have the luxury of being able to go and examine something from a different angle, to see exactly how one object occupies space in front of something else. Anything that looks wrong in a photograph will automatically look wrong in your painting.

Photography does have its merits of course, and is indispensable in its use as a reference tool. The speed at which it can capture dramatic moments that we are unable to record in pencil or paint means that we are able to develop those fleeting moments that we experienced, at a later stage back in the studio. Taking a photo of a scene that we were unable to finish for one reason or another *en plein air* will enable us to bring it to a satisfactory conclusion.

I'm sure many famous and successful painters from previous centuries would have given anything for a digital camera, had they been around then.

Selecting a Viewpoint

Choosing the best viewpoint from which to paint isn't quite as challenging as choosing the scene in the first place. Having set your sites on your subject matter, all you have to do is circumnavigate it and spend a little time considering all the alternatives. Consider both a high or low viewpoint, and where to place your eye level. This is where your thumbnail sketches come into play, and your thoughts on your various options can be resolved.

If it's a bright and sunny day think about the light source and how it may affect the scene at different times. Will

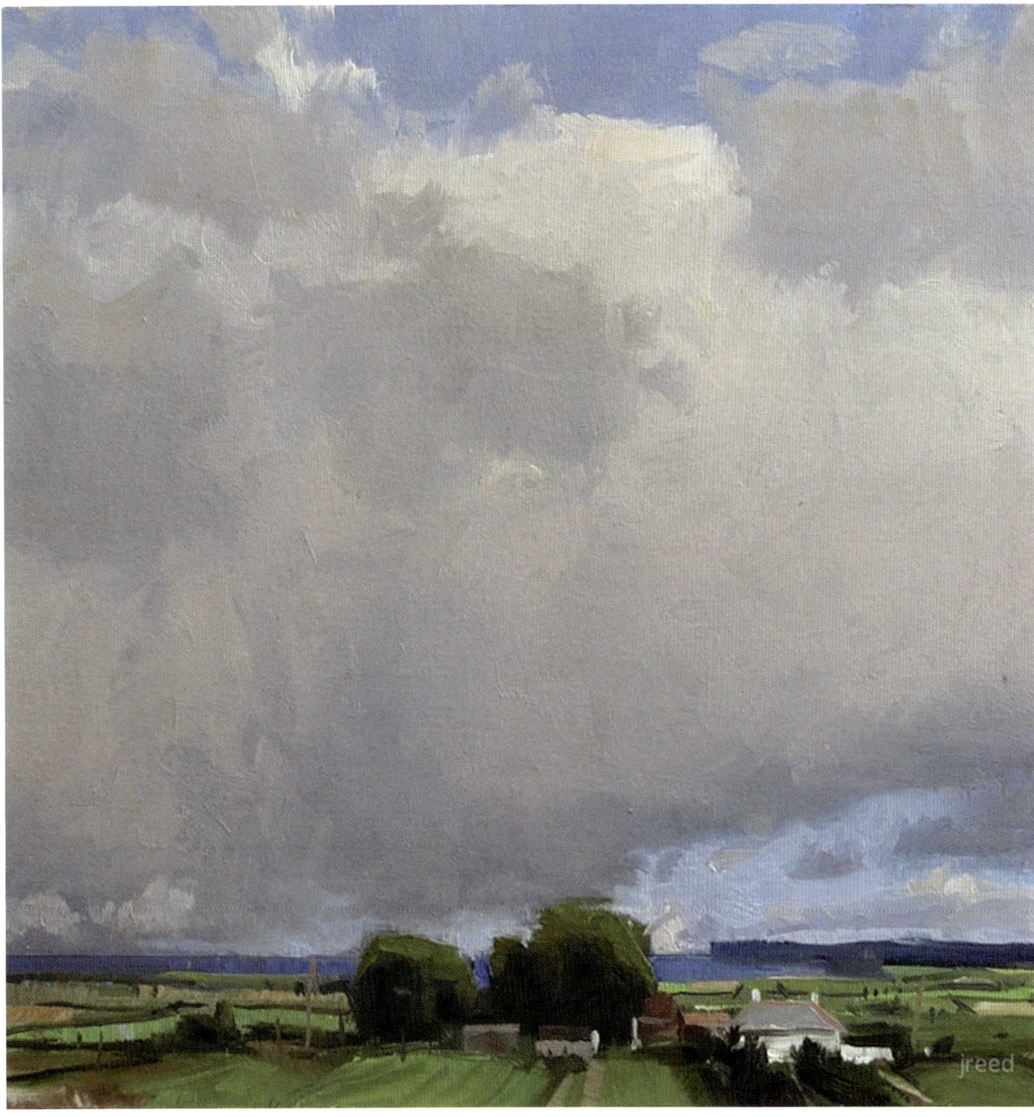

Low Sky, Jeffrey Reed. (8" × 8", oil on paper) The artist always prepares his working surfaces with a warm grey ground of medium tonal value, which allows him to assess degrees of light and dark in either direction of the grey scale. Where the sky meets the horizon is a critical starting point where the relationship of colour and light can be established. Getting this right helps him in his decision-making throughout the rest of the painting. Here, we are immediately thrust into the painting by the absence of any immediate foreground, further emphasized by the presence of the towering clouds, which force the eye down to the landscape and buildings painted in strong, rich colours. The deep shadows give us a clue to the lighting conditions, in suggesting that there is bright sunlight behind the clouds. Painted on location in County Mayo, Ireland.

the painting be more successful if the scene is backlit, or will it be more dramatic with the light source to one side, casting strong diagonal shadows across the foreground? Do you want to depict an early morning scene with diffused light, or a late afternoon one with warmer colours and a setting sun?

If you are inexperienced and intend painting *en plein air* you may want to paint the scene in the middle of the day when the light source is going to be more constant, so that you won't have to contend with fluctuating light and shadows.

There's no reason why you can't pay a second visit to the site, having made some thumbnail sketches and having considered some photographic reference.

EDITING YOUR PAINTING

Just because it's there, don't be tempted to include everything you see in your painting. Nature isn't perfect, and although it can't be physically rearranged, it can be edited in your painting. If a tree is an awkward shape, alter it, or if it is in the way of something behind it, delete it. You can even substitute it for a different tree transplanted from somewhere else in the landscape.

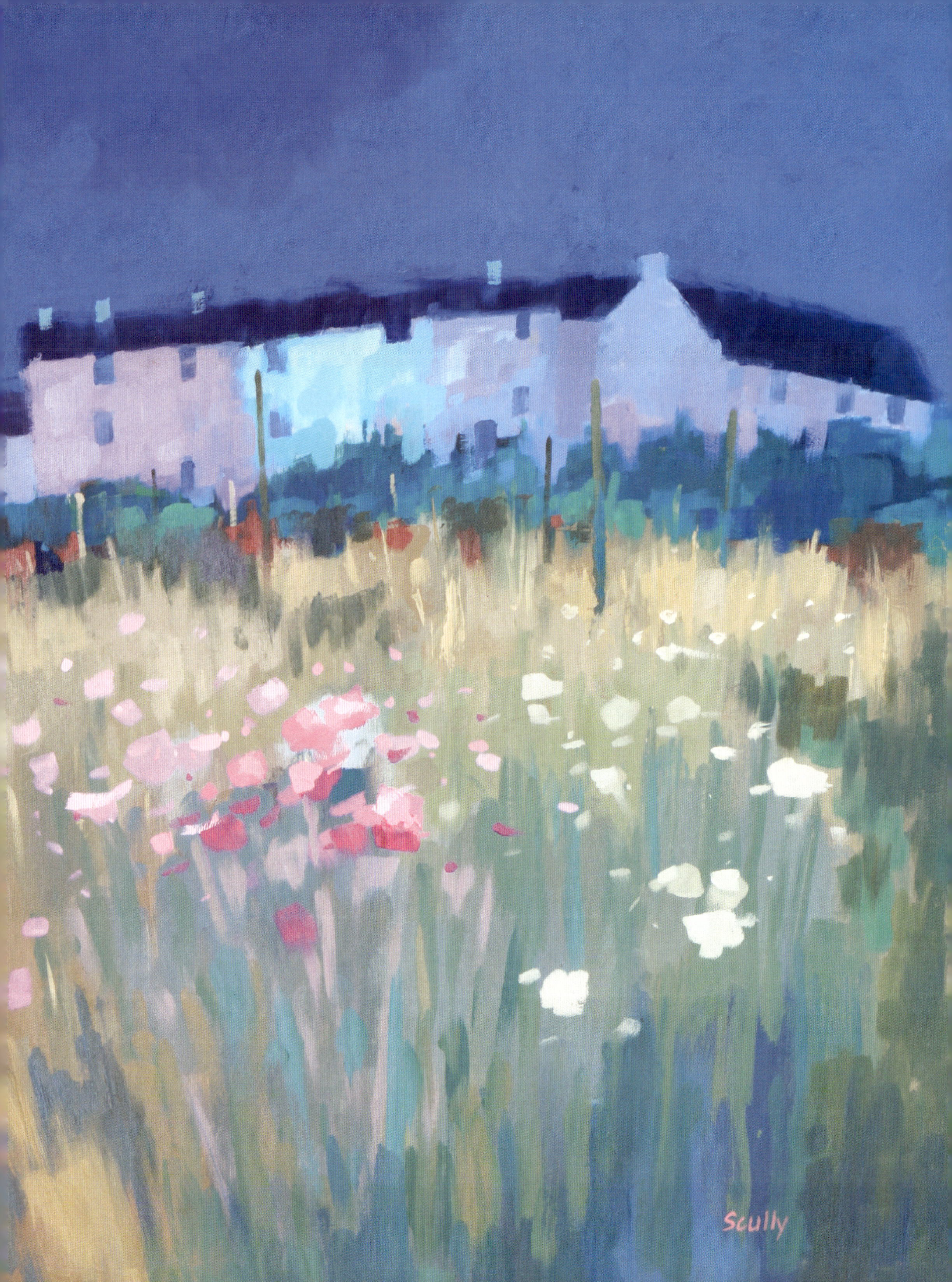
Scully

CHAPTER 5

Colour

Who told you that one paints with colours? One makes use of colours, but one paints with emotions.

JEAN-BAPTISTE-SIMÉON CHARDIN

The colour wheel is a visible system used to identify how colours relate to each other in a continuous, unified spectrum, and this relationship of colours is fundamental to the artist's working language. In essence, the *primary* colours of red, yellow and blue are the backbone of the pigment colour wheel, and cannot be reproduced by combining any other colours, but they can be mixed to produce a multitude of other colours.

The Colour Wheel

When two of these primary colours are mixed together they produce a *secondary* colour: yellow plus blue will make green, yellow plus red will make orange, and blue plus red will make violet. If you mix a primary with an adjacent secondary colour on the colour wheel, you will then h a *tertiary* colour. *Harmonious*, or *analogous* colours are seated next to each other on the colour wheel, for instanc yellow next to orange, or blue next to blue/violet, and are quite happy to be seen in the same company in a painting.

The Field at the Back, Kevin Scully. (23" × 19", oil on board)
This demonstration painting is based on an analogous colour scheme using the green/blue/violet/violet-red range. The colours seen in the centre section of the painting are modifications of the other colours on the opposite side of the colour wheel, and touches of these colours also appear further down the painting amongst the grass. The composition is based on another image seen many years ago by an unknown artist. My apologies to the artist whoever he or she is, and also my thanks for providing me with inspiration for the idea. We can all learn from each other.

Complementary colours face each other on the colour wheel, and can be used to either strengthen colour intensity, or reduce it, depending on where they are placed in relation to each other.

When deciding upon a selection of colours to purchase, it's all too easy to be seduced into buying a tube of every single beautiful colour available, but it's far better to start

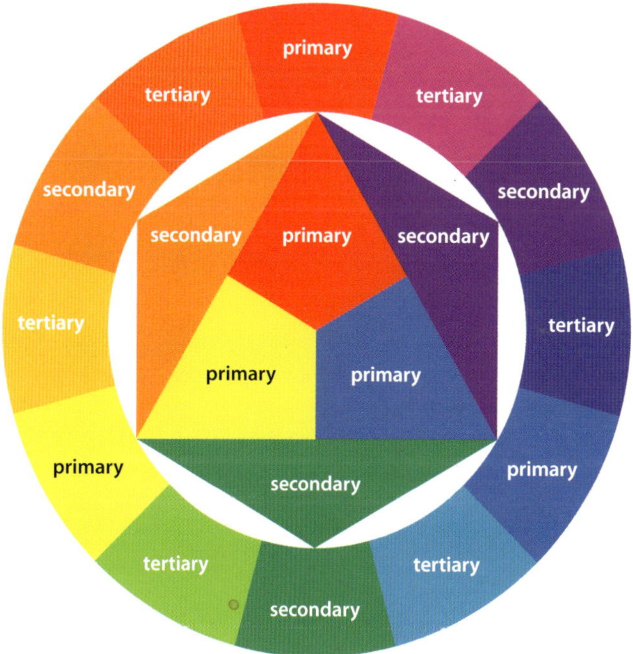

The 12-section colour wheel showing the primary, secondary and tertiary hues.

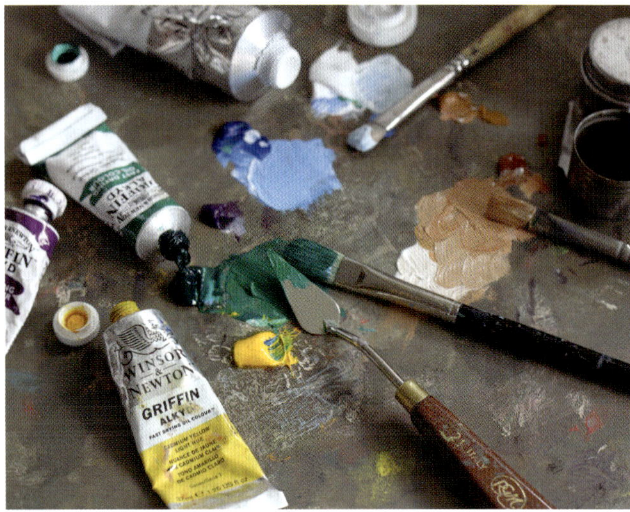

Small amounts of colour are best mixed up on the palette by using a brush, but larger amounts are better mixed with a palette knife. When using alkyd oil paints, which dry fairly quickly, it's imperative that the colour is cleaned from your palette each day, as it will be more difficult to remove at a later stage.

off with a limited selection of just a few. Whilst it's possible to mix a surprisingly broad range of colours using just the primaries of red, yellow and blue, plus a white, this is somewhat limiting, and it would be better to choose a warm and a cool version of each, plus a couple of neutral earth colours. The description of a colour being either warm or cool is relative, so someone's idea of a cool colour may be at odds with another person's perception. But there is a general acceptance of which colours fall into the cooler or warmer category. So a pretty versatile palette might consist of these colours:

- Cadmium Yellow Medium (warmer yellow)
- Lemon Yellow (cooler yellow)
- Hooker's Green (warmer green)
- Viridian (cooler green)
- Cobalt Blue (warmer blue)
- French Ultramarine (cooler blue)
- Cadmium Red Medium (warmer red)
- Alizarin Crimson (cooler red)
- Raw Sienna (warmer neutral)
- Raw Umber (cooler neutral)
- Titanium White

Over a period of time, you may wish to substitute some of these colours, because every artist has their own individual preferences, and there are no right or wrong colours, just different ones. It's often stated that greens are difficult colours to cope with when painting landscapes, and that they are best produced by mixing blues and yellows, but there are some excellent greens on the market that will do the job just as well. Perylene Green and Oxide of Cromium are colours that are particularly suited for use in landscape painting, and provide an excellent, fairly neutral base colour that can be tweaked by the addition of other colours where necessary.

There are a few other colours that are worth mentioning for their purity, as they are very difficult, if not impossible, to produce by mixing two other colours together. Permanent Rose, Dioxazine Purple, Magenta, and Cadmium Orange all have an intensity that cannot be easily replicated. Depending on the manufacturer, these paints may have different names and may be slightly different in their individual chemical make-up, but they all pack a powerful, concentrated punch.

Having chosen your colours, you will now want to squeeze them out of their tubes onto your palette. As a beginner, a logical way of arranging them would be to place them along the top of your palette in the same order as the colours of the spectrum, starting with yellow. Keep your white away from the other colours as it is easily tainted, and leave plenty of room in the middle, and along the bottom for mixing colours together. If you are including some of the earth colours, these can be positioned to the side. This is a good starting point, but it can be adapted to suit your own requirements once you become more familiar with the way colours interact with each other. One thing to consider, however, is which colours will you actually need for a particular painting. If the scene you are painting contains no trace whatsoever of either a warm or cool red, there is little point squeezing either of these colours onto your palette for them to remain unused, scraped off and then disposed of at the end of the painting session.

There is a misconception that blue pigment plus red pigment will make a bright purple, and that a blue plus yellow will make a pure green. This is based on nineteenth-century colour theory and isn't really relevant today. This theory also states that the three primaries when mixed together make black, which they clearly don't. What they do make is a dirty brown. On the other hand, printer's primary colours magenta, cyan and yellow when mixed together will produce pure colours right across the spectrum.

Gordes, Provencal Landscape, David Sawyer. (24" × 36", oil on board)
A large picture painted in the studio composed from two smaller works and drawings made from the subject. The artist was interested in the way in which the buildings of this hilltop village integrated with the organic elements of the rocks and trees. The mass of ochre stone is alleviated by the inclusion of the blue shutters with their direct connection to the colours of the sky. The overall atmosphere was to be defined by the Mediterranean light creating a strong contrast between the lights and darks, and casting a blue haze over the distant hills.

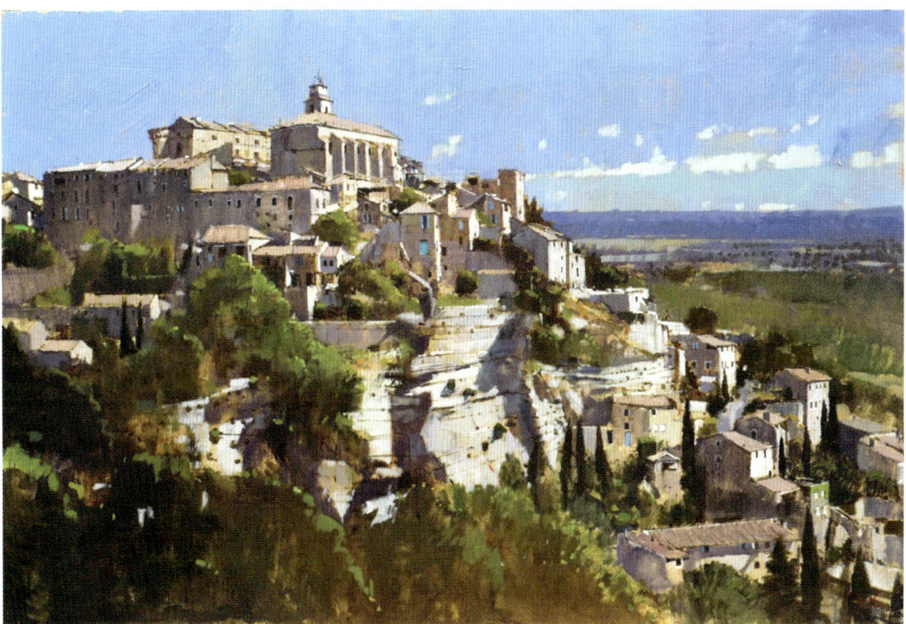

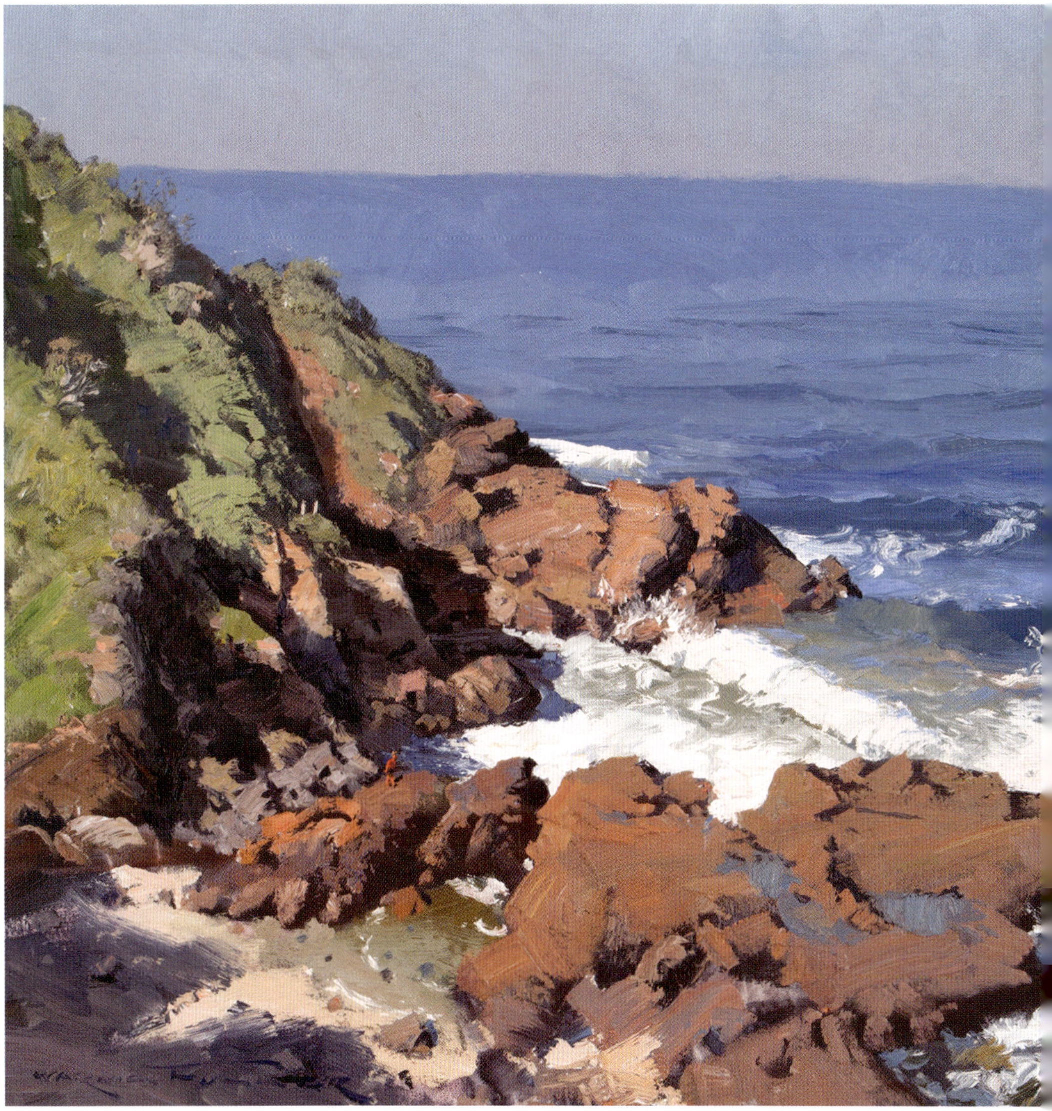

Cliffed Coast, Port Macquarie, Warwick Fuller. (24" × 24", oil on canvas, stretched onto board)
Using a fairly limited palette and pushed for time, the artist has created a painting that contains all of the essential character and feel of this subject without the need to add any further refinement. The mood and atmosphere of the scene has been suggested in simple terms, and any additional detail or adornments would have been unnecessary. The strong diagonal line of the cliffs is counter-balanced by the horizontal line of the sea. The painting was completed on site, in about one and a half hours.

Colour in nature is rarely seen in isolation, and the primary colours are very seldom found in their purest form so they have to be modified, and being able to mix a reasonable facsimile of what we see is something that has to be learned. We know that tree trunks are usually brown, and this is their *local* colour, but more often than not they will appear to be in a different colour, and this colour will have been influenced by other colours around it. What we should be searching for is this *perceived* colour. There may be reflected light present from the leaves, sky, water, grass, or anything else that happens to be in proximity, and the more we train our eyes to seek out these colours, the more colours we see, and the more interesting our paintings will become.

Hue

There is a certain amount of confusion associated with the term 'hue'. Essentially it just refers to a pure colour, and one that has not had either white or black added to it, and more specifically refers to the names of the colours on the colour wheel.

Colour Temperature

As a general rule warm colours appear to advance, whilst cooler colours recede. The temperature of a colour can only really be judged by the relationship it has with those colours around it. A colour normally labelled warm in ordinary circumstances may suddenly appear cooler when placed next to, or on top of an even warmer colour. A painting that contains passages of both warm and cool colours will hold more interest than one that is entirely warm or cool. A sunlit scene containing warm, rich highlights will be further enhanced by introducing cool colours into the shadows, and one that has cool highlights will benefit from some rich colours suggested within the shadow areas. There is much to be observed in nature with regard to colours and their temperature, and there are general rules that apply, but they are not hard and fast rules, and several contradictions can be thrown into the mix, so train your eye to detect these temperature changes and use them to your advantage.

Colour Intensity

Intensity can be described as the brightness or dullness of a particular colour, and this can be adjusted by the addition of other colours to the pure hue. An object of a greater tonal intensity will appear closer to us than one with a reduced tonal strength. Reducing or neutralizing the intensity of a coloured object as it moves further away from us creates the illusion of distance, and this effect can be implied by adding a small amount of complementary colour to the object as it recedes into the distance. Adding a little blue to the far end of a long orange building will reduce its intensity and make it appear further away from the viewer. Areas that are subject to a light source are more intense in hue, whilst those receiving less light or in shadow are usually less intense chromatically.

The Tonal Value of Colour

Colour can vary in tonal value that is not always immediately evident when we look at a scene. This can be demonstrated by taking a colour photograph and then reproducing it in black and white. When placing the two images side-by-side you will find that some of the colours you assumed to be darker than others are often actually lighter in tone. A yellow may be darker in tonal value than a blue, and a brown lighter than a green. Some objects may merge into others in the black and white image, whereas in the coloured image they are separated by a difference in colour. Failing to evaluate tonal differences can have a negative effect on your paintings, and only experience will enable you to discern the different tonal values within a scene.

Shades and Tints

Colour theory informs us that a *tint* is a colour that has white added to it, creating paler versions of that colour in varying degrees. We are also told that a *shade* of a colour is when it has been made darker by adding varying degrees of black. The more black that has been added the darker the shade will be. This is rather misleading for artists; we will rarely use black to darken a colour, as it will undoubtedly make the colour appear rather dirty. In landscape painting, as in all painting, there are many other colours that will do the job of darkening far more effectively and be more visually pleasing than black.

When blue is placed immediately next to orange, which is its opposite on the colour wheel, it creates a striking contrast and has the effect of each colour intensifying the other. This also applies to the other complementary pairs of green and red, and violet and yellow. But when each pair is mixed together they cancel this effect out with the result being a neutral, rather dull and dirty colour. It's unlikely that you would be using these pairs in their purest forms, so they would have to be modified to include a range of intermediate colours.

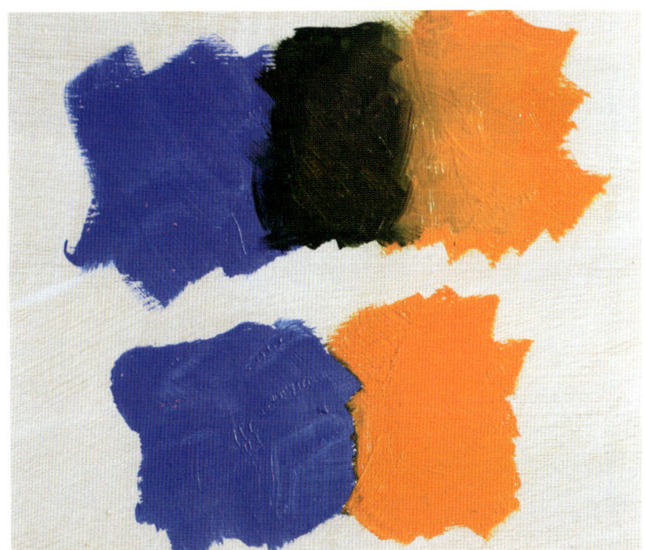

Complementary Colours

When placed next to each other, complementary colours create a dynamic visual intensity that can be used to great effect in our paintings, particularly if both colours are of a similar tonal value. The orange sail of a boat against a blue sky, or red flowers against green grass, and violet hills in front of a yellow sunset are combinations of colour that create real drama, each colour making its complementary appear more intense. When complementary colours are mixed together they tend to cancel each other out and produce a rather neutral colour. In the natural world it's unlikely that you'll encounter complementary colours in their purest form, so they will need to be moderated slightly when implementing this aspect of colour theory. When two complementary colours are liberally distributed throughout a painting they can have more of a disturbing effect, and rather than appearing visually pleasing together, they now clash.

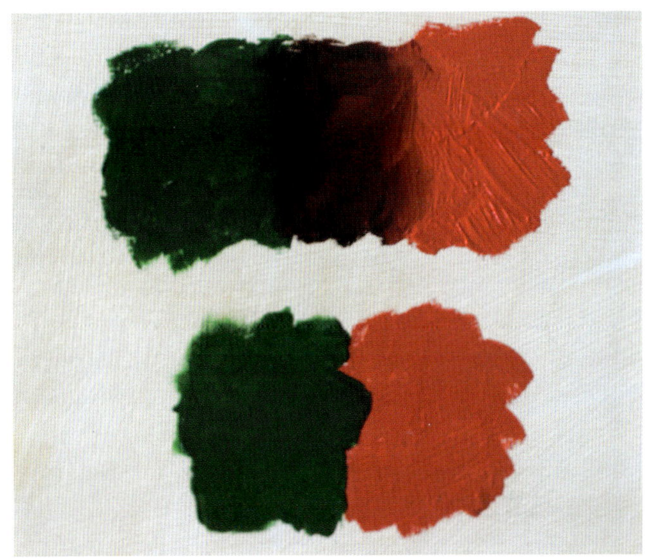

When attempting to paint the shadow of a colour, a common mistake is to make the shadow too dark and devoid of enough colour to make it interesting. When the sun is bright, shadows can be very dark, but when this is translated into pigment on canvas it can appear quite unconvincing. To counteract this, a touch of the colour's complementary counterpart can be added to the shadow, which will enhance it without making it too dominant.

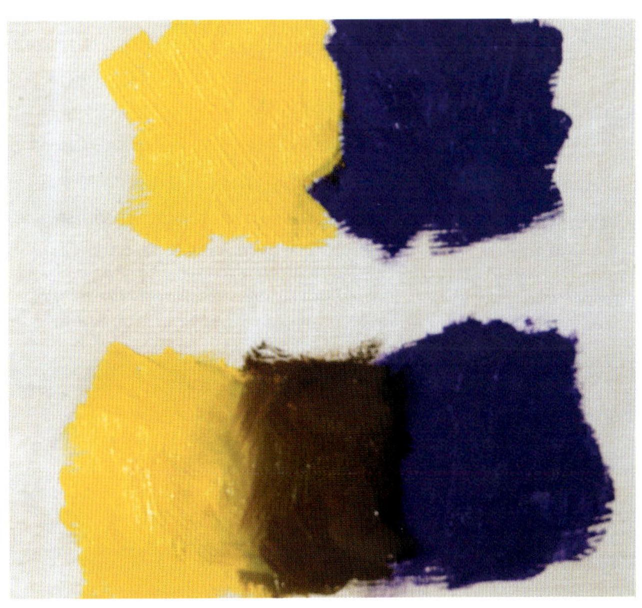

EXERCISE

The Colour of Shadows

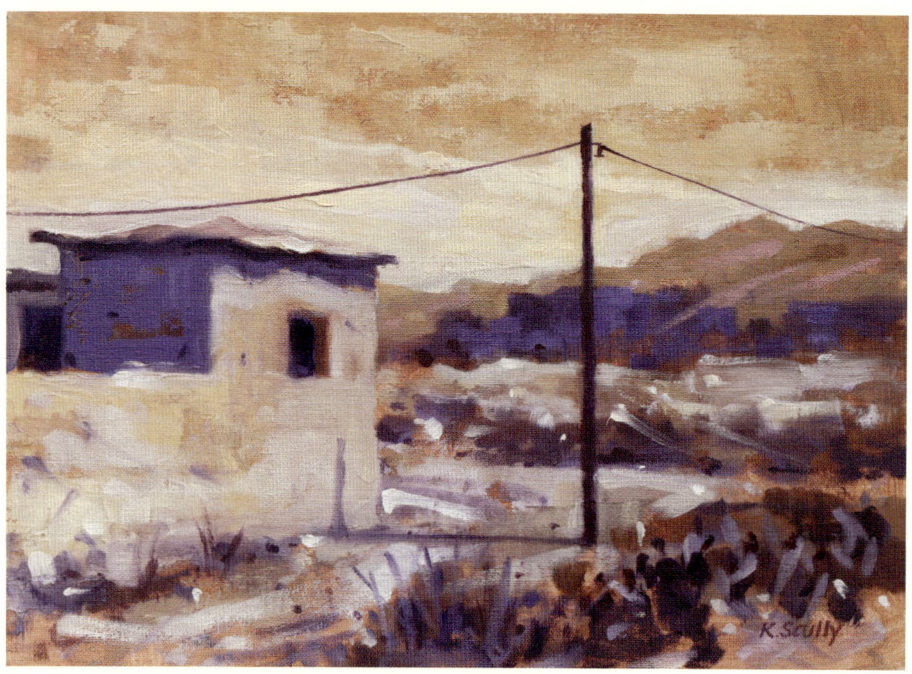

Imagine this building with bright sunlight shining on it from the right-hand side. The left-hand side will receive no direct light, but will attract a certain amount of light reflected onto it from the surrounding local colours in the landscape. Using just a few colours to keep things uncomplicated, complete these stages, to help you think about how to use colour in shadows.

This small study of a building in Morocco was painted with just a few colours: Titanium White, Raw Sienna, Burnt Sienna, and Dioxazine Purple.

1. Draw this simple building, and paint the face of it in its local colour using a mixture of Titanium White, Raw Sienna, Burnt Sienna and a little Dioxazine Purple, adding some texture to it by altering the proportions of the colours in certain areas. If you don't have these colours, any similar ones will do.
2. Paint some of the surrounding sky and landscape using mixtures of the same colours. You don't have to recreate the whole painting.
3. Position a lamp closely on your right-hand side and place your right hand over the painting, without really touching it. This will create a fairly strong shadow on the surface of your painting. Any other coloured objects that happen to be in the vicinity will also affect the colour that you see.
4. This will give you a clue regarding how the colour of the shaded side of the building will look. See how closely you can match this colour, and use it to paint the side of the house and the edge of the window that are both in shade. This colour will probably be a fairly warm neutral brown.
5. This may be a fairly convincing colour for the shadow on this house, but it may not be particularly interesting in artistic terms. As a contrast to the warm colour, paint over part of it with a cooler colour, and in this case a colour that contains more of the purple than anything else. The juxtaposition of the two colours together will give the shadow a livelier appearance.
6. The really dark shadow under the eaves and inside the window can be painted with a mixture of the Dioxazine Purple and Burnt Sienna.
7. Experiment with other colour combinations; perhaps paint the house in a pale pink or blue, and play around with contrasting colours for the shadows.
8. Repeat the exercise, this time using a combination of harmonious colours or complementary colours.

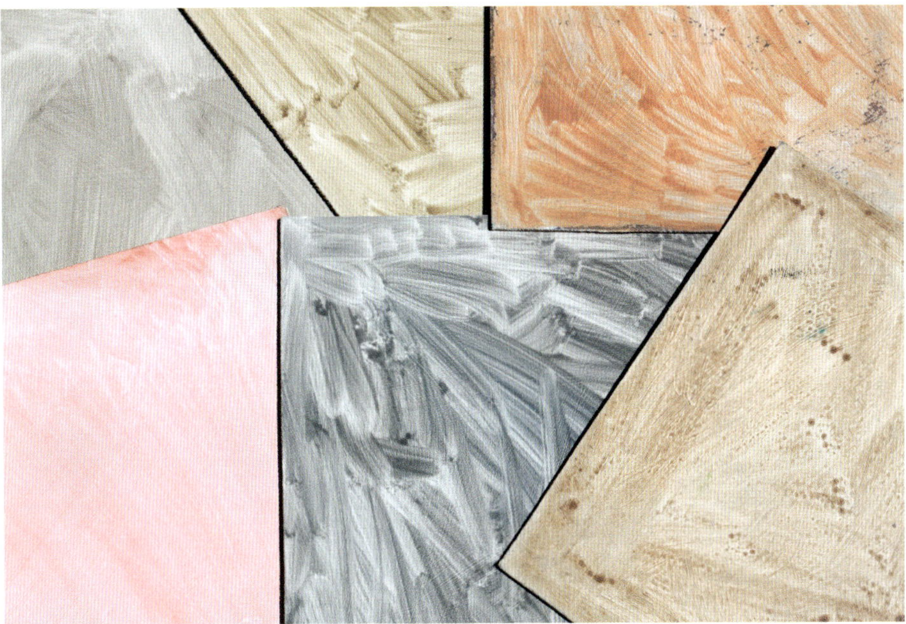

A selection of ready-toned panels, in a variety of colours, ready for use.

Applying Colour

It has always been standard practice to get rid of the white of ready-primed canvas by toning it with a thin wash of an appropriate colour as a ground. This can be a thin mix of oil paint diluted with turpentine, or acrylic diluted with water. Even if you paint in oils, and are in a rush, acrylic will obviously dry quicker. Keep a selection of painting surfaces already prepared, and in a variety of different colours.

Some frugal artists use the remains of oil paint left on the palette at the end of a painting session as a ground for future paintings.

A traditional method of beginning a painting in oil is to create an 'underpainting', and one such process entails covering the whole working surface in a thin, mid-tone colour, often an earth colour such as Raw Sienna or Burnt Umber. The process is partly subtractive, with the lighter parts of the image carefully wiped out with a rag whilst the paint is still wet, and the darker parts painted in with a brush. The image is gradually built up until a monochromatic, tonal version of the painting has been created. This then acts as a base onto which the actual colours of the painting are placed. The benefit of this method, according to those that use it, is that the whole tonal range of the painting has been established before you have to think about the complexities of colour. When this is dry the final painting is created by applying increasingly more opaque layers of paint.

A more contemporary version of this method, and one which is more widely used, is to first tone your surface in a chosen colour, and when this is dry, draw out your image in pencil, charcoal or thin paint, before creating a thin underpainting in the general mid tones of the actual colours that you will be using for the finished painting. In a way this resembles a kind of watercolour wash. As with the more traditional method the paint is gradually applied in a more opaque consistency. The general rule for painting in oils or acrylics is always 'thick over thin'. Eventually this underpainting may be totally obliterated or in some areas it may be allowed to show through.

You will need to thin your paint at some stage, and the vast range of mediums for doing this has been discussed in a previous chapter.

For the finer details in the final stages of a painting, it takes a little practice to mix your paint to the right consistency, but if you liken it to the texture of soft butter, you won't be too far wrong. It shouldn't run off the brush, but neither should it be so thick that it doesn't leave the brush at all.

CHOOSING A COLOUR FOR YOUR TONAL GROUND

Try experimenting with contrasting colours for your toned grounds. This can result in some interesting effects. If you are going to be painting a picture that contains a lot of green, try toning your canvas with a red. The red will make the green really sing out. If you are painting a landscape where the earth is a particular colour, by toning your picture with this colour it will create a sense of harmony throughout the whole image, especially if this colour is allowed to show through in places.

EXERCISE

Transparent, Semi-opaque and Opaque Paint

This exercise will take you through the process of building up your painting in a series of stages, from initial transparent washes through the semi-opaque stage, and finally to the finished stage using opaque paint.

1. Take a photograph of a simple landscape scene to be used as reference.
2. Prepare a small, toned board or canvas using a thin, fairly neutral colour. For this exercise, don't make the colour too strong. You could perhaps use a mixture that comprises a small amount of Raw Umber and Ultramarine, thinned with turpentine.
3. Draw out the image you want to paint. It doesn't really matter what you use for this, as the paint will eventually cover it anyway.
4. Mix up a selection of colours on your palette that correspond to the main colours in your image. These don't have to be accurate matches, as they will be refined later.
5. Beginning with the darker colours, paint in these areas using a thin colour that vaguely resembles the colour in your image. This should be thinned with your painting medium. Do the same with the mid-tone colours. Don't add too much white to the lighter colours at this stage, but treat them more as pale washes.
6. You don't really need to wait for this underpainting to dry completely, although it will do so fairly quickly if the paint has been applied in thin washes. You can now begin to refine the colours a little more carefully on your palette.
7. You can now use the paint in a semi-opaque consistency and add a little more detail to your painting.
8. In the final stage, reduce the amount of medium you use, and the final touches can be added using thicker paint.

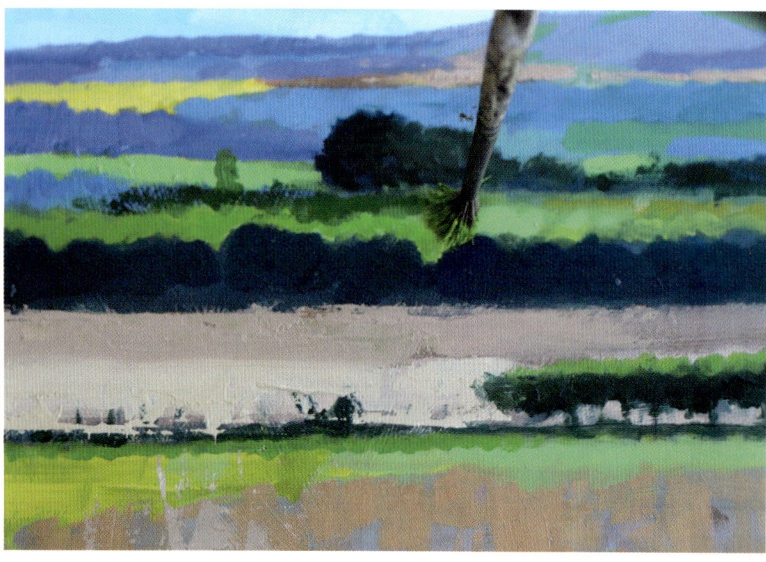

An old brush, well past its sell-by date is the ideal tool for scumbling, which is one of the techniques used in this painting, to add interest to some of the overlapping bands of landscape.

BRUSHWORK TECHNIQUES

Scumbling

In both oil painting and acrylic painting there are a number of techniques that can be used to create different and exciting effects, and because you will sometimes be painting on a rigid and forgiving support, these can be more robust than those techniques associated with watercolour painting. It's not necessary to use all of these techniques in your paintings, but useful to know of their existence.

The technique known as 'scumbling' can produce an interesting texture where small amounts of different colours are placed on top of each other, which partially obscures the underlying colour. By combining both opaque and transparent layers, where one shows through the other, the multiple layers mix optically to create a sense of luminosity and complexity to the painting, in a way similar to the effect of painting small dabs of colour next to each other, as practiced by the Impressionists. Scumbling is a technique that you wouldn't want to use your best brushes for, because the paint is stabbed into the painting surface. It is similar in a way to a dry brush technique, where you don't need too much paint on your brush as you apply different colours one on top of the other with a twisting motion. The colour is applied unevenly producing an irregular quality, and when combined with other techniques such as underpainting and glazing, the effect can be one of incredible depth and richness. In oil painting, underlying layers should be left to dry before subsequent layers of colour are applied. With acrylic's fast-drying properties, this isn't a problem.

Dry Brush

The difference between scumbling and dry brush is the way in which the paint is applied. When using dry brush, you will be dragging the brush across the surface of the painting, where the paint is then deposited on the surface of the grain of the canvas or painting board. With dry brush, you can also build up complex layers of both transparent and opaque paint, and as the name suggests, you will need very little paint on your brush. This technique is particularly effective when rendering rough stone, wood, or any other weathered surfaces. When applied with loose brushstrokes, dry brush can convey a sense of movement in water, hair, clouds, grass and many other subjects.

Alla Prima

An Italian expression meaning 'at the first try,' or in artistic terms it refers to completing a painting in just one session. This involves working wet-in-wet directly onto the working surface in a fairly loose and rapid way. The technique produces paintings that display a liveliness and freedom as the consequence of unfussy brushwork. This is a rapid and direct way of painting that produces bold and expressive paintings. Not the easiest of approaches for the beginner painter, because by painting in this way you are attempting to cope with tone, colour, shape and light, all at the same time. The *alla prima* approach is especially suited to working outside when you often don't have the luxury of time, and when you need to complete a painting quickly, before the light changes.

Blending

Very delicate effects can be achieved by the subtle blending together of different colours where they meet, and oil paint in particular, with its viscous, smooth, buttery quality, is the perfect medium for achieving softly blended colours. When two differing colours are applied side-by-side, they can be merged into each other by using a soft brush in short, gentle strokes, which produces a band of colour that is visually halfway between the two colours. If one colour is darker than the other, it's always best to blend the lighter colour into the darker one and not vice versa. Don't be tempted to overdo the blending though, as this may detract from the painterly appearance of the brushwork.

When creating a soft blend with acrylics, the paint will obviously dry far more quickly, so you will have to adopt a slightly different method of blending. The addition of a little gel retarder will slow the process down a little, which will buy you some more time. Paint your two colours side-by-side but not touching, and then working quickly, use a clean, soft, wet brush to blend them together.

Glazing

Glazing is the layering of successive films of transparent colour one over the other after each has dried, to create a sumptuous and luminous effect. It is a technique that allows you to achieve a subtlety and richness that is impossible to create by simply mixing up a colour on the palette. Although usually associated with oil paint, it can be used in conjunction with virtually any other medium. The reason that glazing produces such luminous effects is because due to its transparency, light passes through the glazes and is then bounced back from the ground colour beneath, through the various layers, each adding a slight variation in colour.

With oil paint, a special glazing medium should be used, which usually contains beeswax. This forms a transparent film giving a gentle lustre to the surface of the paint. A glaze can also be used to alter or enhance a colour. If you find that a colour appears too dull, you can glaze over it with a richer alternative, and this is particularly useful when adding life to shadowed sections of a painting. It should be applied thinly, using a soft brush, and if you are applying several layers, each one must be dry before another layer is added. To speed up the drying time a little alkyd-based medium such as Liquin can be added to the glaze.

Acrylic glazes are slightly different in that the medium used has a white, milky appearance that disappears as it dries, leaving a clear film.

When glazing is used in conjunction with other painting techniques, some great textural effects can be achieved. When the glaze of a contrasting colour sits in the crevices created by scumbling, dry brush or the heavily textured impasto, it can simulate weatherworn surfaces and craggy rocks, with some excellent results.

EXERCISE

Painting Clouds Alla Prima

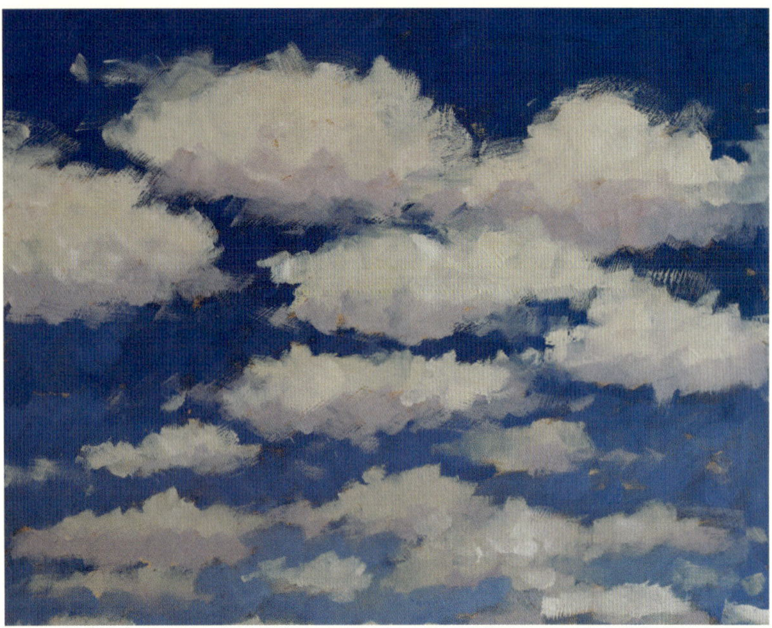

In this exercise restrict yourself to a limited range of colours, which will prevent you from overcomplicating matters. Use only turpentine for thinning your paint slightly, as too much oil in the mix may cause the paint to crack when subsequent layers of thick colour are applied. Use a different brush for each colour. Don't be mean with paint quantities.

You will need:

- Titanium White
- Cobalt Blue
- Raw Sienna
- Alizarin Crimson
- Three brushes
- Toned painting surface
- Turpentine

1. Draw out some clouds on your painting surface, remembering to reduce the size of them as you move down the picture.
2. Create a sky colour on your palette using a mixture of Cobalt Blue and a little Titanium White.
3. Starting from the top of your painting, paint the sky behind the clouds in this blue, alternating the direction of the brushstrokes to eliminate any stripyness. As you move down the picture to your imaginary horizon, create a slightly paler blue by adding a little more white to the colour on your palette. The two different shades of blue can be blended together with loose and varied brushstrokes.
4. Now mix up a colour for the clouds by adding a minimal amount of Raw Sienna to Titanium White. Just add enough to take the edge off the white. Now paint the top three-quarters of each of the larger clouds with this off-white, using a different brush in a circular motion, loosely softening the edges by blending them into the blue sky behind.
5. Mix a colour for the underneath, or shadow side of the cloud. This can be created by adding a little Alizarin Crimson and a little Cobalt Blue to the cloud colour itself. With a third brush, paint in the bottoms of the larger clouds with this colour, loosely blending it with both the lighter cloud colour and the sky behind.
6. Repeat the process with the clouds at the bottom of the picture, but this time making them less dominant by adding a touch of the blue/crimson mix to the colours.

By not creating smooth blends each time, or mixing up too many colours on your palette, you will be keeping the painting loose and expressive. You may find it necessary to wipe your brushes occasionally, as you pick up too much of the existing colour on your painting.

TEXTURAL PAINTING

Impasto

Impasto is thick paint applied with a brush or knife that stands proud of the painting surface, and its use is limited to oils and acrylics. It can be used in certain sections of a painting to simulate different textures, or it can be used for painting an entire picture. When used in small areas, the raised paint catches the light, so impasto is useful for creating effective highlights in a painting. Its use should be tempered though in the darker passages of a painting, where you don't want distracting light being reflected off the raised surface. If you paint in oils and you paint your whole picture in heavy, opaque impasto, it will take a very long time to dry, so you should consider a quick-drying additive such as alkyd medium. If you want to build up further layers of impasto, make sure that the underlying layer is completely dry before adding more paint because the effect of the paint drying at different times will cause it to crack.

Depending on the brand, oil paints may contain different amounts of oil in their constituents. Some paints have a higher oil content than others, which makes it more difficult to apply the paint in a heavily textured impasto. Some of the excess oil can be removed by squeezing the colour onto a sheet of kitchen towel or blotting paper. After a few minutes the paper will have absorbed some of the oil, and the paint can be scraped off onto your palette.

When using acrylic paint, if you want to be extravagant, you can squeeze the paint straight out of the tube onto your painting. The paint will dry quickly, so it can also be built up in more layers if necessary without the fear of it cracking. Acrylic paint can be thickened with the addition of gel medium if necessary.

Sgraffito

Derived from the Italian word 'graffiare', meaning to scratch, sgraffito is a technique whereby you scrape or scratch through one layer of paint to reveal the layer of colour below. You can use any sharp tool for this, from a needle or a scalpel, to a putty knife or the end of a paintbrush handle. For more subtle effects, one colour can be painted over a lighter one whilst it is still wet, so that when the top layer is scratched through, a soft highlight is created. For more pronounced textural effects, dried paint can be scratched through to reveal a colour beneath.

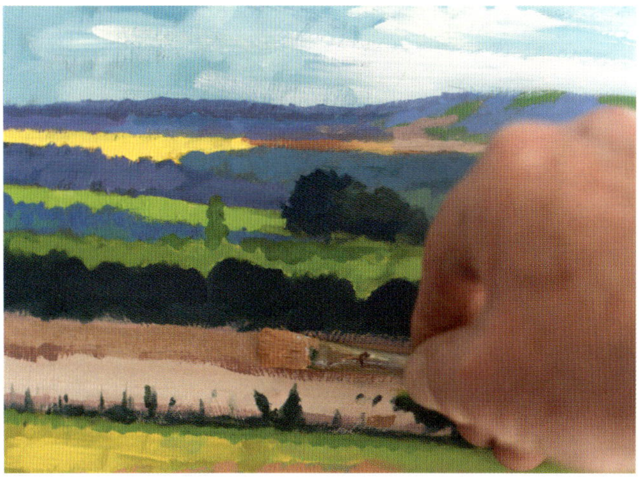

Everybody has their own way of holding a brush, and normally it's similar to the way we hold a pen, but to add variety to your brushstrokes try changing your grip every so often, and it's surprising how different the marks will look. If you hold the brush further up the handle close to the ferrule, so that the brush is under your hand rather than over it, you will be able to lay the paint thickly on the canvas rather than brush it into it. This grip is especially effective when adopting an impasto technique.

Painting with a Knife

Painting knives come in a great array of sizes and shapes, and although less versatile than a brush, they can be used in a variety of ways to create some unusual and exciting effects. They can be used to lay the paint onto the canvas in a heavy impasto, or they can be used to create smoothly blended areas within a painting. The soft, creamy texture of both oils and acrylics make them perfectly suited to painting with a knife. There is a very pleasing way in which canvas yields to the pressure of a knife as well as a brush, but care must be taken when exerting too much pressure around the timber frame over which the canvas is stretched, as this will lead to an impression of the frame's edge being created by the paint.

PAINTING WITH A KNIFE

Painting with knives needs a little practice, because it's very easy to get carried away when ladling the paint on, and you can end up with a terrible mess. During the painting process, it's a good idea to keep the various paint marks made with the knife separate from one another for as long as possible before blending any colours together, and to wipe the knife before mixing up new colours.

DEMONSTRATION

Using a Painting Knife

In this demonstration, a painting knife has been used in conjunction with brushes, where the majority of knife work has been restricted to the areas where the clay has been excavated, suggesting the various planes that have been created by the scraping actions of the heavy machinery. The sky has been painted using brushes to create a softer feel to this part of the painting, as well as to introduce a degree of aerial perspective by pushing it further back.

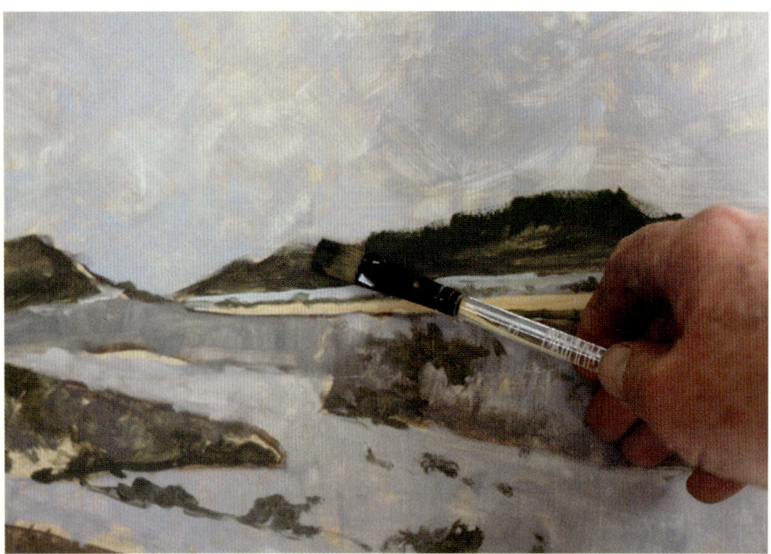

The ground chosen for this painting was a thin wash of Yellow Ochre, as it was a colour that could be seen in certain parts of the scarred landscape. After the initial blocking-in, some thicker colour was added, and here the hills in the distance were painted with a synthetic brush using a dry brush technique to create a soft edge against the sky.

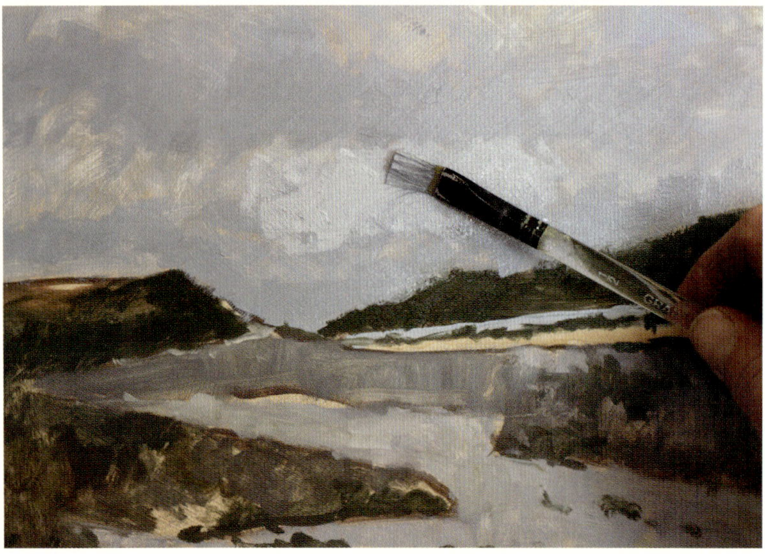

The clouds were painted in thick, opaque colour, using a circular motion to create brushstrokes in keeping with their shape. The colour was also dragged along the tops of the hills in dry brush, creating a soft blend against the sky.

Where the clay had been exposed below the surface, the paint was applied in vertical brushstrokes to suggest the way that the machine had cut into the hillside. By holding the brush almost parallel with the surface of the painting, the colour can be deposited thickly in one stroke and left, with little or no blending. A square brush was chosen for this painting as its shape corresponded with the shapes left in the clay by the machine.

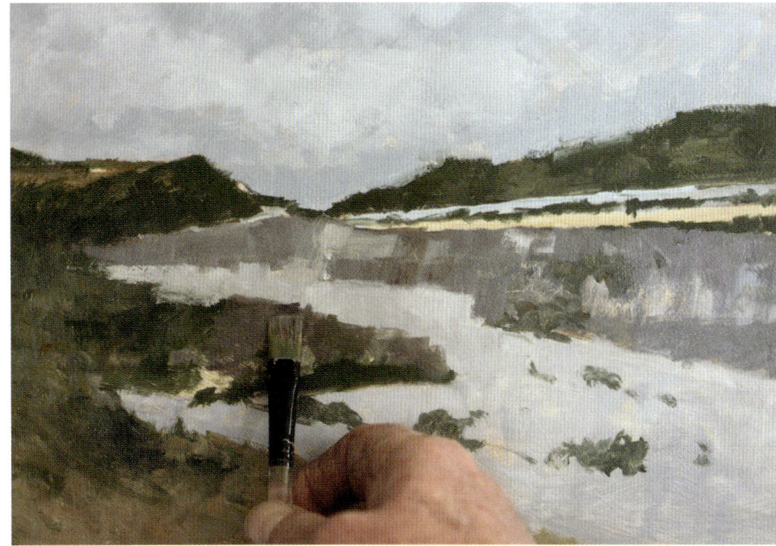

To emphasize this effect further, a painting knife was used to create some sharper edges and create a little texture in certain places. Where the paint was applied too thickly, it was adjusted with the wipe of a finger.

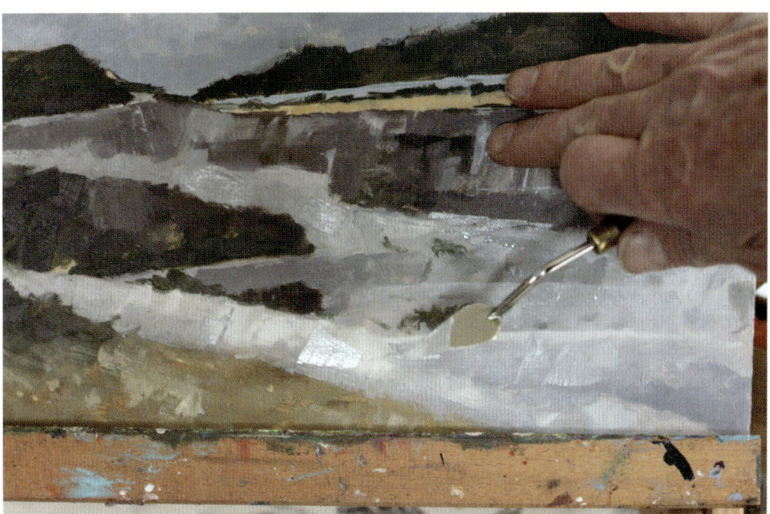

The rest of the painting was completed with a combination of brush and knife, and apart from the sky, much of the loose detail was flicked in with paint on the end of a painting knife. By using a knife, small random shapes can be made that are difficult to produce with a brush.

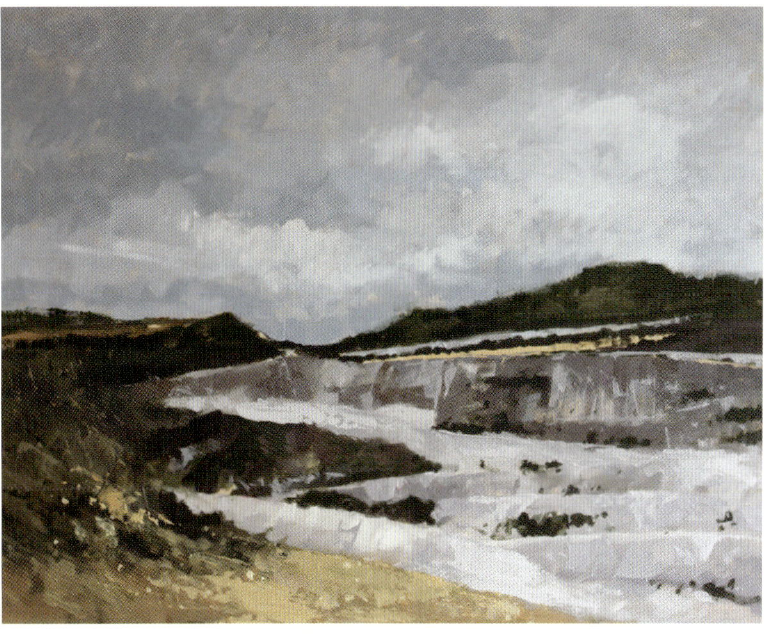

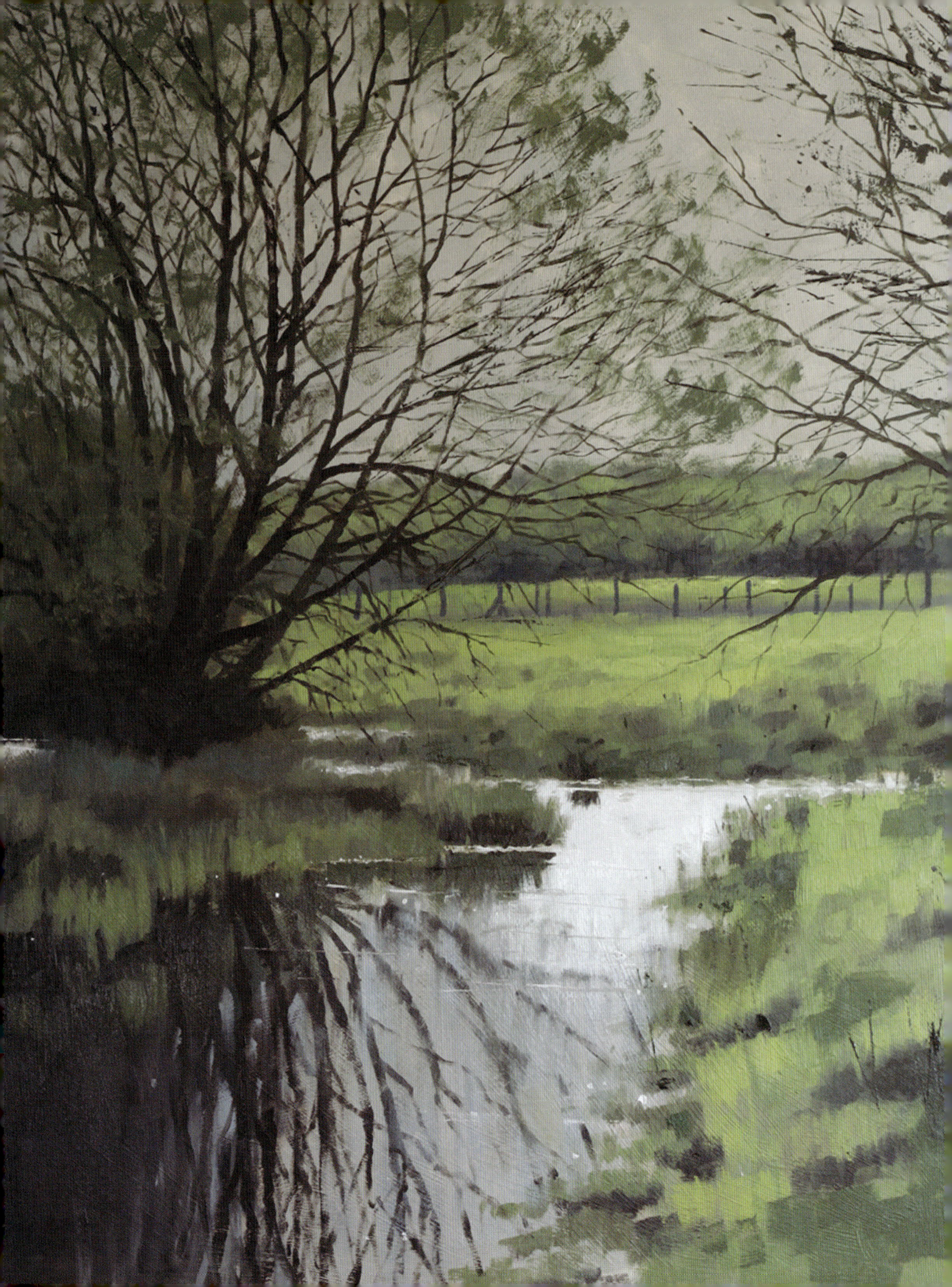

CHAPTER 6

Planning the Painting

Composition, an arbitrary, inexact process, appears to be guided best by intuition and chance rather than science.

PETER CICCARIELLO

The natural world is vast, and so as painters we have to somehow contain a part of it if we wish to represent it in a two-dimensional form. This requires the use of a picture frame or edge, within which all of the components that make up our composition are to be located. Many people instinctively know when something is out of balance, or visually disjointed, but are not always able to pinpoint why that is. A good composition relies on many factors, and they shouldn't be considered in isolation, as they all overlap and influence each other in their interrelationship.

The ability to draw plays an important part in our search for good composition, for by continually drawing, we are observing and dissecting that which we see in front of us. The more we look, the more we see.

Size and Format

More often than not, by using a viewfinder we are able to select a satisfactory composition from a particular scene in the landscape that appeals to us enough to make us want to paint it. Particular scenes will intuitively suggest whether a painting should be in either a landscape or portrait format. A scene with a dominantly tall building as its focus will call out to be painted in a portrait format, whereas a wide-open, flat seascape with some low-lying buildings on the horizon would require a landscape format. If you have an adjustable viewfinder you will be able to alter the proportions of your format by moving the slider up and down, or from left to right. You can also move it backwards and forwards. Don't decide on using a particular canvas or painting board just because you have one handy, if the ratio of height to width doesn't match the proportions of your chosen format. This would mean that you would have to crop your composition where you hadn't originally intended.

But there are occasions when composing through a viewfinder is not the complete answer. Looking at a scene through a viewfinder is one thing but really knowing what it's going to look like when painted is another matter altogether. By actually drawing the scene surrounded by a frame, and this can be done with just a simple line, you will be able to resolve any potential problems in your sketch that may raise their ugly heads later in your painting, especially if you produce a fairly accurate tonal drawing.

Choosing a size for your painting isn't quite as important, and is more to do with how comfortable you are painting on a large or small scale. However, if you are painting a dynamic, action-packed scene with lots of things happening, it would suggest working on a larger scale.

Spring Willows, Kevin Scully. (20" × 18", oil on board)

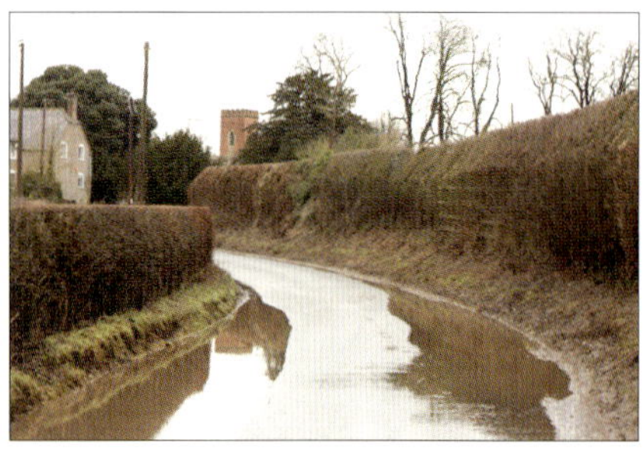

Although the scene in this image has potential, the composition is rather imbalanced, and would benefit from cropping in some way. It's always worth trying a few alternatives before you decide on a composition, as the photograph you took may not look as promising as you originally thought when you print it out or view it on a screen.

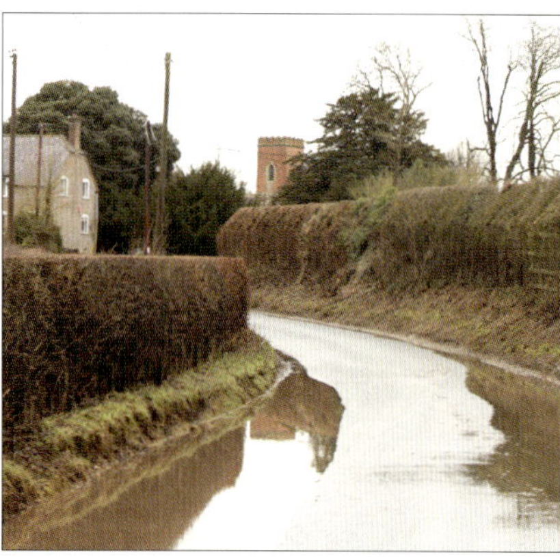

This squarer format is unquestionably a more comfortable arrangement of the existing elements, and with a few adjustments it could be the basis of an interesting painting.

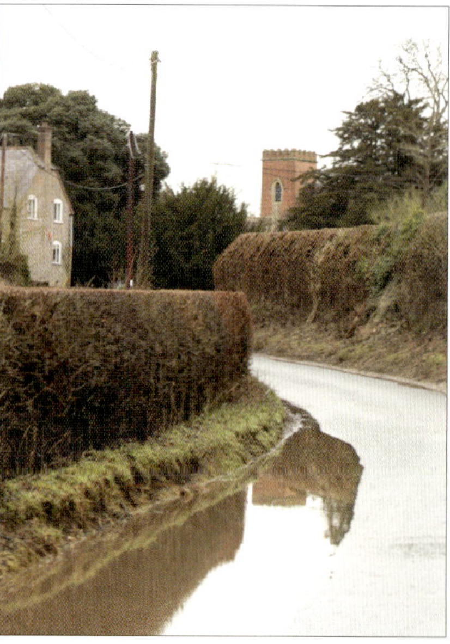

Consideration should be given to a different format altogether, so perhaps by cropping the area of the image on the right-hand side, where very little of interest is happening, more emphasis is given to the church in the background. The reflection of the church and part of the hedge in the puddle creates a rather uncomfortable shape, so this should be altered. By removing the house to the left of the photograph, a simpler but better-balanced composition will be arrived at.

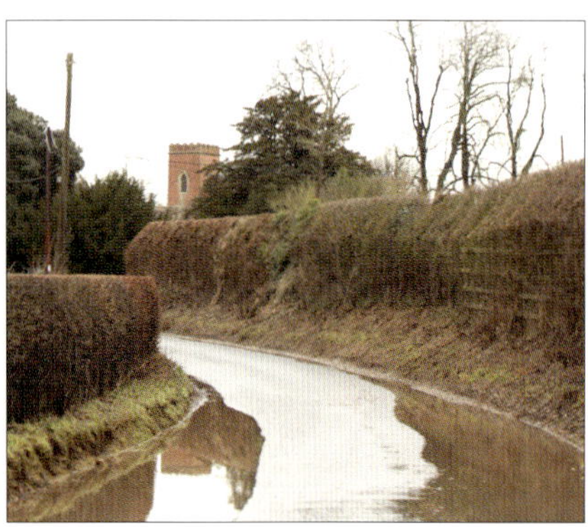

The house to the left of the photograph has been cropped, and the image extended to the right. The reflections still look uncomfortably odd and need to be amended, but the church is now in a more agreeable position in the arrangement of elements.

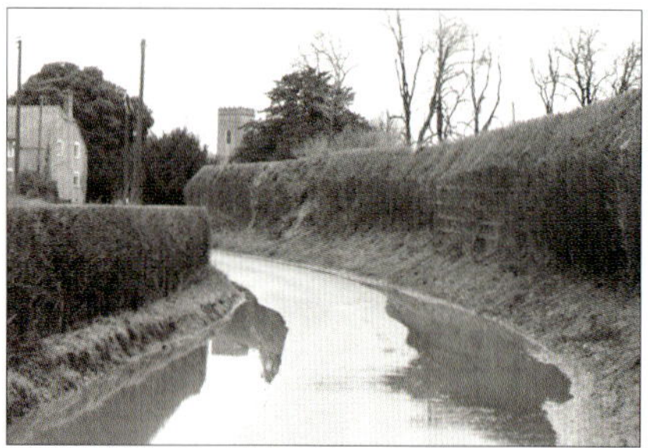

With the colour removed, it is far easier now to assess the differences in tonal values. It's very useful to study these variations, particularly if you are going to impose your own colour scheme on the image.

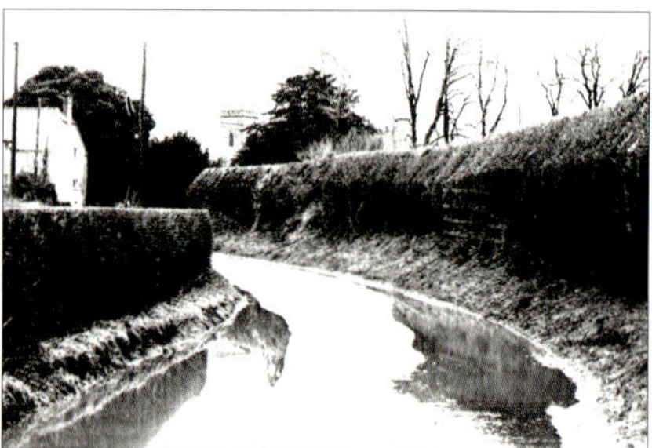

In this version, the number of tones in the black and white photograph have been reduced to just a few by using the Posterization filter on Photoshop. This allows you to see the basic framework of the image more clearly.

Bridge at Callander, Douglas Fryer. (6" × 12", oil on panel) When producing a group of paintings, Douglas Fryer enjoys working on a variety of sizes. The small scale of this painting necessitates smaller brush strokes and passages, and because it requires getting up a lot closer to the image, it allows him to experience a much more intimate involvement within the painting's space. The painting focuses on the relationship between the heavy arch of the bridge, and the way it is broken up by the frail and shimmering veil of trees in front of and behind it. There is a serene quality as the eye follows the gentle arch from one end of the painting to the other, and back and forth through the 'z' pattern of the composition. The success of the painting also owes a great deal to the careful balance and distribution of the various tonal values.

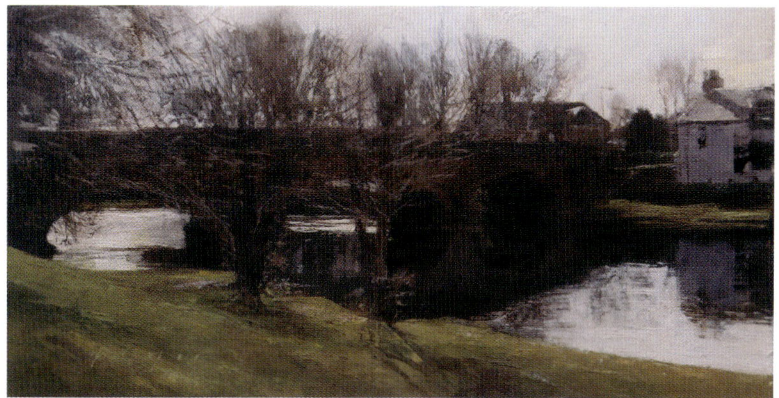

South Fields in March, Douglas Fryer. (16" × 36", oil on panel) This painting depicts the snow finally giving way to the dark earth that has been covered during the winter months. The composition demonstrates a subtle colour play between the restrained blues, purples and golds, with the neutral tones acting as a foil, which allows the colour to read with more intensity than it would do otherwise. The composition is simple, with the painting divided into three sections; the sky, middle distance and foreground. The winter sky is almost featureless, and the middle distance contains a series of horizontals, verticals, diagonals and rectangles, all set within an elongated rectangle. The foreground has been treated simply, so as not to detract from the details suggested along the centre of the picture.

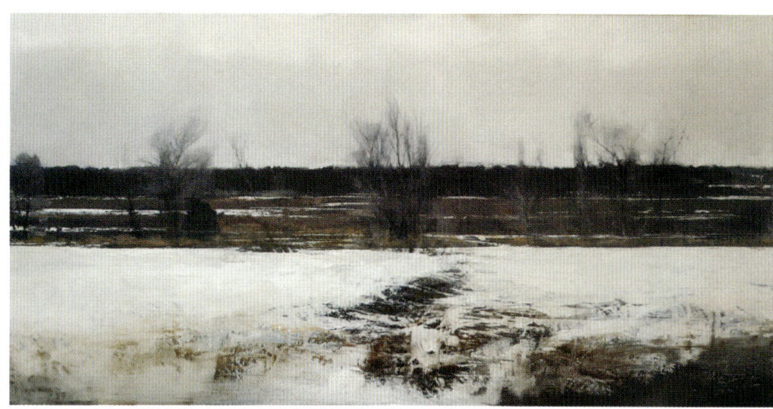

COMPOSITION

When composing a picture, there are a few procedures that can help you achieve an interesting and stimulating arrangement.

The Law of Thirds

The 'Law of Thirds', also known as the 'Golden Mean', divides your image equally into nine sections, creating three rows of three both vertically and horizontally. The points at which these divisional lines intersect produce four 'hotspots', and as a general guideline it is on or very close to one or more of these points where the viewer's attention should be focused. In landscape painting, the horizon line will also look fairly comfortable placed along either one of these two horizontal lines. If the emphasis is to lie with the foreground, then the horizon should be placed on the top line, and if the focus is on the sky then the horizon should line up with the bottom line. There is no need to follow this rule precisely, and positioning things a little further one way or the other can work equally as well. As a general rule this works well enough, but there are many great paintings where the application of this theory is totally absent. Instead, we may see the focus of attention placed squarely and effectively in the centre of the picture, or the composition based on a swirling curve, or a series of diagonals.

If you are making a compositional sketch with the intention of producing a finished drawing or painting, you can divide your page into thirds and begin by roughly drawing your main point of focus on one of the four 'hotspots'. This will immediately create an agreeable starting point for your drawing. If there is another lesser point of interest in your subject matter, try placing this on another point diagonally across the page from the primary point of interest. Providing this does not compete for centre stage with your main focus, this can produce a harmonious balance to your composition, otherwise your focal point might be in competition with a large area of negative space. With experience, you may find that you are creating some wonderful compositions instinctively, only to find that when analysed, they fall into the 'Law of Thirds' concept. On the other hand it may be totally absent. There are many examples of excellent paintings in this book where the artists have followed no known rules of composition.

To intensify this main focus of attention even further, you

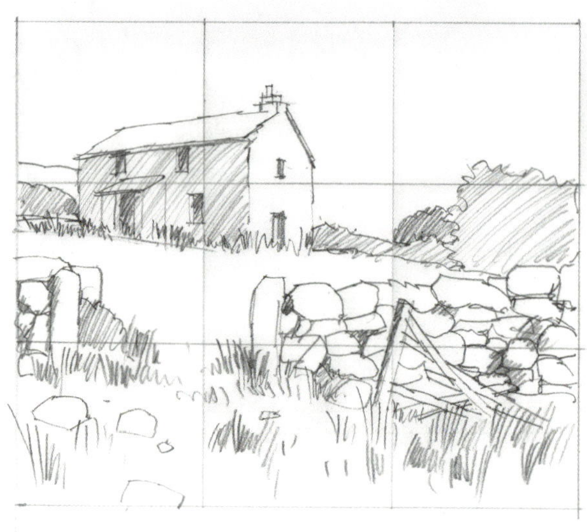

Law of Thirds
In this sketch, the main focus of the composition is the farm building, and this has been placed on one of the 'hot spots' on the grid. A subordinate element of interest is the broken gate, and this has been located on another 'hot spot', diagonally across from the farm building.

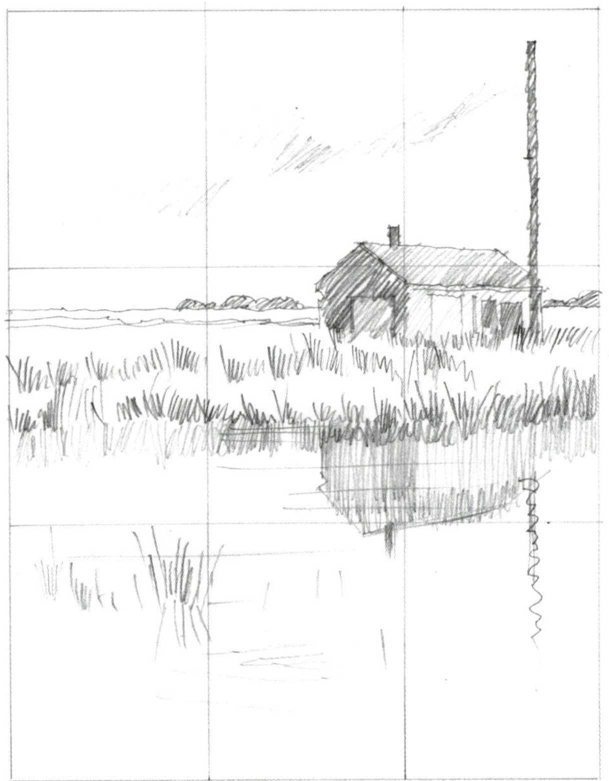

Law of Thirds
This shed is on one of the 'hot spots', and the horizon line has been placed close to the top horizontal line on the grid. To create a visual balance to the shed, some reeds have been introduced in a position diagonally across the composition.

can place both your darkest dark and your lightest light on this spot, which will guarantee a very strong focal point in your picture. A focal point can also be created by including extra detail, more intense tonal value, a dominant contrast in colour or size, in that area where you want your main point of interest to be.

Laws regarding composition are there to be broken, and are useful as a guide, but a drawing or painting doesn't necessarily have to have a single focal point. If you want to emphasize the chaos or complexity of a scene, the viewer's eye can be kept moving around the picture by including many centres of interest. There are several highly complex laws devised by various artists and photographers to aid composition, which could fill a whole book. You may also simply trust your instincts, and if a composition that doesn't follow any rules still looks good, then it is good.

Balance

When positioning your main area, or areas of interest, give them an appropriate amount of space in your painting. There is no point in devising a cunning position for a focal point that's so small no one can really see what it is, and it may even be questioned why it's there at all.

In our compositions, we may all have a natural inclination towards either a symmetrical or asymmetrical arrangement, and depending on the mood of the painting we can choose one or the other. If we are planning a calm and thoughtful painting, a symmetrical composition where both sides of the painting have been given an equal weight distribution of components will provide an appropriate harmonious balance. A balance that is asymmetrical is more suitable for an edgy painting. A balance may take the form of colour, shapes, curves or diagonals, repeated and distributed in visually pleasing areas in a painting. If there is no repetition, or if the repetition is disjointed and its weight imbalanced, an entirely different effect will be created.

Shapes and Edges

When we stand in front of a landscape in which many of its components are in silhouette due to the lighting conditions, we are unable to determine a true sense of perspective, and the volume and colour of these elements within it. We have to rely on other ways of defining these constituents in our composition.

Shapes play a very important part in composition, and the way in which they are arranged and overlapped can inform us about the distance between objects in the landscape. We have to rely on variation in scale and a visual organization

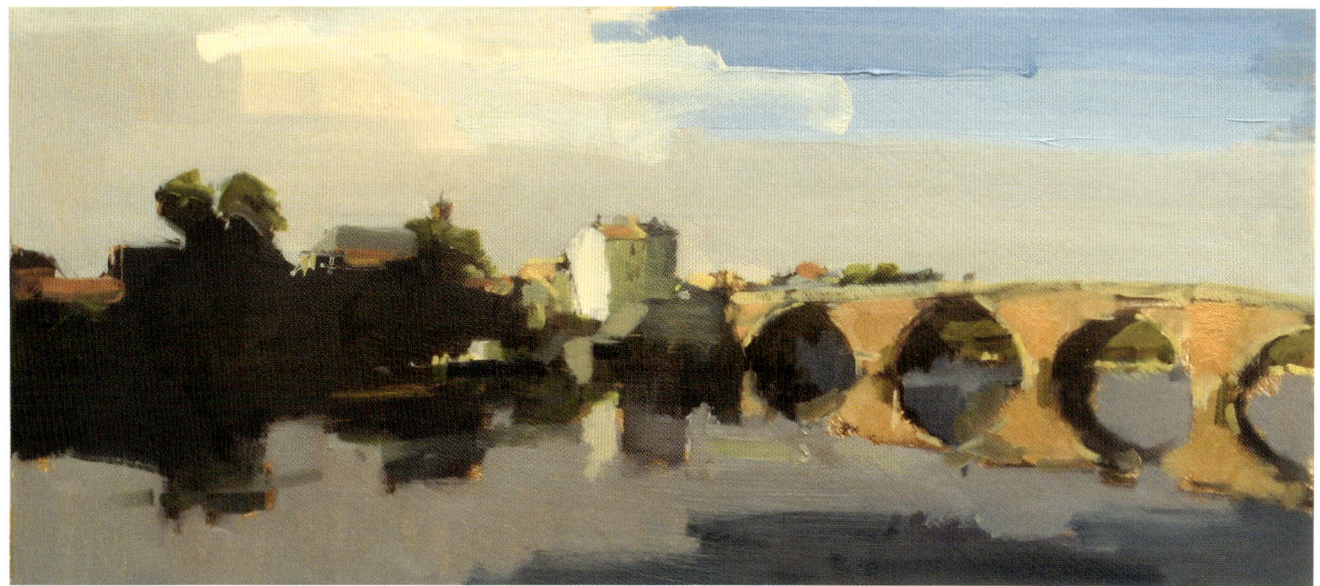

Bergerac, Stephen Palmer. (10" × 22", oil on board)
An intense and high sun provided the strong tonal contrasts that underpin this painting. The area of deep shadow to the left helps to create a balance with the strong shape and colour of the bridge. Although the artist has taken care in the arrangement of the elements within the elongated format, the actual painting itself was completed in very little time. He tends to work as quickly as possible, avoiding unnecessary detail, in order not to lose sight of the initial impetus that attracted him to the subject. He always uses a limited palette, which usually consists of between four and six colours, and in the case of this painting, Cadmium Red Light was used throughout, in order to convey the sensation of heat, and to give a chromatic coherence to the whole painting.

of these shapes. By creating a kind of cardboard cut-out of shapes, and subtle variations in tone, we can instil a degree of logic into the arrangement. We may be able to detect horizontals and verticals, and perhaps directional movement, and these can be emphasized to provide the necessary clues to establish exactly what is going on.

If we are unable to decipher the precise nature of something purely by its lack of form or colour, we will have to identify it by its outline, or edge. If there is a building in our painting, it will by its nature have a sharper edge than a tree, but if the building is in the middle ground, and the tree in the foreground, these edges have to be modified in relation to each other otherwise the spatial difference between the two will not read properly. The mechanics of our vision dictate that objects further away from us will have a softer, more diffused edge, whilst the edges of those closer to us will have a sharper edge. But if we want to place more emphasis on a certain area of our painting, we can give it a slightly harder edge.

Contrast

Contrast can be used to great effect as a tool in creating visual interest in the composition of our paintings. This can take the form of contrast in tonal value, colour, scale, texture or shape. Our eyes will quickly scan over an area of similarity but if we come across an area of contrast, they will linger a while with interest before moving off again. The contrast may be a subtle contrast in colour temperature, or it may be a less than subtle contrast in scale.

Rhythm

If the colours in a painting have been blended together so smoothly that the brush marks have been disguised, the result may be a flat and dull picture. By contrast, where they have been applied with a rhythmical, repetitive action they add greater interest and depth to the work, and can lead the eye around the painting in the desired direction. The landscape provides a great deal of ready-made subject matter where a rhythm of brushstrokes can be used to great effect, from clouds, foliage and grass, to hills, paths and streams, and so utilizing the natural rhythm of nature.

As well as brushstrokes, a kind of rhythm can be suggested by the repetition of lines, shapes, patterns and colour, and these can dictate the speed at which the eye travels around the painting. If taken on a rhythmical journey encouraged by a combination of vividly contrasting brushstrokes or patterns, we will travel with a sense of unease, or perhaps excitement. A feeling of calm and peaceful reflection can be created by the repetition and rhythm of a static shape and harmonious colour combination.

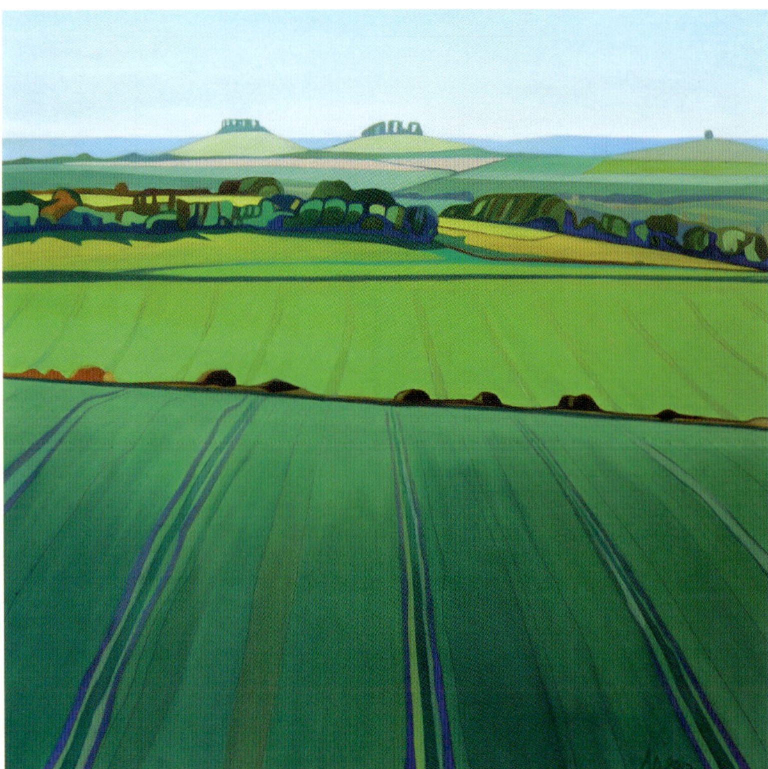

View from Aston Downs, Anna Dillon. (16" × 16", oil on wood)
It isn't always necessary to choose a landscape arrangement when tackling a scene that involves creating the illusion of distance. The artist here has chosen a square format, and by placing the horizon line high up she has been able to create a sense of spatial perspective by dividing the area between the foreground and the pale blue hills in the distance into a series of separate plains by painting them in ever increasing subdued tones. The direction of the ploughed furrows in the bottom half of the painting indicate the downward curve of the field, and those in the centre of the picture suggest a slight curve upwards. Painted primarily in a palette of complementary blues and greens, a subtle contrast has been created with the inclusion of a few touches of yellow, pink and brown.

Focal Point

You can direct the viewer's eye to a particular point or points in many different ways. You can run converging lines towards your desired focal point by introducing a path, road or meandering stream into your landscape. A line of trees or a run of fence posts will result in the same effect, and these don't necessarily need to be in a straight line. A sudden change of colour will make a certain element stand out, as will a distinct variation in tone, shape or texture.

Positioning your focal point following the 'Law of Thirds' has been mentioned before, and placing it in the centre of the picture will undoubtedly demand attention, but moving it slightly off-centre is often a more comfortable option. If your composition includes a grouping of several individual elements, one of these placed in isolation will become a focal point. The inclusion of a slightly unexpected element into the mix, such as an abandoned vehicle, piece of farm machinery, or some other incongruous object will also catch the eye.

Altering and Editing

When painting anything, we must remember that it's our painting, so we are at liberty to change things around as much as we like. We are under no obligation to include everything we see. In an ideal world, it would be wonderful to be able to step outside into the landscape and immediately find the perfect subject to paint. With everything positioned impeccably, there would be no need to even think of changing anything. But this rarely happens, so we have to be prepared to make the most of a slightly imperfect scene. Photographers don't have the luxury of being able to move trees, hills, or the course of a river on the spot, but artists do. If something is obscuring the view of our intended focal point, we can move it to one side or remove it altogether. We can alter the scale of individual elements to draw attention to them, or make them less dominant. If the colour of a tree clashes with surrounding specimens, it can be tweaked to appear more harmonious, and a dull, grey sky can be injected with a little brightness and a cloud or two.

Many inexperienced artists find it difficult to do this when painting outside, and are more comfortable making alterations back at the studio when they have more time for considered thought.

Scale and Proportion

When we consider scale in a painting, we must think of the size ratio between all of the elements within the picture. There has to be a logical relationship between the sizes of the objects to make them appear credible. Mistakes in these size relationships can make objects appear too large or too small, and this is particularly critical when including figures

This simple illustration demonstrates two-point perspective. Although each box has its own two vanishing points, they will both be located somewhere along your eye level, which is that imaginary line travelling horizontally immediately in front of you when you are looking straight ahead. Each box is turned at a slightly different angle to the other, so their vanishing points are in different places. If they had been placed in parallel, they would share a common vanishing point, no matter which angle they are viewed from. Vanishing point 2 has to be estimated, as it falls some way off the page. Note how the lines above your eye level are travelling down to it, whereas those below your eye level are travelling up.

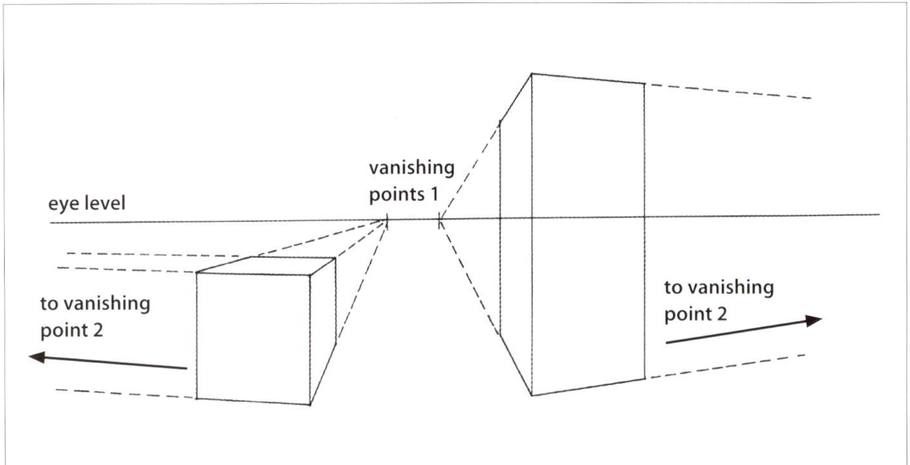

in the landscape. Nothing looks more blatantly wrong than a human who seems to be the same height as a house in the distance.

Linear and Aerial Perspective

A basic understanding of perspective is essential with all forms of drawing and painting. If the basic rules of perspective haven't been fully comprehended, no matter how beautifully something has been drawn or painted it will all have been in vain.

There are a few basic principles to get to grips with that are the cornerstone of understanding and describing perspective as we see it. These rules make sense of the physical way in which our two eyes work, and how they focus on objects. There are two ways in which this three-dimensional visual phenomenon can be translated into two dimensions when drawing or painting, and they can be described as linear and atmospheric perspective.

Linear perspective is used to make sense of the way in which the scale and location of objects can be determined as they recede into the distance, or advance into the foreground. The three essential components of this system are the vanishing point, the horizon, and parallel lines, and it is used in creating the illusion of depth on a two-dimensional, flat surface. Aerial perspective does this by describing the way in which colours and tonal values change and how atmospheric conditions create blurred edges to objects that are further away from us. By combining these two theories, we can create a sense of three-dimensional credibility in our drawings and paintings.

Any object, whether it's a tree, a building, a car or a person, will appear smaller, the further away it is. If that object, for instance a farm building, is viewed at a slight angle, part of that object will appear smaller in size as it is further away than another part, which is closer to you.

Aerial, or atmospheric perspective, can be introduced to suggest distance, even though there may be no linear perspective present. When first viewing something briefly, we tend to focus on the middle distance, which is the area at and around the level of our eyes. This is usually along the centre of a picture. If we look down slightly, we will see more detail in the objects immediately in front of us as they are closer, but this is not where our eyes normally look first. If we were to record this area in great detail, it would prevent us from focusing on that natural band of vision lying in the middle distance, so this should be painted in a slightly looser way as if in our peripheral vision. We can suggest distance beyond our focal point by painting this part of the picture in a more obscure way where objects have diffused edges, and their colours are more muted.

The two forms of perspective can of course be used simultaneously to great effect, and there is nothing to stop you using exaggerated perspective to create an added sense of drama in your pictures. Once you have grasped the basic principles, perspective can be manipulated to suit your own needs and doesn't have to be an obstacle in the way of creativity.

Choosing a Colour Scheme

Colour... a pigment of my imagination.

ALAN BENNETT

Deciding upon a basic colour scheme for a painting will be dependent upon the visual mood you wish to convey. No one colour scheme is better than another; it may simply be more suitable. If the mood you want to portray is one of calmness and tranquillity, you may choose a harmonious

Monochromatic colours
An infinite number of tones can be produced from using just one colour, as in this example based on Dioxazine Purple. To produce a more subtle colour, the base colour can also be made from mixing two or three different colours together to form the darkest tone, which can then be lightened progressively with the addition of white.

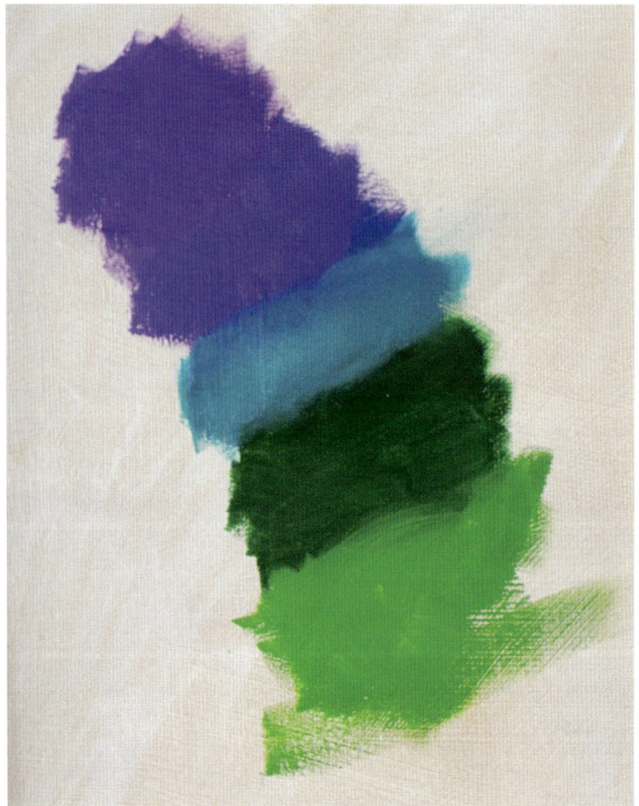

Analogous colours
These colours are analogous, as they sit together side-by-side on the colour wheel, and this combination would provide the basis for an acceptable colour scheme. On the other side of the colour wheel, the grouping of yellow, yellow/orange, orange, orange/red, and red/violet could also be combined.

arrangement. You could choose a *monochromatic* scheme that involves the use of one colour, altering its intensity with a variety of tints and shades to produce a painting that is both well balanced and visually appealing. You could perhaps choose a blue-violet or a blue-green for this.

An *analogous* colour scheme uses colours that are next to each other on the colour wheel, and this would usually consist of a combination of between two and four colours, and maybe five at a push. A suggestion for this could include blue, blue-violet, violet, and red-violet. To prevent any visual imbalance, restrict your group of colours to either the cool or warm range. Choose one of these as the main colour, whilst using the others to add variation and richness. This scheme will provide a more colourful and varied solution than the monochromatic scheme.

If you want to produce a painting that is vibrant and animated, choose a scheme of *complementary* colours, which are those placed opposite each other on the colour wheel; red and green, blue and orange, blue-violet and yellow-orange and so on. Placing these colours side-by-side intensifies them, but if they are mixed together, this results in a neutral brown being created. When placed together and viewed from fairly close up they offer the highest contrast, but when viewed from further back, they can neutralize each other, producing a rather dull colour, so if possible it's best to keep them slightly apart. It should be noted that it's quite difficult to achieve an acceptable colour balance with this scheme.

A more adaptable and successful version of the *complementary* scheme is the *split complementary* scheme. This uses one colour, together with the two colours either side of its complementary on the opposite side of the colour wheel. For example, you could combine violet with yellow-green and yellow-orange. This produces a degree of contrast less violent than the *complementary* scheme. Another alternative is the *triadic* scheme, which combines any three colours that are equally spaced around the colour wheel, such as orange, green and violet. In their purest form they could be too intense, so they can be combined with the neutral greys produced by mixing them with their complementaries. For the best results choose one colour to be the most overriding, and the others to be subservient.

DEVELOPING A *PLEIN-AIR* STUDY

Your *plein-air* painting may have been created just for the pure pleasure of it, or it may have been a dress rehearsal

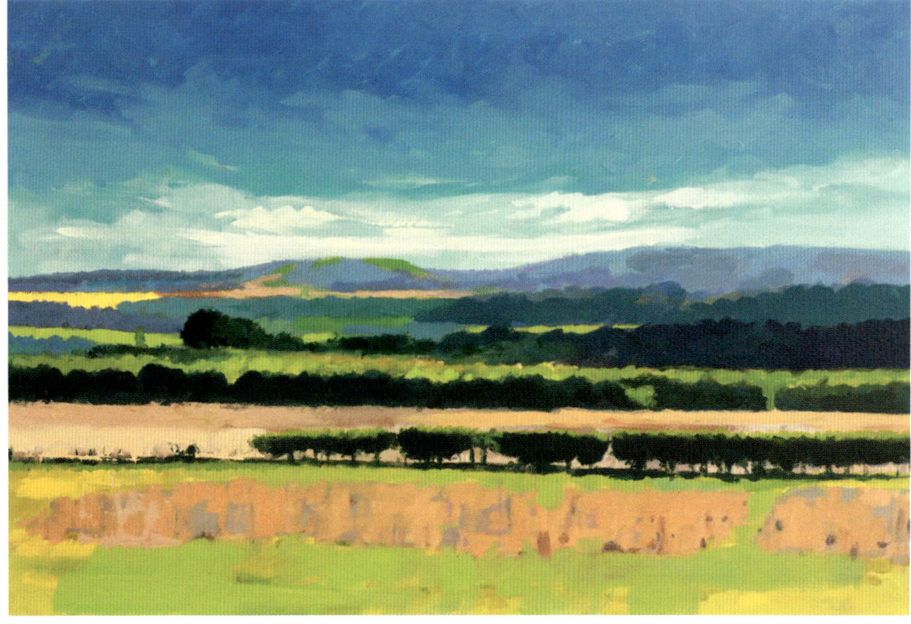

Beacon Hill, Kevin Scully. (10" × 22", oil on board)
An oil sketch for a much larger studio painting. The finished painting was to be concerned primarily with colour, and was to be painted in a semi-abstract style, with the layers of the landscape depicted as flat, cut-out shapes rather than trying to suggest any aerial perspective.

for the main event – a full-size, scaled-up studio painting. You may have made sketches, and you may have taken photographs, but the painting that you created on the spot was produced following that which inspired you to tackle it in the first place. Hopefully, your painting will display an immediacy and vibrancy brought about by the constraints of time, and recreating that sensation in a scaled-up version in the studio isn't always easy. You will of course have time on your side, which will allow you to adjust, reconsider and refine the detail. Sometimes though, this can have a detrimental effect on the final version where your original spontaneity has evaporated. But your spontaneity can always be practised!

So when working on your studio painting, don't burden yourself down with too much detail that will now be evident from any photographs you may have taken; attack the canvas with the same verve and vigour that you employed when outside, perhaps modifying and refining some of the colours and brushstrokes.

If your *plein-air* painting didn't involve too much detail in the way of perspective or buildings, you will probably be able to draw out the studio version by eye, but if there are elements that require more considered drawing, you may need to scale-up your small painting or initial sketch proportionately to a larger size. To do this, cut a sheet of clear acetate or tracing paper to size and lay it over your painting, or sketch, and trace off as much detail as you wish. If you are using acetate, you will need to draw with a fine fibre-tipped pen. Draw a grid on this, dividing it in half horizontally and vertically as many times as necessary, which will leave you with a series of uniform rectangles. If for instance your small painting is 10" × 12", and you want to double, or even treble the size of it in your studio painting, prepare a canvas or board 20" × 24", or 30" × 36" respectively.

After you have toned your painting surface with the appropriate colour, and when it is dry, you can then draw a similar grid on it using an ordinary pencil or coloured pencil. As with the tracing, draw the grid by dividing it in half horizontally and vertically, the same number of times. Each of the rectangles on your painting surface will now be the same proportionately as those on your tracing. You can now transfer the image by copying the detail into each corresponding section.

COLOUR SCHEMES

These colour schemes are based on traditional theory and scientific and optical research, but implementing them can be a little tricky. Although there are of course certain connections between art and science, the overriding factor distinguishing the two is that of aesthetics. There are some things that we as humans and artists find both visually and emotionally pleasing, that cannot be explained by scientific theory. So if you have produced a painting that follows none of the generally accepted methods of devising colour schemes, and it still looks fantastic, so be it. They are included as a guide only.

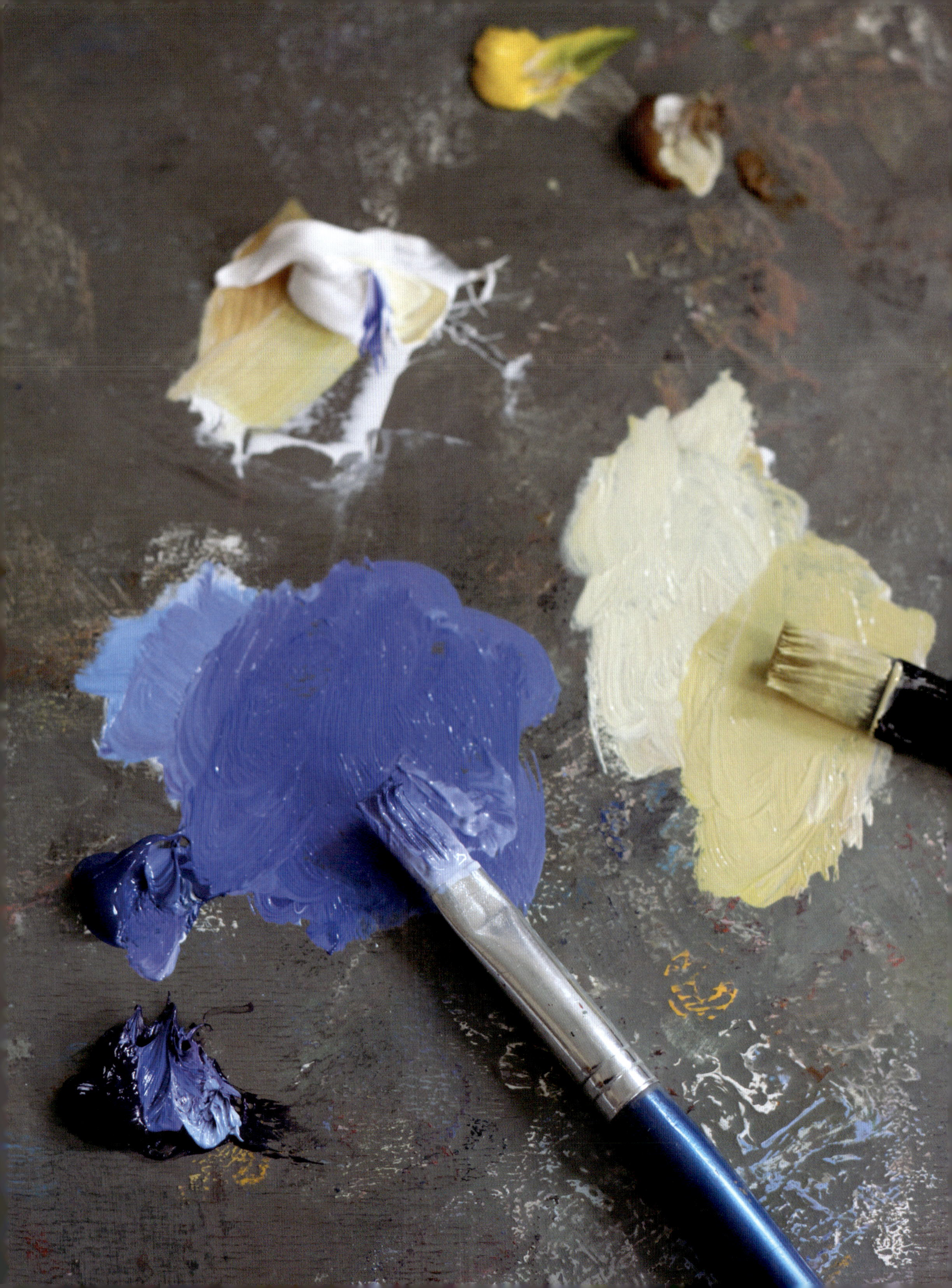

CHAPTER 7

Starting to Paint

When you start a painting, it is somewhat outside you. At the conclusion, you seem to move inside the painting.

FERNANDO BOTERO

Although it's generally acknowledged that a painting surface is toned with a colour of some description before starting the painting itself, it's not a criminal offence to paint directly onto the white primer. Some artists do this and produce perfectly good paintings, but it does make life more difficult than it need be.

By toning a surface in a mid-tone value, you are establishing a base from which you are able to judge both the lighter and darker tones of your painting far more easily than you would against white. Particularly in the landscape, there is virtually nothing that is white, so it seems illogical to use it as a starting point. Watercolour painting is different in that it's a transparent medium, and relies on the white paper to reflect light back through the colour. Both oils and acrylics are primarily opaque mediums, so when painting the landscape it would make sense to use a colour that is more in tune with the colours of the natural world.

For the painting *Vapour Clouds at the Power Station* (frontispiece), a limited colour range was chosen to emphasize the dramatic effect of the water vapour in the sky. On the palette a few colour combinations were tested before deciding on a suitable colour range. Shown here are Titanium White, Winsor Yellow, Raw Sienna, Cobalt Blue and Dioxazine Purple. A touch of Cadmium Red was later added to the lighter colour, so it became more in keeping with the orange/blue complementary colour combination.

Choosing a Ground Colour

The earth colours are a good starting point when choosing a colour for a toned ground, simply because of the fact that the pigment comes from the earth, and this is where most of what we see in the landscape springs from. Raw Umber is a fairly neutral colour, and it can be made even more neutral by the addition of a little Payne's Grey, Ultramarine, or one of the violet/purple colours.

Having chosen a colour (or two), squeeze some into a jar and dilute it with either white spirit, or a 70/30 white spirit/turpentine mix to a ratio of about 60/40, liquid to paint. Use a fairly large brush, especially if you are toning a few canvases or boards at the same time, and apply the colour. As this will be fairly transparent, you'll end up with a rather streaky finish. This can be left as it is, because most of this ground will be painted over, and it may also add liveliness to the painting if left to peep through here and there. If you prefer a smoothly toned ground, wait a minute or two, and then wipe the canvas or board with a clean rag, gently rubbing the paint into the surface. This will lighten the colour, and the result will be a rich and luminous smooth ground. If you find that it's still too dark for your taste, remove some more of the colour with a rag dipped in a little white spirit. It's best to leave this for at least twenty-four hours to dry, before beginning your painting.

Your choice of colour may be influenced by the general lighting conditions of the scene you are painting, so if you are painting a landscape bathed in a warm, sunny light you might choose a colour based on Raw Sienna, which

DEMONSTRATION

David Mensing

When mixing a colour for your toned ground, make up enough for several canvases or boards so that you will always have some ready for painting, rather than having to wait for one to dry. If you don't want them to be all the same, divide some of the colour up into several tins or jars, and add some different colours to each. You could add one of the other earth colours to create a little variety. If you don't use the entire colour, you can store it in a screw-top jar for further use. As the colour is diluted, it will keep for some time without drying out.

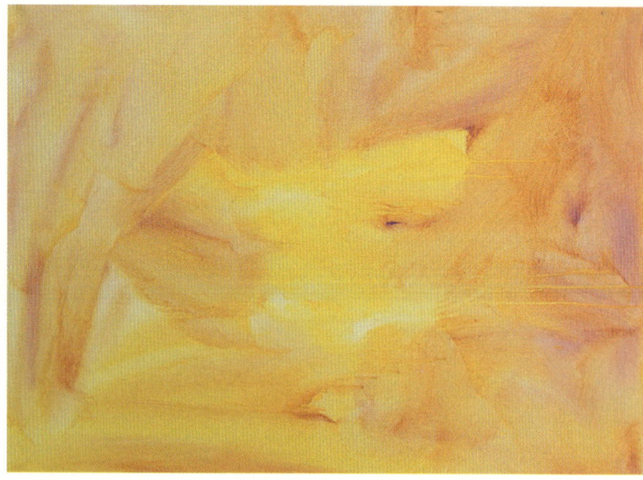

Bound for Freedom, David Mensing. (30" × 40", oil on canvas)
Stage 1: Prior to beginning a painting, David Mensing will typically tone his canvas with intense colours. For this picture he has applied a wash of thinly diluted oil paint comprising two colours, red and yellow, mixed loosely together to produce an overall warm orange, of a mid-tonal value.

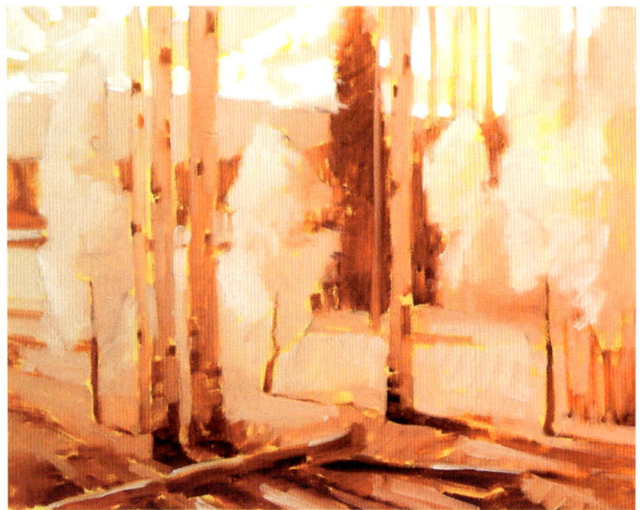

Stage 2: He began with a loose drawing primarily to locate specific points in the composition. He then produces a monochrome, tonal underpainting, mostly in thinner paint applied with a brush. This provides colour harmony and establishes the various tonal values. Some of this intense colour will still show through as highlights and reflected light when the painting is complete. He chose Burnt Sienna tinted with Titanium White for this underpainting.

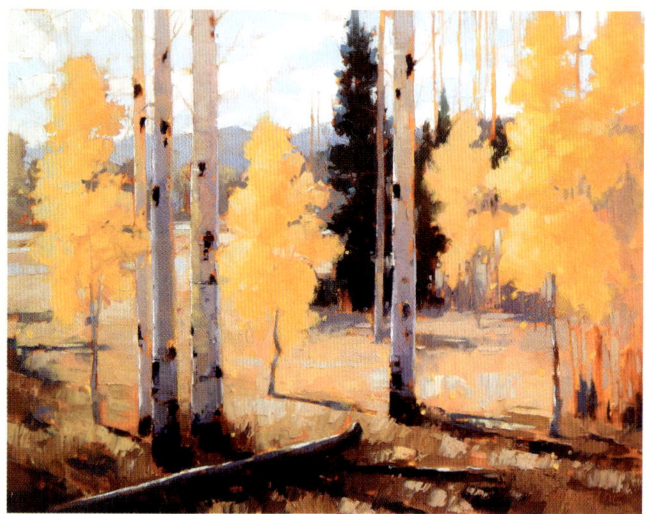

Stage 3: Finished Painting
Once the monochrome painting had been completed, he used a painting knife and undiluted paint to apply the final colour. He employs a technique of scraping and mixing the paint already on the canvas, to neutralize and 'marble' some of the existing colour. He then revises the edges around the different elements, and works on improving the negative shapes. With a final touch-up here and there, the painting is complete. The painting depicts the brilliance of autumn in the Sawtooth Mountains of central Idaho.

is warm. If your scene is misty or foggy you could choose a colour that leans towards grey. These colours used for these paintings could be based on the analogous colour scheme, and so harmony will be established at the outset, but if you want to create a more vibrant effect, you could choose a ground colour that contrasts with that of your overall painting. For instance, if your painting is going to be predominantly blue, you can tone your ground with an orange-based colour.

If you're in a hurry, it's perfectly acceptable to use acrylic for the ground, and if your painting is going to be in acrylic, this is what you will be using anyway.

Drawing the Composition

You may be confident enough to draw your composition straight onto your support, or you may need to transfer your sketch by using the grid method.

It's a good idea to practice drawing straight onto the support, as all drawing by eye will be beneficial in the progression of your drawing skills, and remember that any mistakes made can be corrected by simply drawing over them in a different colour and will eventually be painted over anyway. Traditionally, charcoal was the preferred tool for this as it could easily be erased, and then lightly brushed over to remove the loose dust. More recently this has been considered to be a rather outmoded and imprecise method, and charcoal can be substituted by pencil, coloured pencil, or by drawing with a brush dipped in thin paint. If a pencil has been used for drawing, any mistakes or alterations that are necessary can be corrected with a coloured pencil or brush.

Mixing Your Colour

Having arranged your colours on your palette, and attached your dippers containing a painting medium, you're ready to paint. Unless you are painting *alla prima*, you will need to begin by using the paint in a fairly thin mix. The process you should follow involves painting 'fat over lean', which means that as the painting progresses you will be using less medium to thin your paint, so the mix becomes progressively thicker.

As the initial stage of painting uses thin colour, you won't need to use a palette knife for mixing colours, and instead you can just pick up individual colours and mix them with your brush. Mix a pool of each of the main colours that you will be using. For instance you may have sky, trees, rocks and buildings in your paintings, so mix a general colour for each of these individual elements that can be used as a base for further modification. This means that you won't have to keep mixing up new amounts of colour all the time.

First Brushstrokes

Begin by blocking-in the massed shapes with fairly large brushes, without attempting to paint any details at this early stage. There are no hard and fast rules about working from dark to light, or light to dark because the paint is opaque, so each can be painted on top of the other, but most artists will probably adopt the former approach. The colours used for this blocking-in don't have to be an exact match of the finished colour, and it's even preferable for them not to be, as further applications of pigment of a slightly different hue will create an interesting juxtaposition of colour. By using varying thicknesses of paint throughout the process, varying from semi-transparent to opaque, you will be able to create different levels of depth in your painting.

At this early stage, keep the brushstrokes loose and adopt a lively approach to the way in which you apply them. Alternate the direction of them rather than making them all horizontal or vertical, and add areas of colour all over the canvas, rather than completely filling-in any one area, so that the whole painting proceeds at the same steady pace. By taking this route, you are able to keep the whole image at a stage where it is easy to make adjustments and alterations. As your paint is fairly diluted, it will dry fairly quickly, but if you are keen to keep painting and want to continue adding more layers of paint you can add a little Liquin medium, or one that is alkyd-based, which will speed things up. Alternatively, if you need time for a little contemplative consideration, you can continue at a later painting session.

Remember to stand back from your work at regular intervals, so that you can assess its progress, as it's all too easy to get too comfortable and carried away without realizing that things might be going wrong. Remember that paintings are usually viewed from a certain distance, so try to imagine it hanging on a gallery wall. By doing this it's a lot easier to spot any areas that might need adjustment. Sometimes we are not the best judges of our own work, so it's a good idea to obtain the opinion of others who may pinpoint any weak or uncomfortable areas in the painting. If all is going well, you can now begin to add more detail and the finishing touches. Even when steering a painting to completion, keep moving around the image, adding touches of colour here and there, so there is a unity in the degree of finish.

DEMONSTRATION

Spring Willows

The intended mood of this painting was to be one of calmness and tranquillity by using a very limited colour range. When tackling a scene such as this, which contains little else but green, it's very tempting to include too many different colours when endeavouring to create a sense of space and distance. However, by analysing the subtle transitions in tonal values, it can be made possible. It's not always a good idea to paint a scene as overly green as this one, but a valuable exercise nevertheless. An alternative and less traditional approach would be to choose one of the previously mentioned harmonious colour schemes, perhaps based on a green/blue/violet palette.

The colours used in this exercise were:

- Titanium White
- Oxide of Chromium
- Winsor Yellow
- Cobalt Blue
- Payne's Grey

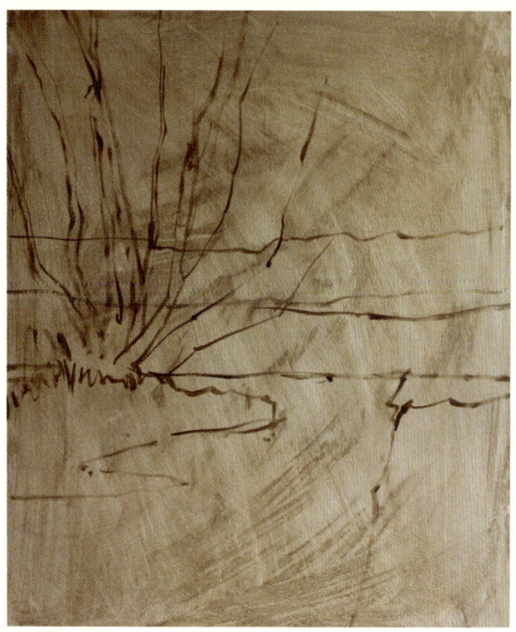

The MDF board was primed with three coats of acrylic gesso, rubbed down lightly between each application. This was one of several that had already been prepared with a toned ground of thin Raw Umber and wiped loosely with a rag to remove some of the more definite brush marks. The composition required very little drawing, so the general position of the different elements was indicated with a brush.

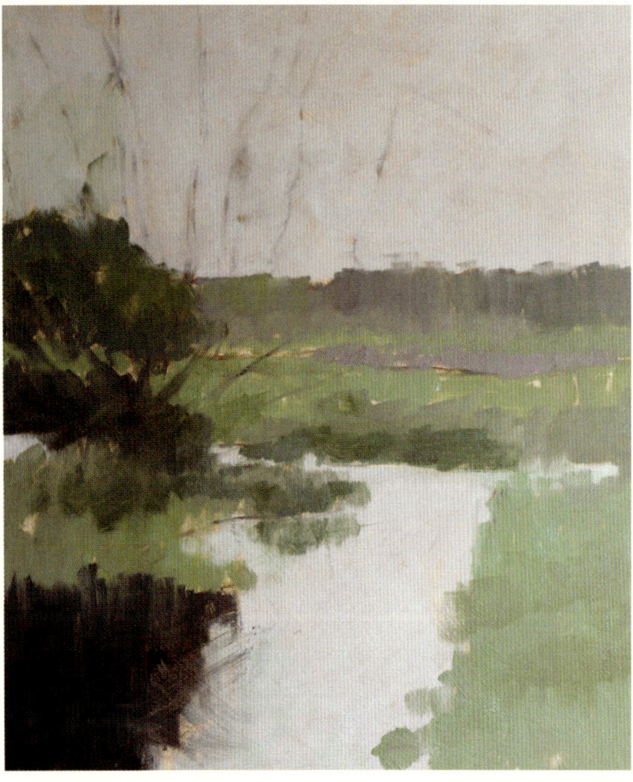

The large willow was going to be left until a much later stage of the painting, so this was ignored during the initial blocking-in process, which was painted using some filbert brushes, one for each colour. In this scene, the water was noted as being lighter in tone than the sky, so this was used to set the tonal key.

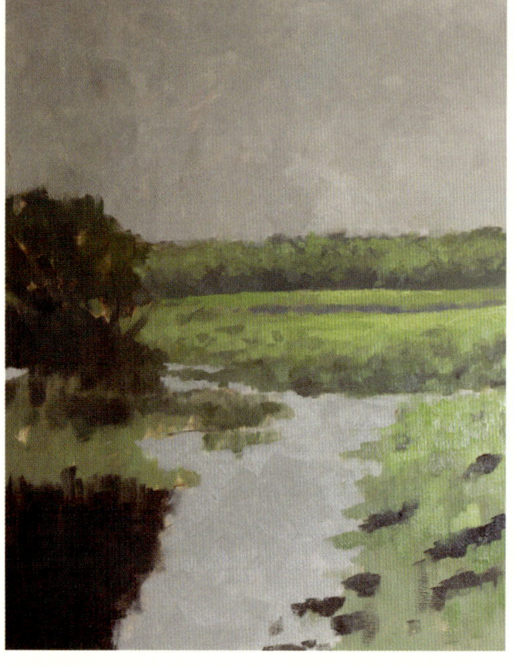

As the painting progressed, and still keeping the relative tonal values, some blue was added to the shadow part of the trees in the distance.

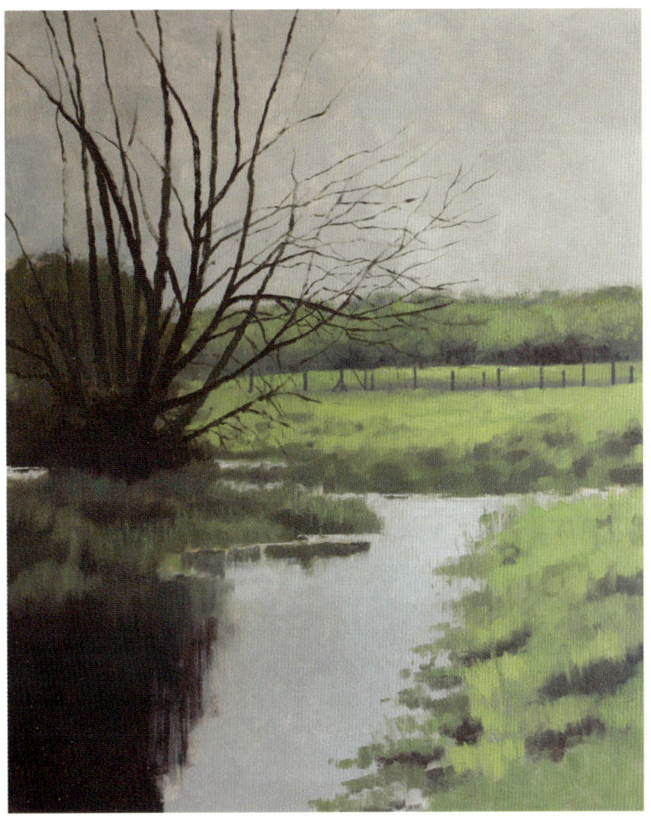

Satisfied with the tonal value and colour of the featureless sky, trees and fence posts, the main stems of the willow tree were painted carefully, ensuring that they tapered towards their ends. A few small branches were added in a slightly lighter colour to see how they looked against the sky. The rest of the painting was built up using both round and filbert hog brushes.

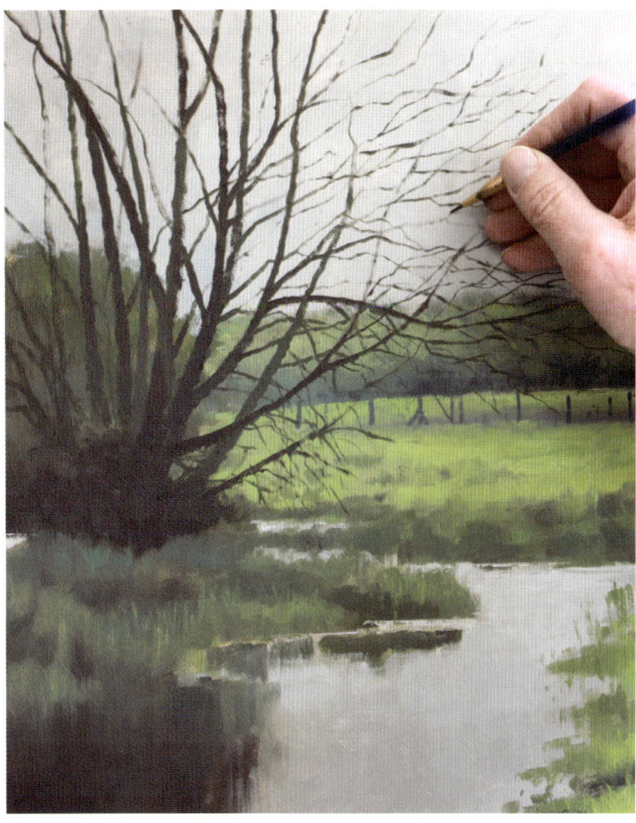

Using a small round synthetic brush, the finer branches and twigs were carefully added, some by using the dry brush technique so that they don't appear too regular. The dark reflection in the bottom left-hand corner was lightened slightly, and some extra colours were added to the grassy areas.

The water was now painted, and whilst the colour was still wet, the reflections were added and softened with a soft, clean brush. The colour of the water was seen to be lighter the further away it was, so this was adjusted, and the reflections in this area sharpened up a little. Leaves were added to the willow using a dry brush, and some branches were painted in the rather empty top right-hand corner to create a balance with the reflections in the bottom left-hand corner.

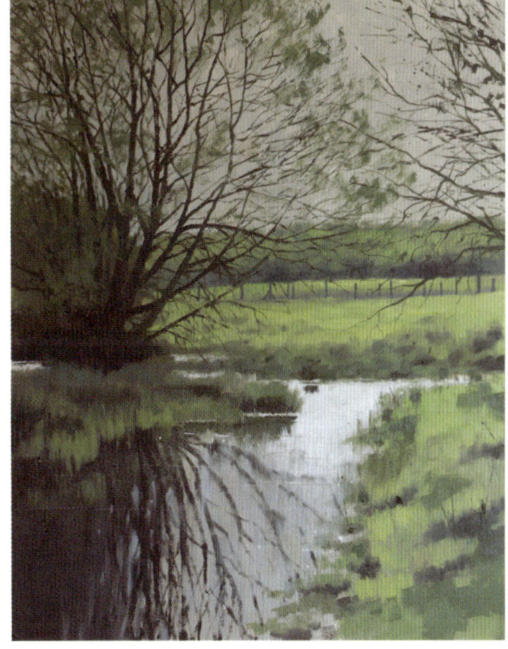

DEMONSTRATION

Fiveways

The winter months provide great material for paintings, and on a grey and overcast day you will find yourself using a completely different palette of colours.

The colours used in this demonstration were:

- Titanium White
- Burnt Sienna
- Oxide of Chromium
- Raw Umber
- Raw Sienna
- Payne's Grey
- Dioxazine Purple

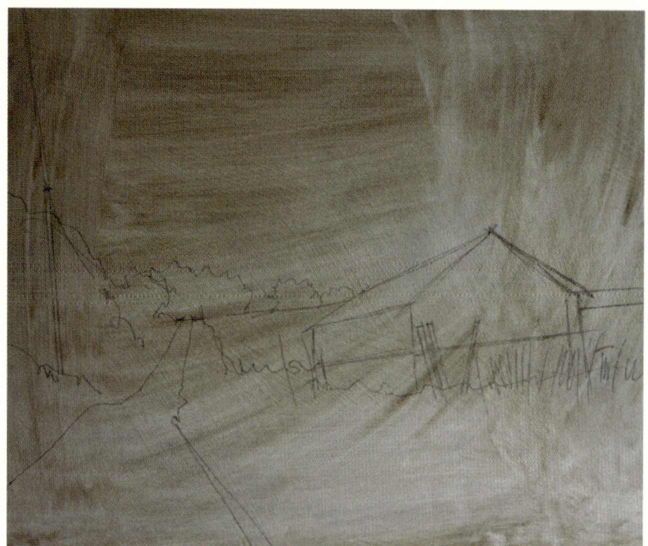

The board has been toned with a mixture of Raw Umber and Ultramarine, which provides the ideal neutral base for this painting in a rather low-key colour range. The image has been drawn out with a simple pencil line.

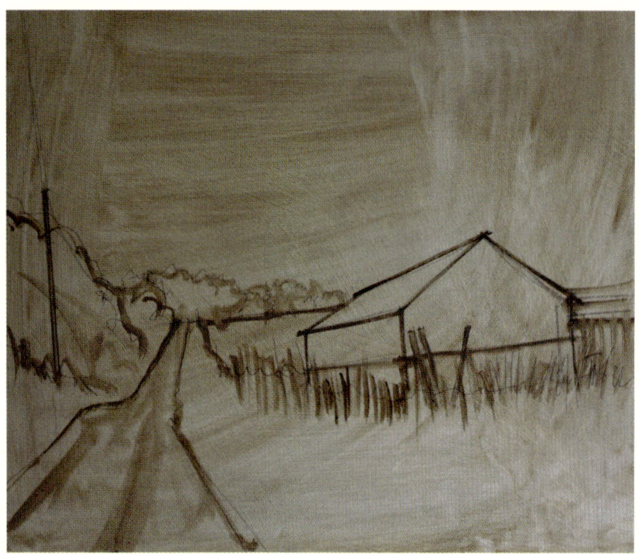

Having been satisfied with the positioning of the key elements, the drawing has been strengthened by painting it in with some diluted Raw Umber. Once dry, this prevents the drawing being lost as colour is washed over it.

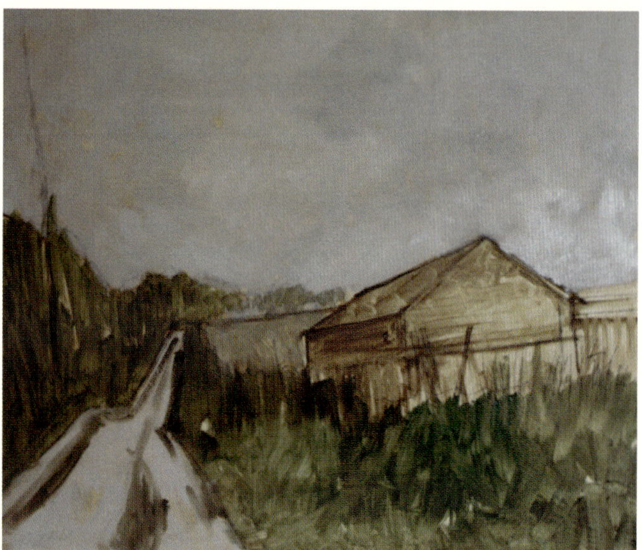

The sky was painted first in a thin wash of Payne's Grey and Titanium White to set the tonal key for the rest of the painting. The large areas of grass and foliage were painted with a mixture of Oxide of Chromium and Raw Umber, and the shed in straight Raw Umber. The snow-covered track was washed in with a lighter version of the sky, resisting the temptation at this early stage to make it too white.

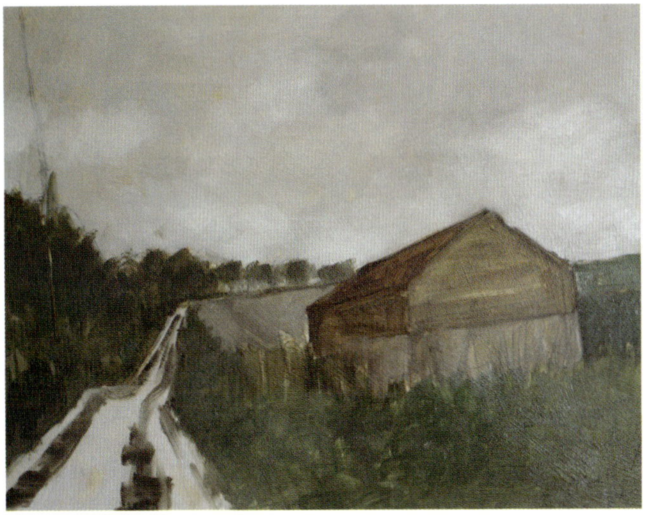

Initially using fairly thin paint, the tonal values were beginning to be established before the addition of patches of semi-opaque colour.

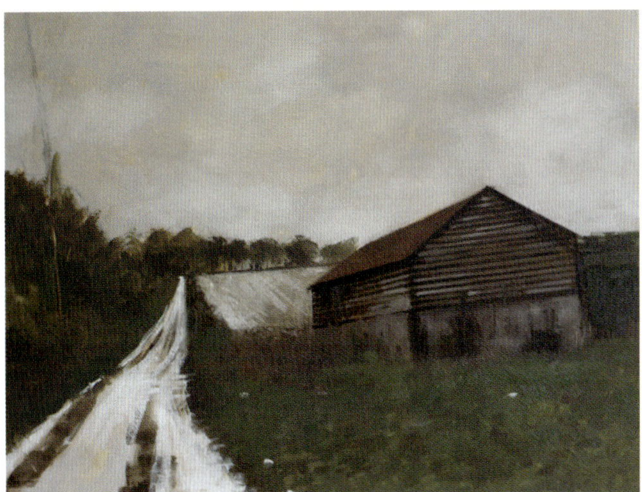

A later stage in the painting where the detailing on the shed has been painted more carefully with the aid of a ruler, and a variety of tones and colours introduced into the foreground.

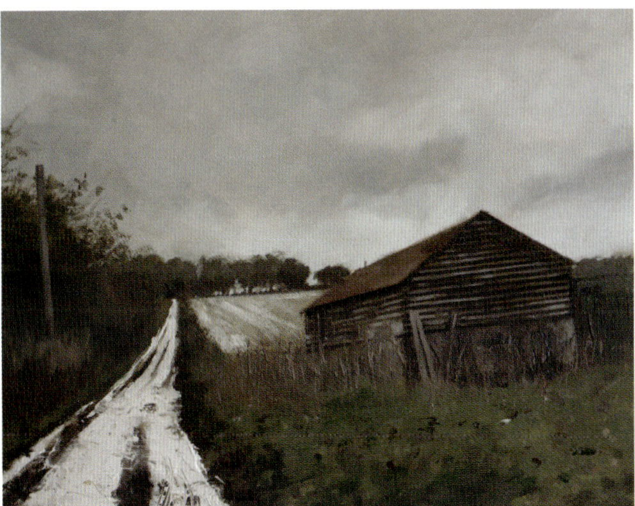

The finished painting displaying a combination of brushstrokes, painting knife marks, and scratching out.

Finishing a Painting

Art is never finished, only abandoned.

LEONARDO DA VINCI

One of the most difficult stages of painting a picture is to know precisely when it is finished, and this is a question that's almost impossible to answer. During the journey along which a painting travels there can be many times when you are elated with its progress, but there are other instances when you feel as though it's on a downward spiral. When this happens it's time to turn the painting face to the wall, and leave it there for a day or two and turn your attention to something else. It can be reviewed at a later time when your feeling of despair has lifted.

VARY YOUR TECHNIQUES

In your painting, combine a variety of treatments in the way you apply the paint. Unite passages of broader, flat colour with small, broken brushstrokes, and add variety in your brushstrokes by using different brushes to produce both squarer and more rounded marks. Use a combination of wet-in-wet techniques with a dry brush treatment, and if you are comfortable using a painting knife, use it with discretion in conjunction with brushwork.

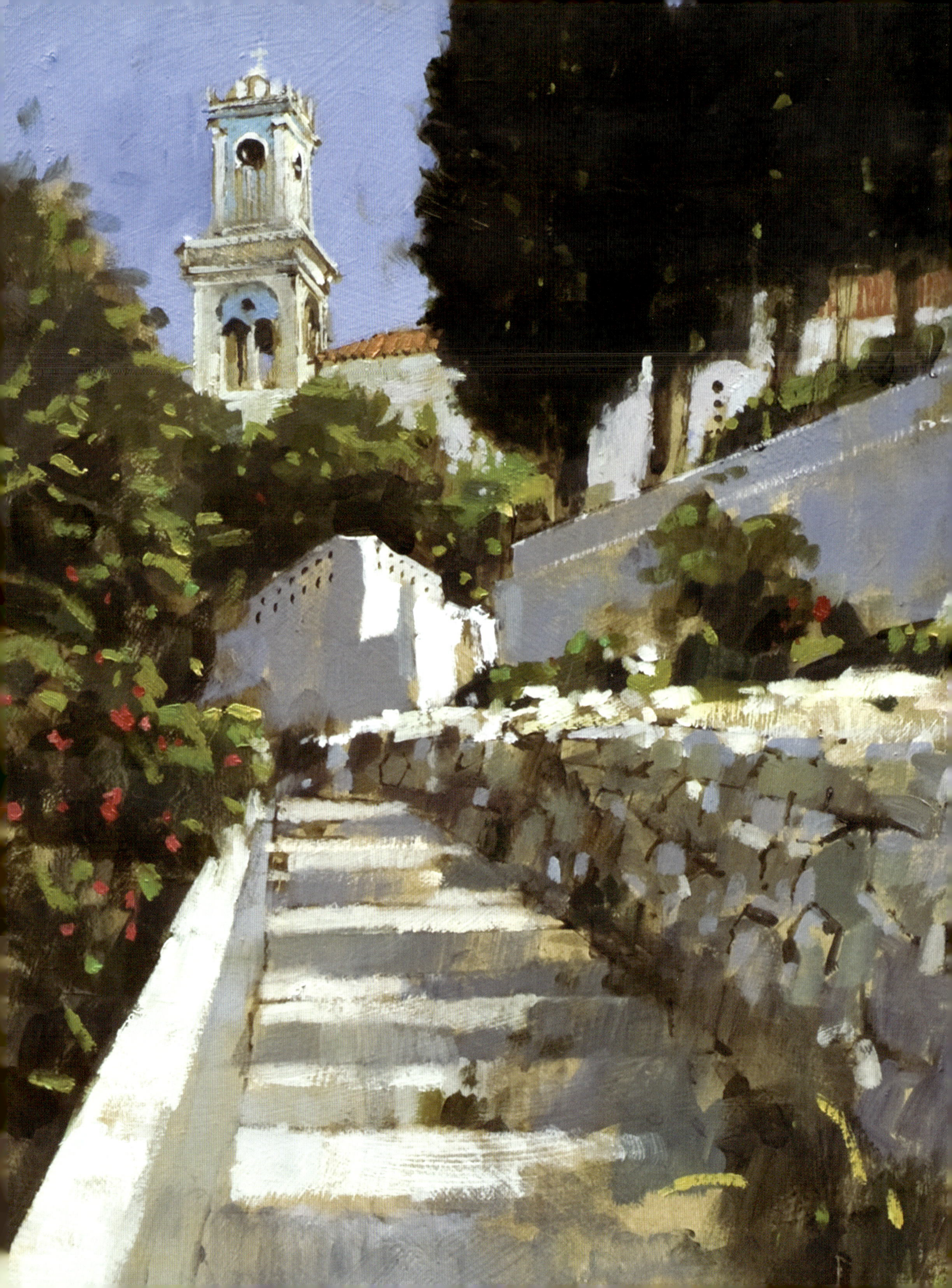

CHAPTER 8

Painting *En Plein Air*

A grey day provides the best light.

LEONARDO DA VINCI

If you are going to be using oils or acrylics, prepare your painting surface the night before, whether it's a painting board or canvas. If you're not entirely sure what your subject matter is going to be, it's probably best to tone your board or canvas in a fairly neutral earth colour. It's a good idea to have a few of these in reserve so that when you're inspired to set out on a painting session on the spur of the moment, you'll be ready for action. The same goes for your other painting materials, so have them all ready well in advance. Don't be too ambitious regarding the size of your painting, as a small painting completed successfully will be far more rewarding than a large one hurried and unfinished. You might consider taking two small panels with you. It's worth knowing that the vast majority of artists who work *en plein air* choose smaller panels or canvases to work on.

Before you venture outside, it may be wise to check the weather forecast. There'll be no point being dressed for the beach if rain or cold weather is predicted. If you are only going to be drawing, you won't really need to worry about what time of day you'll be out and about. But if you're inexperienced and are going to be painting in sunshine, it may be wise to choose the middle part of the day, providing it's not too hot, as the shadows won't change as dramatically than as they would in the morning or late afternoon.

Steps to the Church, Ormos, Samos (detail), David Sawyer. (24" × 10", oil on board)

If you have never painted outside before, an overcast day might be a better choice as a starting point, and although the scene might not be as interesting as one where the sunlight casts dramatic shadows, you won't have to worry about them constantly changing during your painting session. The light and the fairly flat tonal contrast will remain steady over a longer time period and will give you a chance to depict them more accurately. It's possible to spend two or three hours painting at this time of day before the light starts to change at an alarming rate.

If you are really keen to paint the early morning light, or the lengthening shadows of dusk you will have to practice working at speed, because the colours will change all too quickly. Depending on your location and climate, you may be lucky enough to find the same weather conditions at the same spot at the same time over a period of two or three days, which will allow you to capture the essence of the scene. If you choose to do this you'll have to set yourself a time limit for painting, so that you won't be tempted into constantly adjusting your painting as the lighting conditions inevitably change.

If you are painting for the pure enjoyment of it, there is no necessity to set yourself a time limit, unless you are trying to capture fleeting lighting conditions in an atmospheric landscape. Everyone is comfortable working at his or her own pace, and art shouldn't be a race. Just because someone has captured the spirit of a scene at breakneck speed, it can still be a less than successful painting than one that has been painted in a leisurely way. Consider what you want to achieve. If your painting has suffered a bit from some too hasty or careless brushstrokes whilst painting on location, there is nothing wrong with tidying them up a bit later on. Many painters in the past who extoled the virtues of painting in the open air were not immune to finishing their pictures back at their studio. When questioned on this subject, Monet was very cagey about whether or not his paintings had been completed entirely *en plein air*. In fact there is evidence that some of them were fiddled about with a long time after they were originally painted. So, if Monet and some of his contemporaries weren't averse to doing a bit of touching-up of their work when back at home after a day's painting in the field, neither should you be.

Working at Different Times of the Day and in Different Seasons

Painting in different seasons will mean that different challenges will present themselves, and you'll probably need to alter your colour palette accordingly. Snow in winter will require an entirely different set of colours to those you will need on a bright autumn day in October. Even painting snow on a grey and dark January afternoon will involve the use of certain colours that will be absent from an early morning snowy and sunlit landscape. Although it may be more agreeable painting outside on a mild summer's day, there is much to be gained by braving the elements, even if it means a few raindrops on your work or cold fingers and toes.

An interesting exercise is to paint the same scene at different times of the day and at different times of the year. You may also consider painting the same scene in different mediums. As well as familiarizing yourself with a particular location, you will be able to note how changing light and weather conditions alter the appearance and colour of objects. You may not want to do this too often as it could become rather tedious and repetitive, so changing your viewpoint at some stage will keep your interest alive. The time will come to move on and seek out new inspiration.

Preliminary Drawings and Photographs

If you're happy just sketching, keep a sketchbook and pencil handy at all times, as subject matter may present itself to you when you least expect it and in the most unlikely places. Weather conditions and the time of day are not

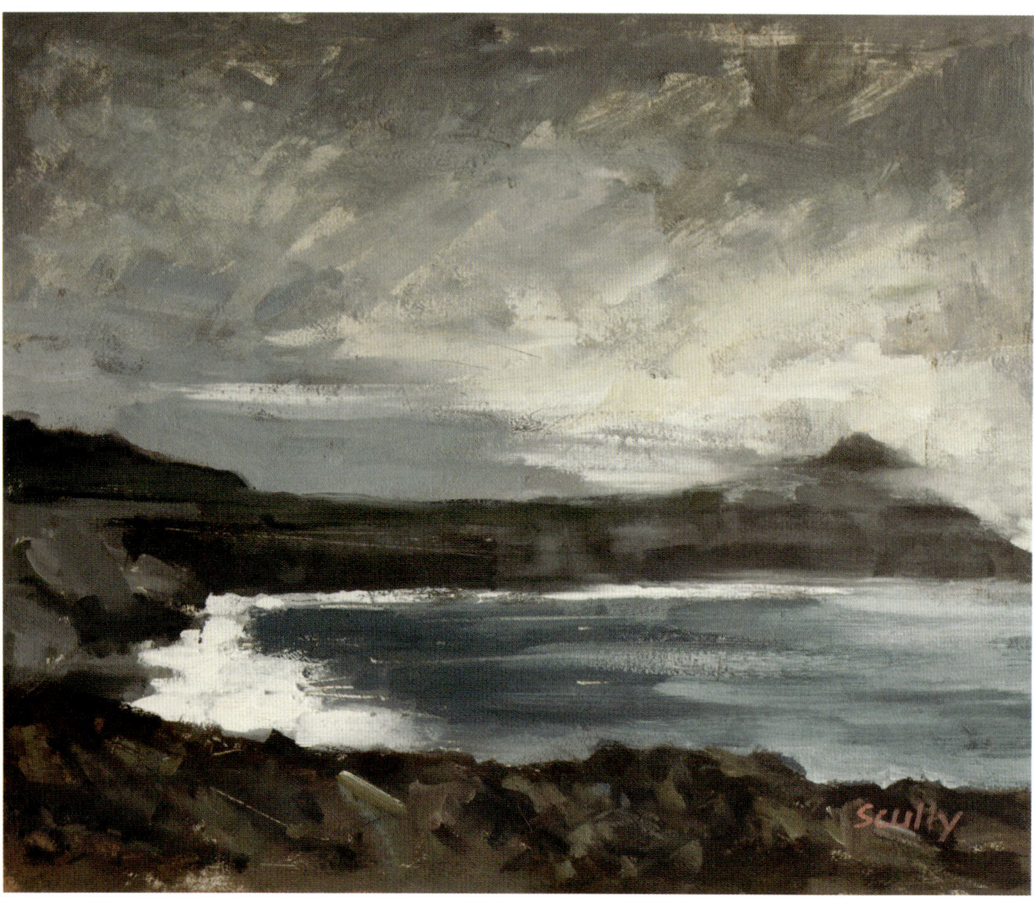

Cape Cornwall, Kevin Scully. (10" × 12", oil on board) A fast and furious oil sketch capturing the wild climatic conditions often encountered in this part of the country. The sketch was to be used as reference for a large studio painting, and contains all the information needed to produce a picture where sea, sky and land combine forces to create a dramatic and atmospheric scene.

particularly important if you are limiting yourself to simply drawing, and although the time of day factor is less relevant, you may on occasions have to work at speed.

Having spent time drawing your chosen subject, you may decide at some stage that it would actually make a good painting. Or you may have already elected to make some preliminary drawings with the intention of producing a painting either on location or back in the studio. The benefit of compositional sketches, those drawings that detail your thought process whilst evaluating the various possibilities regarding where to place objects in your picture, which ones to eliminate, or which ones to move elsewhere, are twofold. If arranged neatly on a page in your sketchbook, they can be a work of art in themselves. They can also help you visualize which compositions will be more successful as finished paintings than some of the others.

How you go about these initial sketches is up to you. Pencil sketches may be sufficient, or you may choose to use colour. If they are merely pencil sketches, they will be more beneficial if they are tonal drawings. Additionally, you can take some photographs. One of the advantages of a digital camera is that you can crop the image at a later stage to find the most agreeable arrangement. However, the camera is no substitute for drawing because when you are drawing, you are looking and thinking more intently and absorbing what is in front of you. The process of connecting eye to brain to hand to paper involves a thinking process more complex than that which we experience when composing an image through the viewfinder of a camera. A drawing can be both informative and expressive, a compositional aid or created simply for the pure enjoyment of it.

When making compositional drawings, you must think about the shape you are going to choose. Whilst a rectangle in either portrait or landscape format is probably the easiest to use when producing a comfortably balanced arrangement, consider also a square, or even an elongated landscape format. This can be particularly effective when tackling a panoramic view, and a square format lends itself to a more contemporary, even abstract look.

Positioning Yourself

If you are painting at an easel, you will need to position yourself appropriately, giving careful consideration to the way in which the light will change during your painting session. Ideally placed, both your painting and your palette should be in semi-shade, which will create a diffused and equally balanced light. This of course is not always possible when your best possible vantage point is in direct light, and if the sun is shining on your easel, it makes matters even worse. An umbrella clamped to your easel, and strategically tilted so that it creates an even light is probably the best solution, and if the umbrella is large enough it may also ensure that you are in the shade. It almost goes without saying that the more comfortable you are, the more efficiently you will be able to operate, which is critical when painting *en plein air*.

An alternative to this option is to place your easel at an angle as the sun moves around, so that both your painting and your palette are always in the shade. This means that you won't be facing directly opposite the scene that you are painting, but at least you will be working in an even light.

Even in the studio, it can be noticeable that the same colour mixed on a palette that is lying horizontally on your work surface will appear darker when applied to your painting. The reason for this is because more light will be striking a horizontal surface than a vertical one. This is even more evident when you are working outside. A way of combatting this is to clamp your palette to your easel so that it is on the same vertical plane. Any colour mixed on your palette will then look the same on your painting. Some artists paint with a large palette, hinged in the middle, with the top half positioned vertically, which dispenses with the need for a clamp.

The Alla Prima pochade box has a clever attachment called a sunshade that allows you to attach a panel above your painting, which casts both the painting and the palette area in shade.

If you like to be comfortable when painting and prefer to work seated, remember to stand up occasionally and to look at your work at a distance from which you can assess its development.

Beginning Painting

Make sure you have chosen a site that will allow your goal to be achievable. Don't choose something vastly complicated, or the chances are that the end result will be a disappointment. Your scene should contain elements that are distinguishable from each other in tone, shape or colour, and there must be enough evidence of spatial variation present to allow you to create the illusion of depth in your painting. Ensure that everything you hope to achieve is manageable; choose a scene that can be painted using a limited range of colours. If particular areas of your scene are slightly imbalanced, rearrange them, and if there are areas that are overcomplicated, simplify them. Or if a section looks confusing and difficult to paint, leave it out altogether.

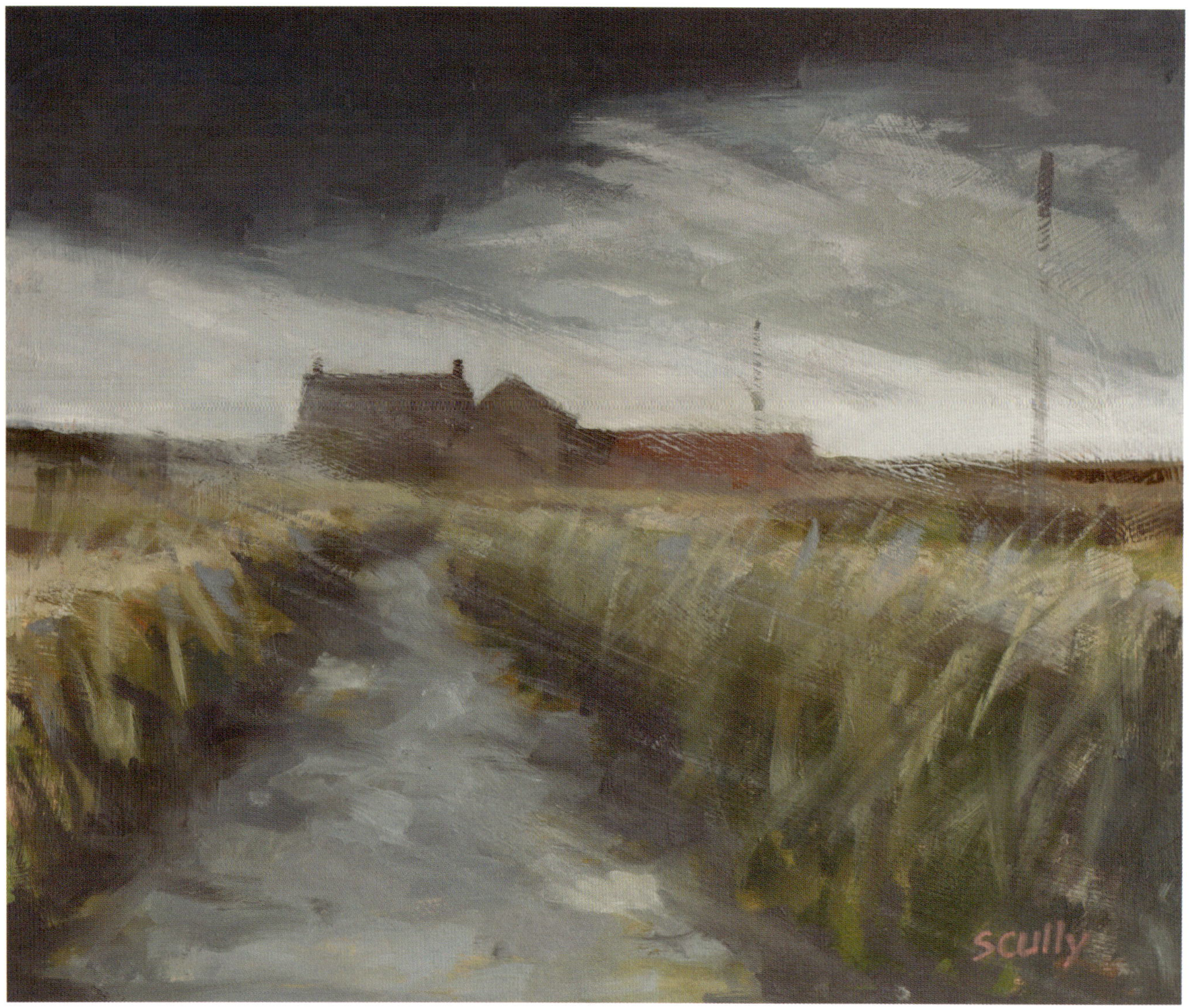

Southwesterly, Kevin Scully. (10" × 12", oil on board)
Occasionally a painting takes a turn for the worse, and rather than discard it completely, this situation can sometimes provide the opportunity for experimentation. This was such a painting, which had begun quite well as a demonstration but soon got into difficulties. Sometimes things just don't work out as planned, so drastic measures were called for. It seemed the only way to perhaps rescue it was to alter the weather conditions from rather nondescript to stormy, so some dark clouds were introduced, followed by driving rain, which was added by dragging some thin paint diagonally across the picture, partially obscuring some of the landscape.

Having drawn out your composition, it's time to start painting. Begin by establishing the initial tonal key from which to assess your other tonal values. The sky is normally the lightest part of the landscape, so this will be a good starting point. Unless you are painting wet-in-wet, you could begin by laying-in your main shapes using fairly diluted paint. Depending on weather conditions and the air temperature, you may want to speed up the drying time of your paints by adding a little alkyd medium to your mixes. This will ensure that the initial layer of colour will later be dry to the extent that you can add more opaque colour on top. Apply your subsequent layers with a minimum of brushstrokes, laying the paint down without blending the colours together too much. The more definite these brushstrokes are, the more interesting the result will be. Once you begin to stir up the semi-dry colour underneath, the duller the painting will look.

Because of the time element involved, a good strategy to adopt would be to first of all establish the general, local colour of things, taking care to keep the whole painting moving along, without trying to finish off any one area too soon. Whilst doing this, make sure you don't lose the tonal relationships that you first recorded.

Give yourself a time limit of perhaps two, to two and a half hours. This will allow you enough time to record the essence of the scene without being tempted into including too much detail. Also, the light will be changing, and you don't want to be forever chasing shadows. Keep in mind the inspiration you experienced when you first encountered the scene, and emphasize this in your painting. If it was an area or object in the middle distance, focus on this and don't be tempted into painting too much detail in the foreground or distance.

If you have chosen a scene that is generously endowed with greens, make sure that you add variety into your colour mixes by adding touches of other colours, remembering that as greens recede into the distance they often become increasingly blue. This may not be particularly evident in your scene, but by adding increasing amounts of blue to the receding layers of the landscape, you can create this illusion. By squinting at your scene and staring long enough, you will eventually see hints of other colours present; perhaps a touch of red here, or a suggestion of ochre there. Look for colour in the shadows, and if necessary exaggerate it for effect – if you can't see any colour, invent some!

If you have decided to paint wet-in-wet, you probably won't need as much time to complete your painting, but this doesn't mean you have to rush it. If you have never painted outside before, this technique is trickier than it looks, and to implement it successfully requires a fair amount of practice. Because the whole painting is completed in one hit, it allows you less thinking time than one that is painted by gradually building up layers of colour. It is more important therefore to be well prepared beforehand, so that before you begin you have already made the important decisions about composition and how you will be going about it. You would be wise to have already completed a tonal sketch, and to have familiarized yourself with the process by having a few practice runs. Remember, you will be trying to cope with several things at the same time; tone, colour, shape, form, lighting and so on.

If you intend to use the paint in a fairly thick consistency, and will be painting one colour over another, you will have to adjust the way that you apply the paint. By loading your brush with a reasonable quantity of colour and merely laying the paint down with your brush at an angle almost horizontal with your painting, you will be picking up less of the colour that has already been applied. You may need to wipe colour off your brush fairly frequently, so that too many colours don't accumulate on it, mixing together and making your painting look muddy.

Steps to the Church, Ormos, Samos, David Sawyer. (24" × 10", oil on board) The main focus of this painting, the church, occupies a relatively small area of the overall image. The steeply rising steps, which fill the bottom of the painting, serve to lead the eye towards the subject, and then the area created by the dark shape of the Cypress tree stops the eye from wandering out of the picture, but at the same time entices the viewer into imagining what is just around the corner at the top of the steps. A comfortable composition has been created by counter-balancing the loosely painted area of foliage in the bottom right-hand corner, with the stronger tone of the shrubs on the left of the painting, behind the wall.

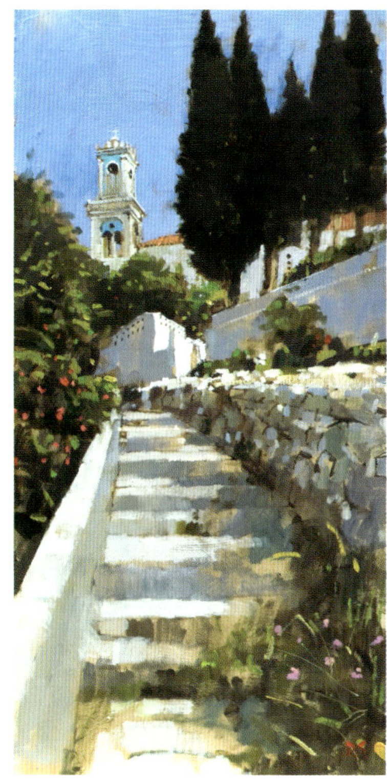

By applying the colour with a painting knife, wet-in-wet, you will be able to create a very different look to that when using a brush, but it is even more difficult and will require a fair amount of practice. If you have never used a palette knife before in anger, it will probably involve a great deal of paint being wasted. One of the advantages of using a knife is that it's very easy to keep clean in between using different colours by giving it a quick wipe with a rag. If you are using oils, you can use the paint straight from the tube without adding any medium, and if you are using acrylic, you can add an impasto paste to thicken the paint. When using acrylics, it's best to work as quickly as possible, because once the paint underneath dries it's difficult to control the colour application, as the ridges that are made by the painting knife will cause further layers to skid over them.

Having completed your painting *en plein air*, it might require a few minor adjustments here and there back at the studio, and this is better carried out a day or two later when it can be assessed with fresh eyes. It's best not to overdo this, as it will detract from the freshness and immediacy of the painting. You could even revisit the site to make a further evaluation. To paint the same scene at a different time of day, or in contrasting weather conditions would be a worthwhile comparative exercise, and you could even return in a different season when the trees are bare and the light levels are low.

DEMONSTRATION

Manstone Farm

A simple composition, with the image divided into just two areas, in which all of the interest is contained in the top half of the painting.

The colours used in this painting were:

- Titanium White
- Oxide of Chromium
- Raw Umber
- Burnt Sienna
- Dioxazine Purple

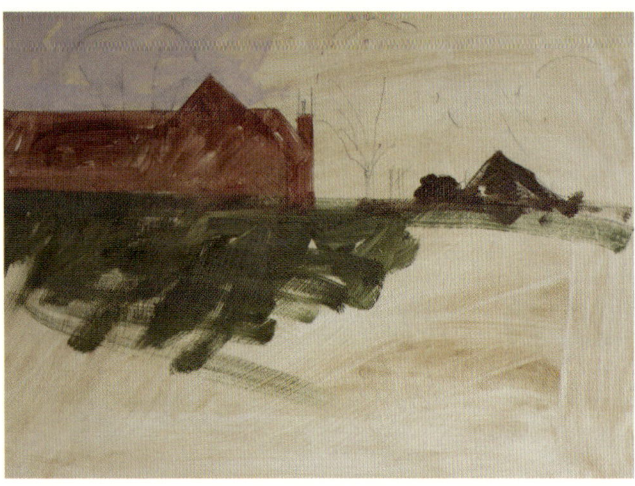

By simply establishing these three main areas of colour and tone, it immediately sets the scene for the following stages of the painting. The colours represented an approximation of the local colour of each element.

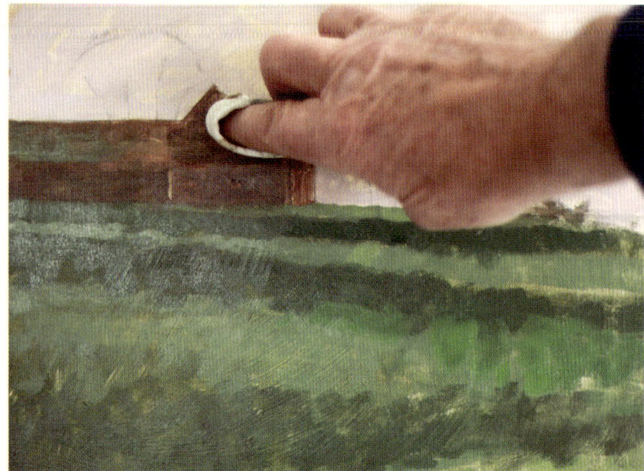

These three colours were extended into their respective areas, with the addition of some variations in colour. Some of these colours were blended with a rag, a technique that can sometimes prove more effective than doing so with a brush. And don't forget that one of the most useful tools readily available to you is your fingers and especially your thumb, if you don't mind getting them dirty.

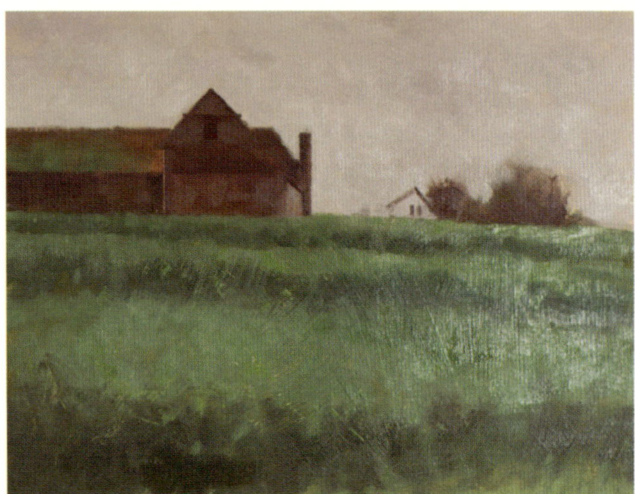

Working forward from the elements furthest away, the sky colour was refined and lightened in the area closest to the horizon. The house, just seen over the brow of the hill, was indicated by merely painting the roofline and windows on top of the sky colour. The trees and shrubs to the right of it were painted the same colour as the barn and their edges blended delicately against the sky. A little more detail was added to the barn, just sufficient to prevent it from jumping forward.

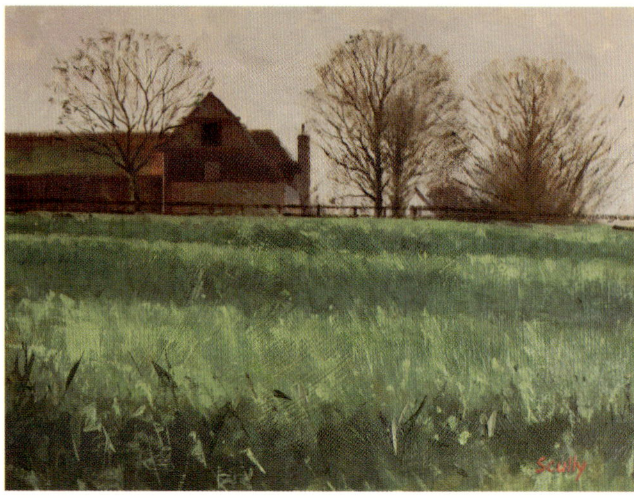

Once the barn and sky were dry enough, the trees and post and rail fence were added, the former with a dry brush technique, and the latter with a ruler and small synthetic brush. Some variation was added to the immediate foreground with colour on the edge of a painting knife, to indicate just enough detail in the rows of crops. In this painting the centre section of the image has been left relatively featureless, to encourage your eye up to the farm buildings at the top of the hill.

DEMONSTRATION

Goring Lock

An elongated landscape format was chosen for this image, so that the lock gates and their mechanism could be included along with the lock keeper's house.

The colours used in this demonstration were:

- Titanium White
- Cobalt Blue
- Yellow Ochre
- Burnt Sienna
- Burnt Umber
- Cadmium Red
- Phthalo Green
- Payne's Grey

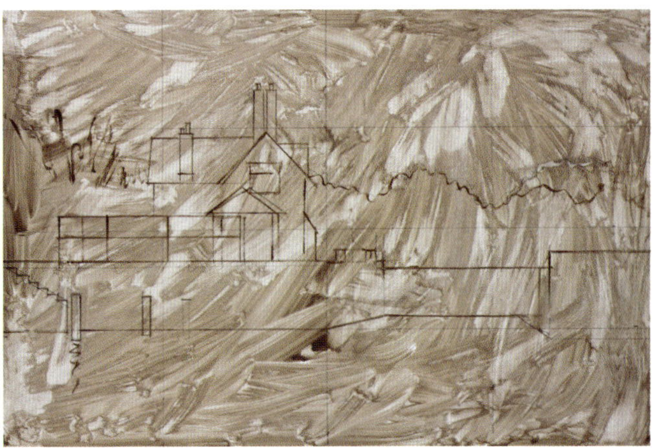

As this painting featured a building, the drawing required a degree of accuracy, so a compositional drawing was transferred onto the board using the scaling-up method. The drawn lines were then painted over with a small brush, using a ruler where necessary. As this autumnal painting was to be mainly warm in colour temperature, the toned ground was painted with a mixture of Burnt Sienna and Raw Umber.

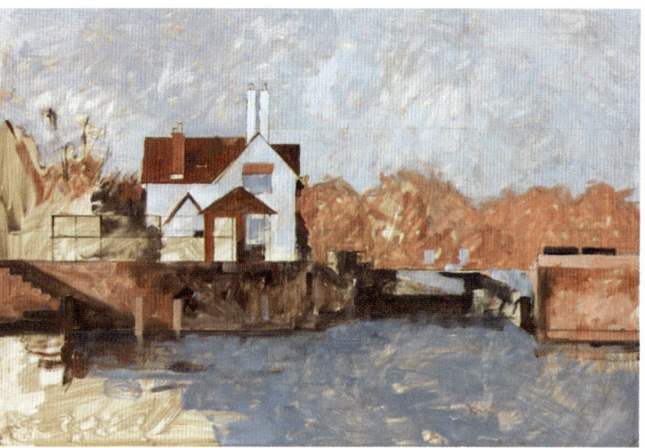

Taking some degree of care with the building, the main colours were blocked in with their local colour with some shadows indicated here and there. In this scene the white house was lighter than the sky, so it was this element that established the tonal key for the rest of the painting.

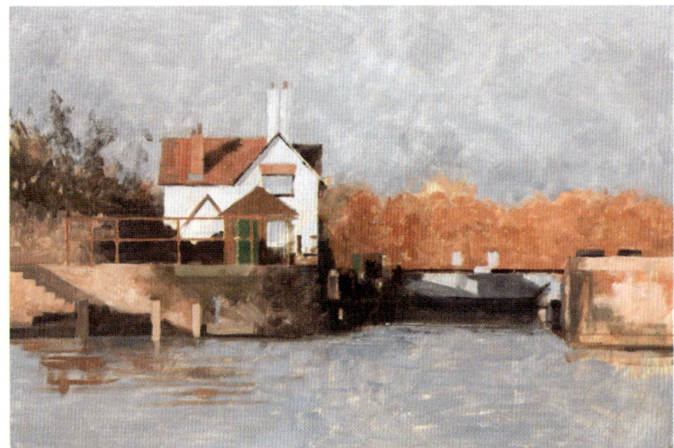

The painting uses the orange/blue colour scheme as its base, with the addition of a selection of neutrals to tie the whole image together. The only other colour that appears in the painting is the green of the door and a piece of the lock's mechanism.

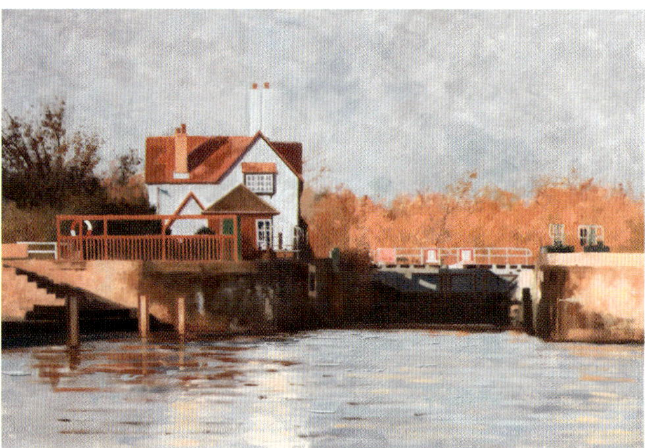

In adding all the final details to the building and the lock gates, the ruler was put to good use. This contrasted with the loose painting of the trees in the background. Some thicker colour was added to the water with the edge of a palette knife to catch the light.

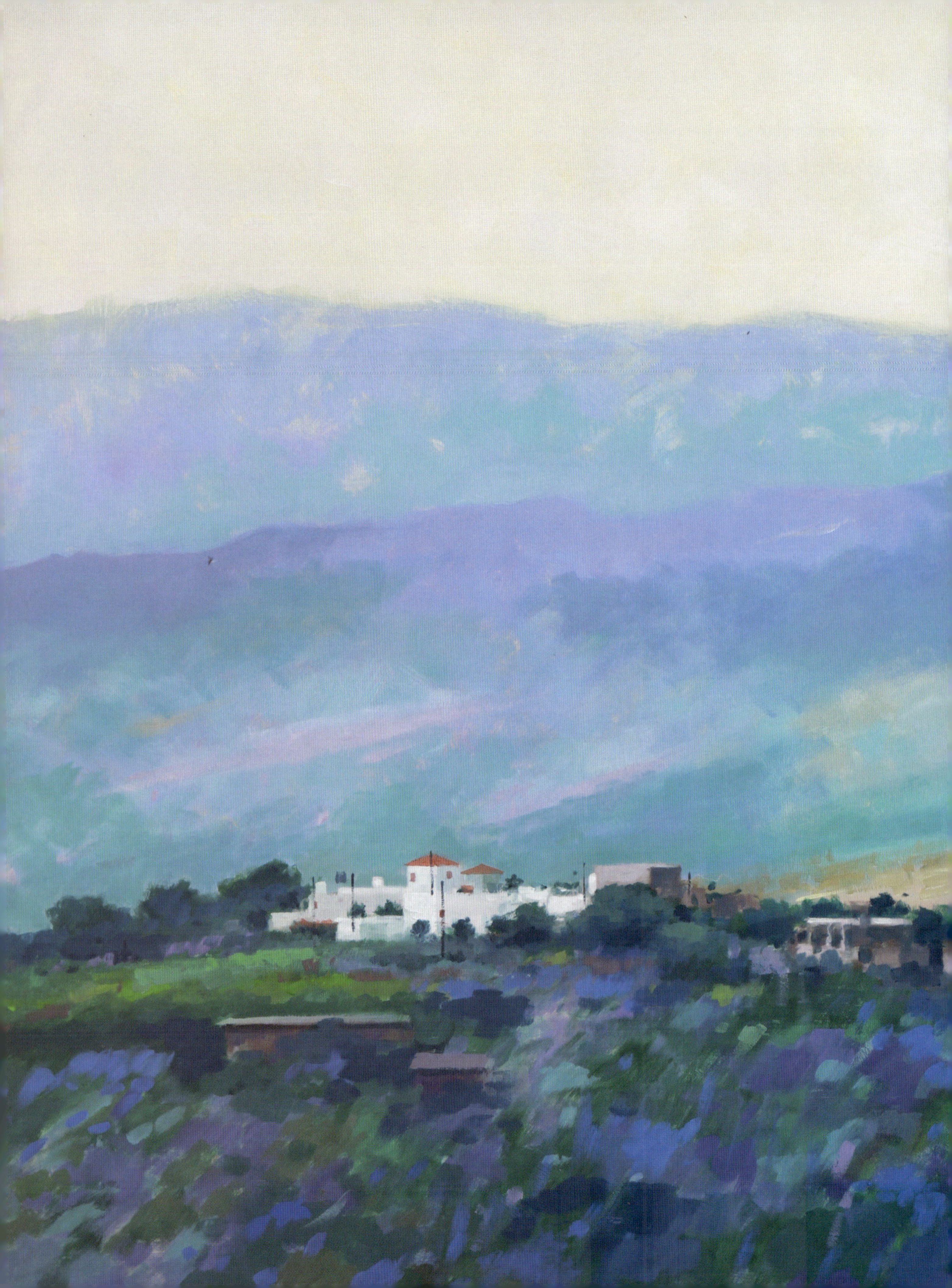

CHAPTER 9

Working from Photographs

Photos can be referred to when accuracy is required but not as our final composition. We must develop our minds to see and retain for later use.

MARION BODDY-EVANS

Although some artists regard the digital camera as the enemy, it does have a place in the toolkit, as long as we are aware of its limitations. Its plus points are numerous; it is practical, fast, detailed, accurate, adaptable and realistic to a point.

It is also a tool, and unable to make aesthetic and creative judgements. It is inferior to our eyes in that it records colour in a different way, often eliminating it from shadows, which it records as dark recesses. It documents what it sees with indiscriminate cruelty, and it can also distort colour and depth of field to a degree that is far inferior to our own eyes. Having said that, many a famous landscape painter from centuries past would undoubtedly have given their non-painting arm to own a digital camera. Edgar Degas hated painting outdoors and declared that anyone caught doing so should be shot. He often worked from photographs, but it can be seen when comparing his photographs with his paintings that his paintings weren't copied indiscriminately from the photos. Because the photographs were all in black and white, the colours in the paintings were those selected by the artist. Emulating unintentional photographic effects can sometimes be a source of inspiration and a sounding board for exciting colour combinations. However, more often than not by including common photographic effects such as blurred backgrounds behind an object in super-sharp focus, or camera 'flare', suggests that these have been directly copied, and diminish the integrity of the painting. A painting that exactly resembles a photograph isn't really a painting in the true sense of the word, but merely a skilful version of a photograph executed in paint.

Karydi, Crete, Kevin Scully. (22′ × 18″, oil on board)
The analogous colours of green, blue and violet that sit side-by-side on the cool side of the colour wheel are dominant in this painting, with the reds, oranges and browns on the opposite side providing a complementary warmer balance. The buildings have been placed low down in the composition to emphasize the height of the distant mountains. The foliage in the foreground has been painted with a minimum amount of detail so that it doesn't detract from the main focus of the painting, which is the group of buildings along the ridge of the foothills.

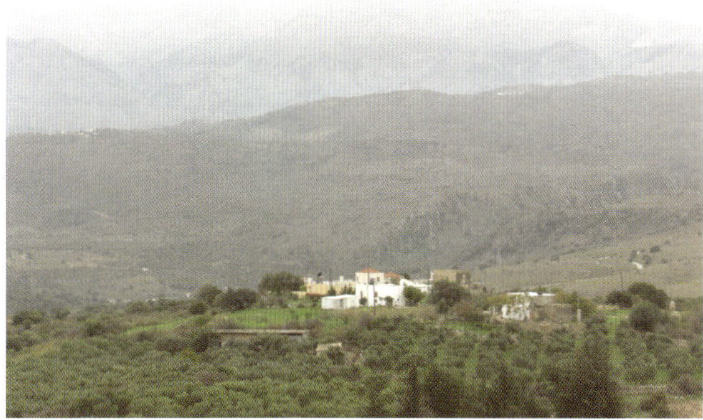

This photograph was taken early one morning on the island of Crete, having been struck by the beauty of a hazy sunrise where the landscape was ablaze with the white light of the sun, casting a blue and violet veil over the distant mountains. When the photograph was viewed some time after, none of the beautiful colours had been recorded. But the photograph was later used as a reference for a painting where the colours of that scene were painted from memory, whilst taking a few liberties with the actual detail.

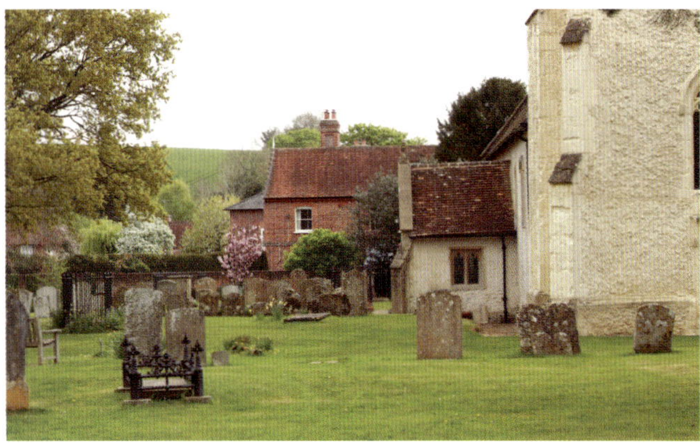

A photograph taken at midday in mid-spring with no sun in the sky. The image appears rather flat as there are no clues to inform us of the distance between objects. The tonal range is limited and so the forms of each of the elements are not fully described.

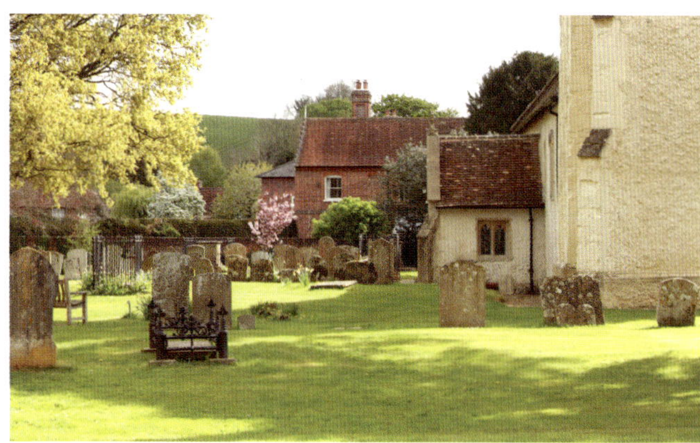

Here the sun has arrived at midday and is positioned at the top right, and out of view. Because it is fairly high in the sky, the shadows cast are merely those from the tall church and some unseen large trees behind us. The tree to the left is in full sun but still appears flat and devoid of form.

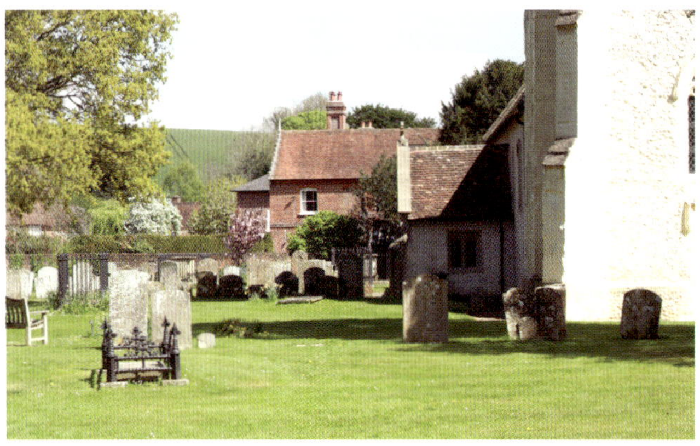

Later in the day, the sun has moved around and presents us with a much more interesting aspect. It has created deep shadows and bright highlights, and some interesting shapes have emerged, including the tombstones at the end of the churchyard where some are now in silhouette. It's possible to see the form within the tree to the left.

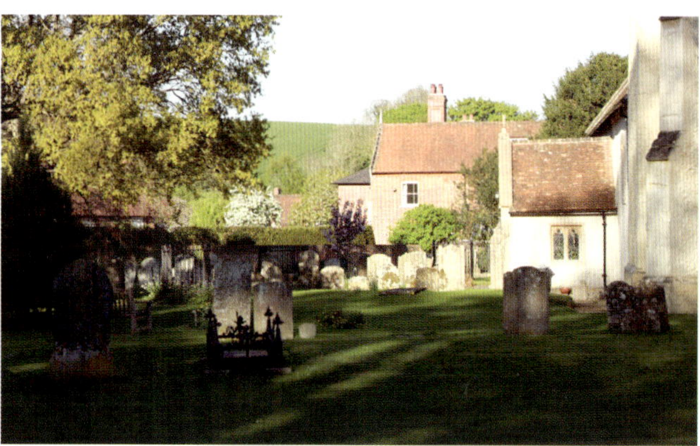

The sun has now moved around behind us and much of the scene has been cast in shade from large trees not in the photograph. The way in which the camera has recorded the scene has now bleached out much of the colour previously seen in the houses in the distance. These four photographs demonstrate how different a scene will look in sunlight at various times of the day, and how the camera records it.

Photographs are great when used as reference material, but they should never be slavishly copied, which results in rather flat and uninspiring paintings. It's far better to interpret into a painting what we experience in real life than to copy what a camera interprets as real life. Once you fall into the trap of copying a photograph you cease to think like a painter, and unless you are a professional photographer, your photos will never tell a true story. If you rely on an automatic focus when taking shots, everything will be sharply in focus with a shallow depth of field, which is not how our eyes record things. There will be an unrealistic contrast between highlights and shadows especially on a bright day. Some of these failings can be adjusted and manipulated with digital software, but the adjustments are far better made by the artist.

A painting takes on a life of its own as it goes through many transitional stages, whereas a photograph has a very short and uneventful life that is over in a fraction of a second. It needs bringing back to life. So when we use photographs as reference material we should only consult them to a minor degree, after which time they should be placed back in the drawer. It makes an interesting exercise to produce a painting outdoors, noting as accurately as possible the subtleties of tonal change and colour saturation. If you then take a photograph of the scene you have painted and then compare the two, you could be forgiven for thinking that you haven't matched the real life colours particularly well, for they will vary greatly from those in the photograph.

Don't be tempted to use other people's photographs to paint from, because as well as it being unethical, you will have had no personal or emotional response to the scene, and as such will be unable to put your own interpretation into the painting. The temptation to include everything you see will be greater, and your ability to edit the contents will be diminished. It's only from your own experience that you can truly and honestly interpret what you experience into a painting.

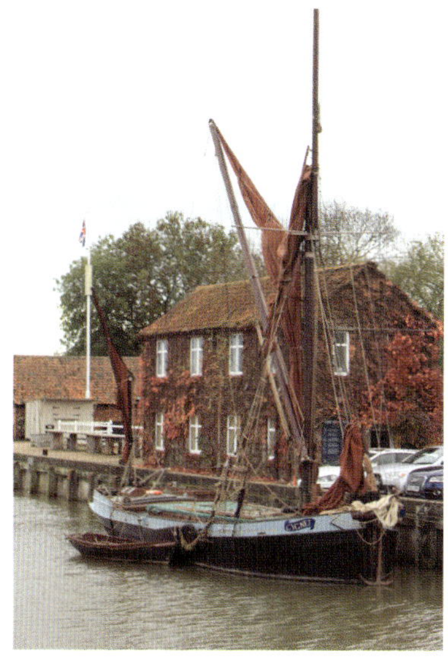

Whilst this sailing barge is undoubtedly a great subject for a painting, this photograph could only ever be used as reference for the vessel itself. If the building behind it were to be included, its colour and tonal value would have to be altered. The cars to the right of the picture add nothing to the composition, and should be removed.

Selective Editing

Photographs are often disappointing in that they don't truly represent the feeling we had when we took them. We may also spot things in them that we hadn't originally noticed. There might be branches from an unseen tree in the foreground that have crept into the picture, partly obscuring our intended focal point. Instead of a single, directional element that leads the eye into the picture, there may also be the confusing suggestion of another one, at first unseen. There might be two strong verticals of exactly the same height, taking your eye confusingly across the picture from one side to the other. Perhaps there are two horizontal elements, one behind the other but at the same height, and of the same tonal value and similar in colour, so that they are indistinguishable from each other.

Some of these elements will have to be repositioned or deleted to form a more comfortable arrangement, so this can be done in our thumbnail sketches. You may also need to crop the image to reposition your focal point, or you may decide that the format you chose wasn't really the right one. Some time spent resolving these problem areas at an early stage will pay huge dividends later on.

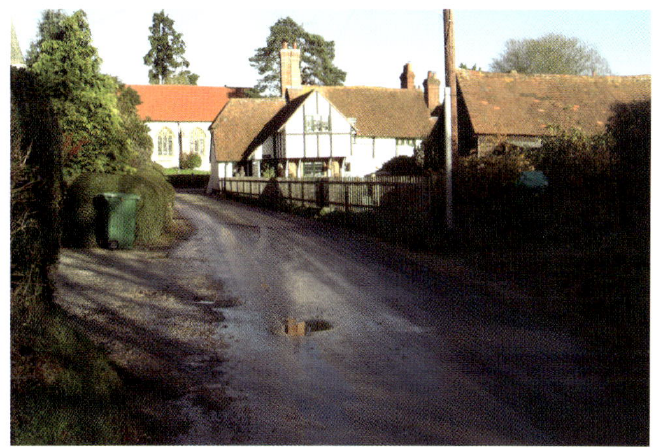

Although this image is a fairly well-balanced composition, it would benefit from being cropped. The areas to the right and left of the photograph add very little interest to the overall scene, and the green bin and reflection in the road are a distraction. The deep shadow to the right is far too dark, and some colour should be introduced into it to make it less dominant.

Altering Images Digitally

If you consider the use of a camera as acceptable in your creative endeavours, you might want to take a step further along the path of technology and use the computer to manipulate your photographs. There are a number of Photoshop filters that can be used to create different effects, and although many of them are for converting photographs into what are supposed to look like paintings, there are others that are quite useful for compositional purposes. There are some filters that separate and exaggerate tonal distinctions as a by-product of producing a different effect in a photograph. There is a danger though in relying on technology too much, as it's all too easy to get sucked into alternative ways of painting, when perhaps what you should be doing is just painting. In Photoshop Elements you will be able to balance the colour saturation, adjust the lighting levels and contrast, convert to black and white, and many other things. There will probably be a feature somewhere on your computer that allows you to lighten the shadow areas of an image, to reveal some of the colour hidden therein that would otherwise be mysteriously absent from your photograph.

But what if by some miracle of divine intervention the photograph you have taken is perfect? There might be a temptation to alter nothing, and simply reproduce it in a painterly way, which would be regarded as acceptable, but another alternative would be to recreate it in a completely different colour scheme. Consider taking a black and white photocopy of your image and use it as a tonal guide for an alternative colour range. Choose from one of the colour schemes detailed in a previous chapter, or perhaps paint a monochromatic version of it.

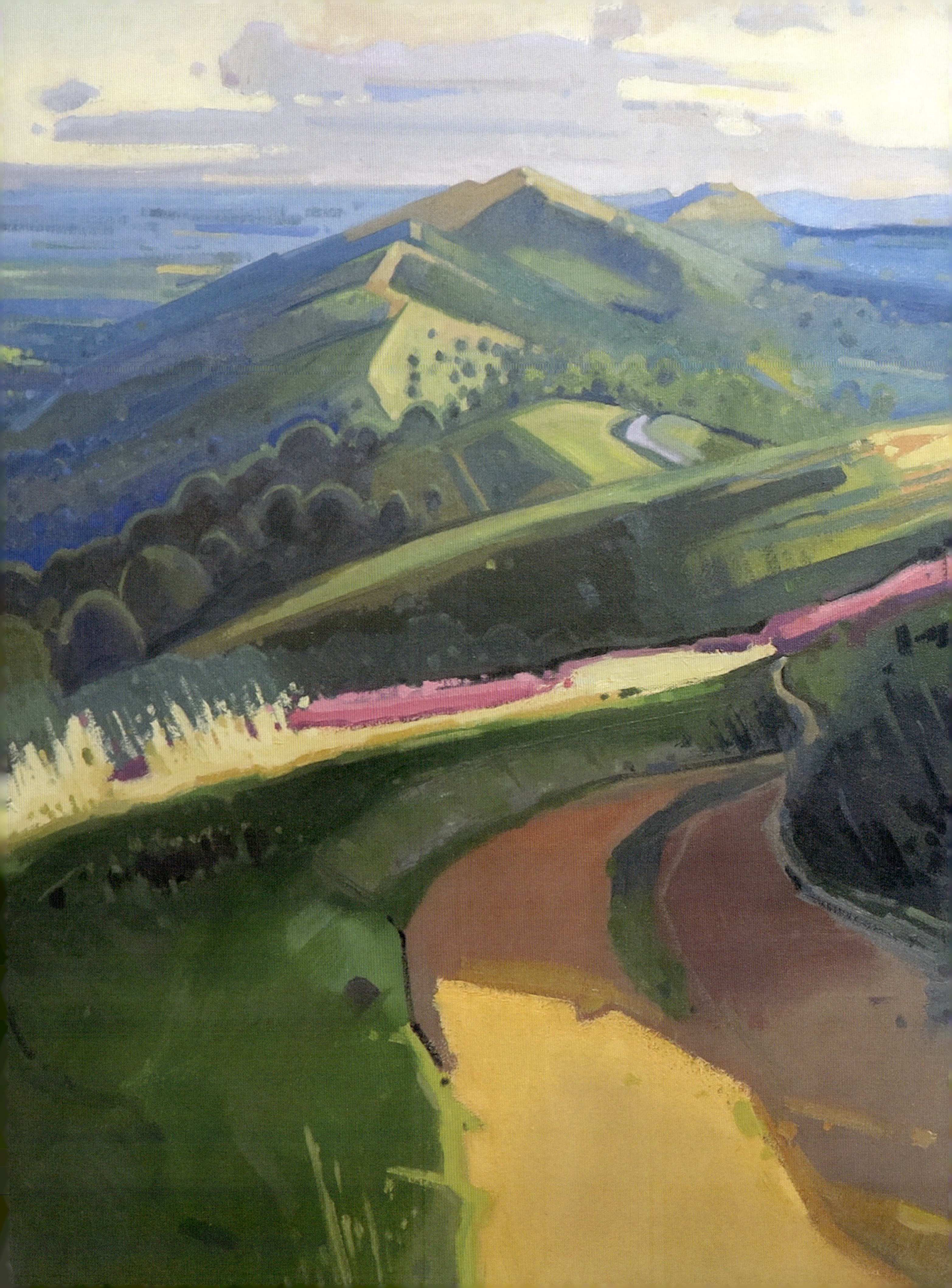

CHAPTER 10

Natural Progression

Without fail, three or four hideous paintings down the road, an absolutely wonderful painting appears. A painting that is a better painting than I know how to do. A painting that feels effortless.

ELEANOR BLAIR

For most of us, success as a painter doesn't come easily, and there will always be many failures on the way, but failure is something that can't, and shouldn't be avoided. To be able to produce successful paintings is difficult, but we can learn from our failures. Without pushing the boundaries and taking risks our creative spirit would become stagnant, and progression would be halted. By going just that step further, there will always be potential for the odd disaster, or joyous success.

In the world of innovation, invention and experimentation, failure is expected, because by failing over and over again, the process of discovery and development gradually exposes the reasons why something doesn't work to reveal a way of ensuring that it does work. And so it is with painting, or any art form for that matter. When your ideas fail, they may give you other ideas that lead you towards those that might succeed. Producing a successful painting may just mean that you are satisfied with your own work, and if you're satisfied with it, then it can be regarded as a success. No matter what we elect to paint, there will be problems to solve, and part of the attraction of being an artist is how we go about finding the right solutions to those problems. The challenges are endless and there is always room for improvement, and we will never stop learning.

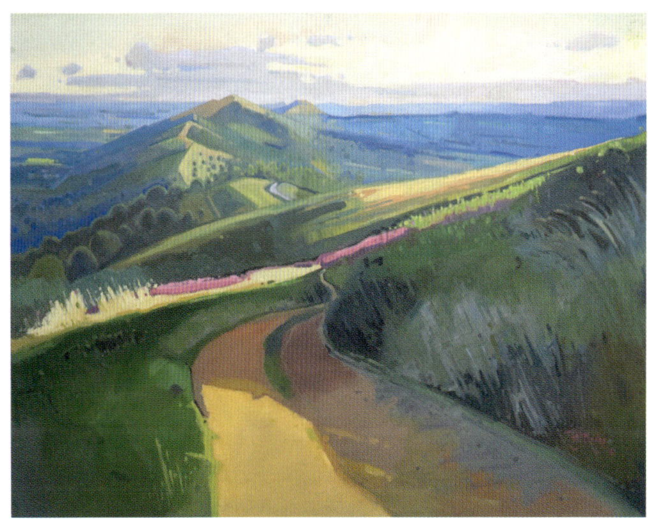

Malvern Southwards, Path, Antony Bridge. (30" × 40", oil on canvas)
A large studio painting that plays with contrasting areas of both warm and cool passages. The predominantly warm colours in the foreground gradually become cooler as your eye travels into the distance. Subtle mixes of the complementary colours yellow and violet are present in the sky, unifying the entire composition.

Malvern Southwards, Path (detail), Antony Bridge. (30" × 40", oil on canvas)

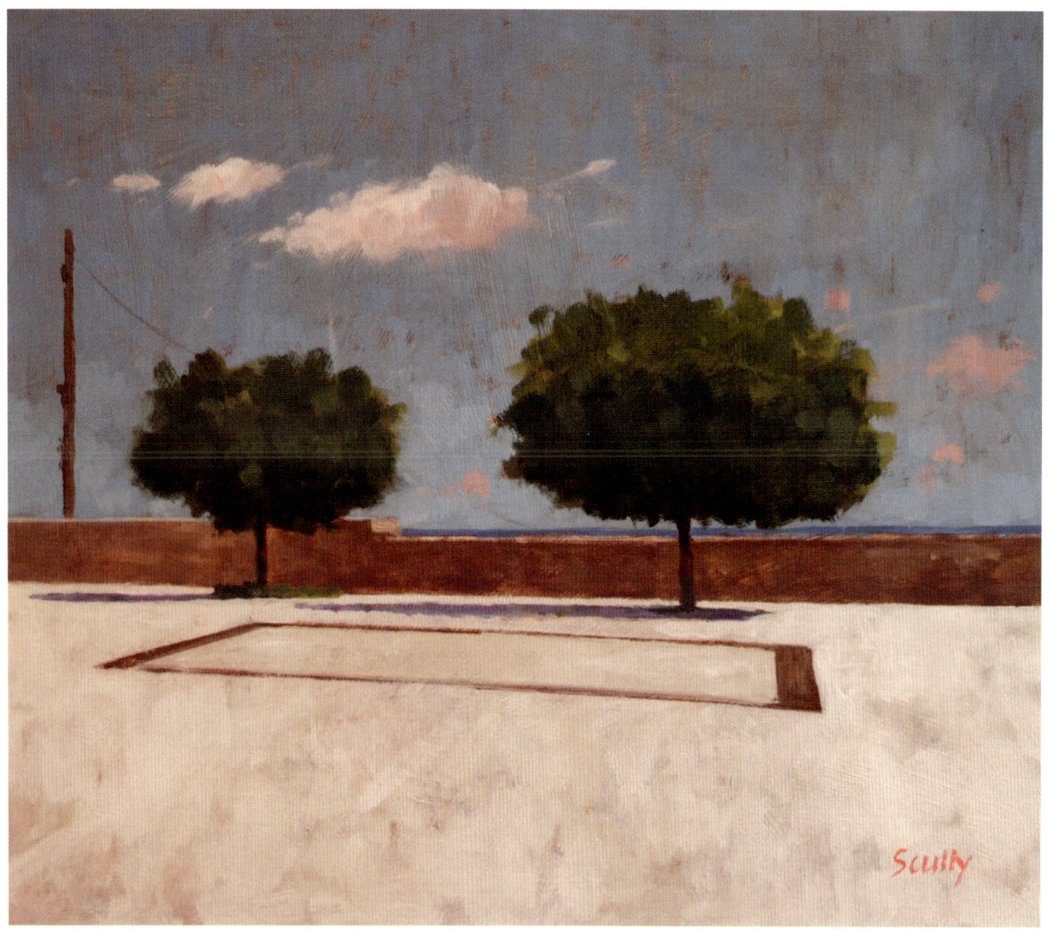

Santa Maria di Luca, Puglia, Kevin Scully. (10" × 12", oil on board)
This scene provided a ready-made composition that needed no amendment or alteration, and was painted as seen. The appeal lay in the variety of shapes within such a simple arrangement. The large rectangular pattern in the paved area added a semi-abstract touch to the scene, as did the stylized appearance of the trees. The cool violet shadows cast on the ground contrast with the warm greens of the trees. The warm tones of the paving have been repeated in the clouds.

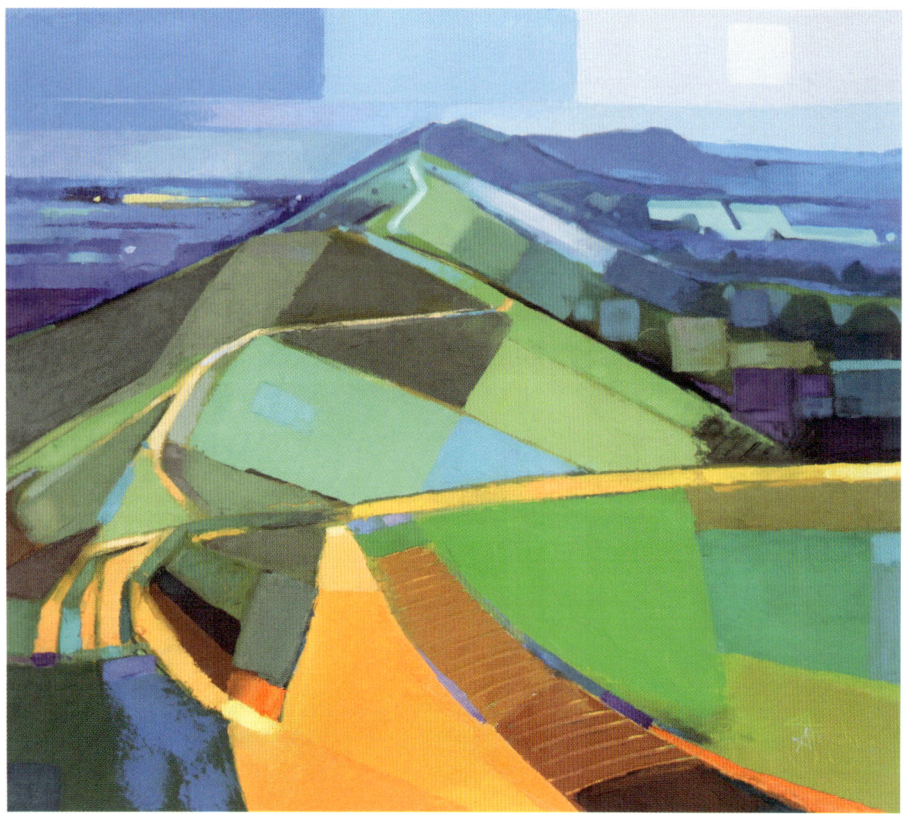

Malvern Southwards – Colour Memory, Antony Bridge. (20" × 24", oil on canvas)
When working *en plein air*, it can be difficult to paint anything other than that which you see in front of you. In this painting, Antony Bridge has created an image from memory after visiting a particular location. He has reproduced what he remembers of the scene in blocks of colour in their simplest form, rather than in specific detail.

Evaluation

Every now and again we should adopt a strategy for self-evaluation, which should involve analysing both the positive and negative aspects of our progress, and this is especially relevant if we work in splendid isolation and don't have the benefit of any independent assessment. It's all too easy to become totally engrossed in our painting and forget to judge it objectively. When asked to critique another artist's efforts we can approach this with fresh eyes and an open mind. Initial impressions are the most important ones, and having never seen someone's painting before, there are certain things that jump out. Some may be good, and some not so good, and so it is when someone looks at your work for the first time.

Because we become so absorbed in our work, we have to find ways of evaluating it ourselves, and doing this with thorough truthfulness. There is no point glossing over things that are obviously faulty, or covering up some suspect perspective by painting a tree in front of it. We have to be honest with ourselves, and there are certain ways in which we can do this. These suggestions apply mainly to figurative or representational painters, but even if you are an abstract painter, or if your work falls into the category of stylized or decorative art, some will also be relevant to you.

Even if you are a starving artist, living alone in a garret, invite people up occasionally to view your work, especially if they are artists themselves. They will be used to looking at paintings and will be visually aware, so will quickly home in on things you may have missed. Unless they are brutally honest, try to avoid asking friends and family of their opinions, as they will usually be flattering and not of much value. You will benefit also from painting in the company of others, especially if they are painting the same subject matter as yourself. You will be able to assess the way that they approach the task, and it may lead you along another path of discovery.

Developing a Style

We all have our own individual inherent way of writing, drawing or painting, but the way that we go about things doesn't have to remain static. We can develop it into our own style. We may initially emulate the style of another artist because we admire their work so much, but gradually something else will emerge. A recognized style of painting doesn't usually manifest itself overnight, particularly if you've never painted before, although there are exceptions to the rule. Many artists are not especially content with the way they paint and are constantly striving for that elusive style, which sometimes may take years to evolve.

ASSESSING YOUR WORK

- Make a point of retreating from your work as often as you can, and view it from a distance. This is something you may do naturally if you paint in the standing position, but if you prefer to work whilst seated, it's even more important, not only for the benefit of the painting, but also for your physical and mental wellbeing.
- Even if you feel as though you have created a masterpiece, before you frame it and take it proudly off to an exhibition or gallery, take some time out to reassess your opinion of it. By turning it to face the wall for a few days and viewing it with a fresh eye, you may decide that it is still a masterpiece, but on the other hand you might notice that there's something not quite right about that sky, or the angle of that roof.
- When you turn a painting upside down, you'll be surprised at how different it looks, but it should still hold together as a composition in the arrangement of its shapes, colour and tonal variation. If there are any slightly suspect areas they will quickly become evident. Don't dwell on it for too long, as some details will of course look strange the wrong way up, but in general the painting should appear to be well balanced.
- Even more telling is when you look at a painting in a mirror. What you have been used to looking at in the normal way suddenly looks very strange, but again, it should appear as a cohesive composition.
- Even though all paintings don't necessarily need a definite focal point, if you have one it should be evident. Your eye should be led to it by some means that is either obvious or perhaps more furtive.
- Determine whether or not your painting has the right amount of tonal variation. A strong composition will have four or five distinct areas of varying tones. If there are too many of these scattered about the painting, from a distance it will appear fragmented and disjointed.
- Your painting should have just one main dark area and one main highlighted area. If there are too many of these, your eye doesn't really know where to look as it searches around for somewhere to rest.
- It's interesting to note that when we look at the three-dimensional landscape with half-closed eyes, we are able to accentuate the differences between the broad tonal masses far more easily than we can by viewing it with fully opened eyes. But when we squint at our two-dimensional painting, it looks exactly the same as when we look at it normally.

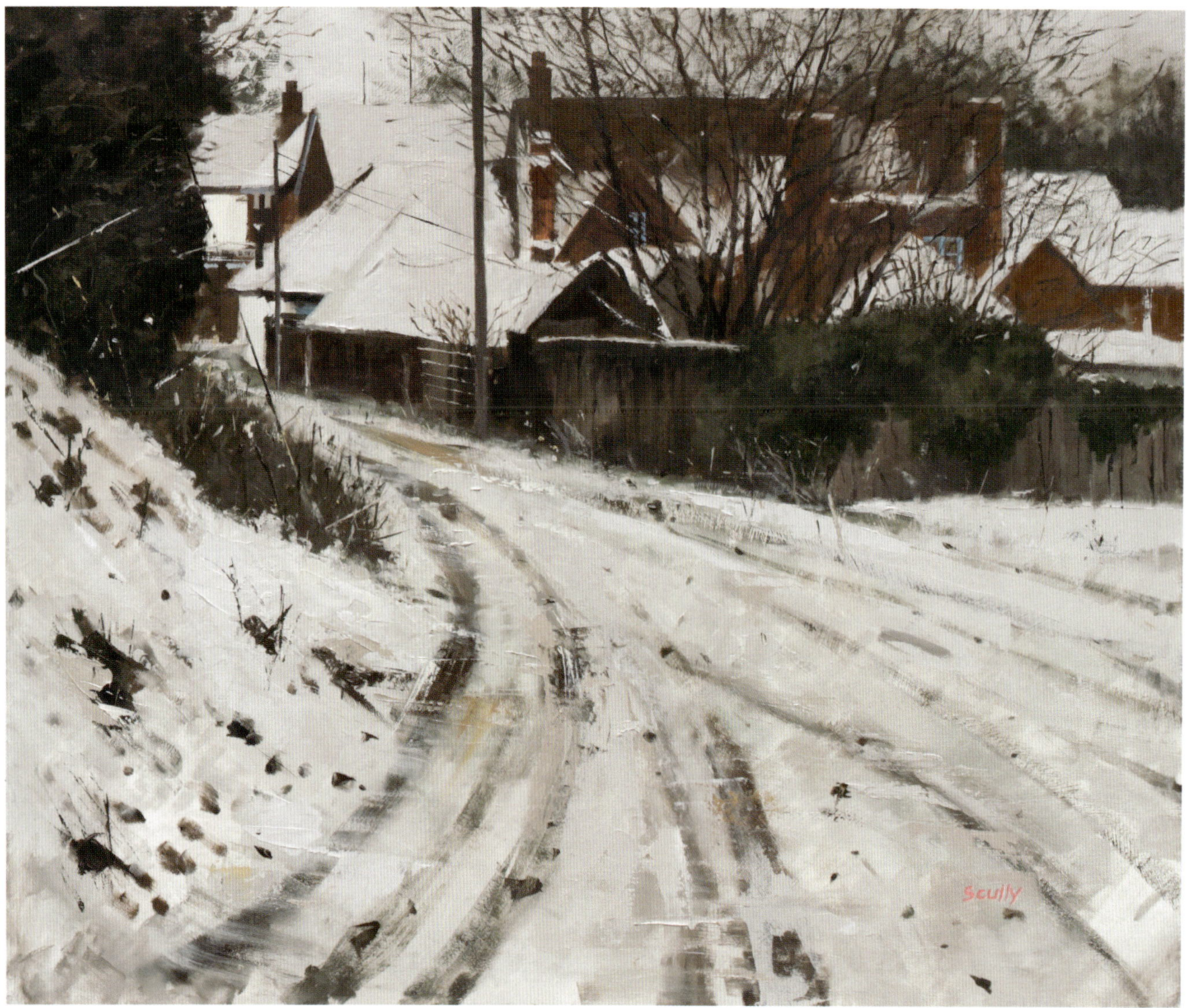

White Hart Track, Kevin Scully. (22" × 24", oil on board)
A painting combining several techniques in one picture. Although most of the painting was executed with a brush, including dry brush and impasto, there are also large areas where a painting knife has been used. The assortment of buildings in the background could have been a distraction to the main focus of the painting, which is the track sweeping around the corner, but they have been afforded less prominence by the veil of winter trees behind the fence.

Unless you are irretrievably set in your ways, and entirely happy with your painting method, one way of finding your own individual style is to experiment with as many different styles of painting as possible. If you are inclined to create very small, detailed paintings, abandon your tiny brushes and reach for ones a couple of sizes larger than you would normally use to make you produce a painting that has more vitality. With experience comes confidence, and this can influence the way that you physically apply the paint to canvas. The once hesitant brushstrokes may now be more dynamic and animated, and the once subdued colour selection may become vibrant and energetic. By adopting different approaches to your work you will be teaching yourself a whole new set of visual skills. These can be used as weapons in your armoury when you next do battle with the paints and canvas. Until you let your hair down, you will never know what you can be capable of.

There are many artists who are perfectly at ease with the way they paint, and are content to produce much the same picture over and over again in a rather low-key manner, and there is nothing wrong with that at all. But if you want to be distinguished from other artists by producing work that is professional, distinctive and unique, you have to create your own style, and this can only be done by exploration and experiment. But by developing a style, it doesn't mean you have to stick to it, and many artists throughout history and in modern times have reinvented themselves, and their work has evolved into a different style. But the process takes time, and being an artist is a time-consuming and an all-absorbing way of life.

Figurative or Abstract (or somewhere in between)

There are many figurative or representational artists, and by that we mean artists who paint things in a recognizable way, who have at some stage in their life dabbled with the notion of abstract art. Abstract art can be defined in many ways, but in its simplest terms it is more concerned with the aesthetics of form, pattern and colour, than it is with how things can be represented in a realistic way. It could be argued that nature itself is abstract, and that it is just a collection of textures, colours, pattern and form.

Both figurative and abstract art concern themselves with these fundamentals, but for the abstract artist their work can mean anything they want it to mean, so there is infinite territory to explore and the boundaries are limitless. The abstract artist attempts to express what other visual art styles cannot, and addresses concepts that are theoretical, intangible and sometimes provocative, existing in the realms of mind and spirit, rather than in outer reality. Abstract art can use pure colour, shape, and form to express its meaning, without resorting to a representation of the superfluous objects that exist in reality, and can influence the emotions in a powerfully direct way. It can perhaps be based on reality, or simply the imagination of the artist. The process of painting in an abstract way need not include any carefully constructed compositional pre-planning, and may be created spontaneously, following random lines of inspiration as they occur.

There is a broad, outlying area of art that crosses the boundary between figurative painting and abstract painting that can be termed as semi-abstract, or semi-figurative, depending on which side of the boundary you're viewing it from. Described in simple terms, it combines the two disciplines, blurring the edges and leaving much to the imagination of the viewer. Many artists, and almost exclusively those artists whose background has always been as a figurative painter, will at some time or other want to take on new challenges, but have no interest in pure abstract art. Not wanting to abandon figurative painting altogether, but having a desire to take their work in a new direction, they will begin to develop new techniques that instil a degree of mystery into their work. Objects will be less defined, edges will be softened, shapes overlapped, brush marks disguised and realistic colours replaced by alternative ones. Objects will still be recognizable but they may merge one into the other, creating a sense of the enigmatic.

New Inspiration and Keeping Motivated

Very few of us can truly say that we are consistently inspired, and many a professional artist will testify that they have produced paintings without the motivation of inspiration to help them. There are occasions when having taken on a commission with unbounded enthusiasm, by the time the painting process has begun, the enthusiasm has ebbed away, to be replaced by apathy. The pressure of completing a large number of paintings for a forthcoming exhibition can induce a mild state of panic, which is a sure way to produce motivation, but where will the inspiration come from? The thought of revenue from possible sales is a great motivator.

Not everyone has the benefit of a studio or permanent workspace, which may mean you are unable to leave your art materials out and need to put them away at the end of every painting session. This situation can quickly induce a state of frustration that can eventually lead to inertia. Ideally, before we begin a painting we should be feeling both enthusiastic and optimistic, but this is often not the case. But what can we do about it?

There are a few options, one of which is to simply wait for inspiration to strike, and eventually it probably will. Another is to simply get out your art materials and put a canvas on the easel. There is the danger though that staring at a blank canvas can of course induce the opposite of the desired effect, which is the same as the writer staring at a blank page. You will probably have some sketchbooks containing drawings that you made in the past, thinking that one day they would make good paintings. You could also trawl through your photographic references, and perhaps some images that were dismissed in the past might ignite the flames of an idea. By engaging in the simple act of drawing something, your brain may uncover latent artistic thoughts just waiting to be revealed.

I learned… that inspiration does not come like a bolt, nor is it kinetic, energetic, striving, but it comes into us slowly and quietly and all the time, though we must regularly and every day give it a little chance to start flowing, prime it with a little solitude and idleness.

BRENDA UELAND

If you have seated yourself at the easel, and arranged your paints and brushes in a way that suggests you know what you are about to paint, why not paint a still life, or even a self-portrait? It may not be your preferred subject matter, but by merely going through the process of painting something, it may start the ball rolling. Even if you abandon your painting halfway through in favour of beginning one of a landscape, the exercise will have been worthwhile.

Looking through books and perhaps some postcards at the work of other artists that you admire, whether famous or not, is one of the best routes to take, and will often produce results. Remember also that these artists have spent their fair share of time uninspired, and staring at a blank canvas or two. Visit a couple of art galleries or museums, where you will be surrounded by other artists' work, where just the sight of paint on canvas may have you scuttling off back home to reach for your brushes.

If all else fails, take your sketchbook and camera out with you on a rejuvenating and invigorating trip into unfamiliar countryside. There is sure to be something out there to inspire you.

Avoiding Clichés

It's becoming increasingly difficult to be totally original when it comes to painting, because so much has already been said by so many artists, which means we have to try and find a way of depicting things in different ways. There are many hackneyed subjects that have been trampled to death, so are best avoided unless we adopt a truly original line of approach. This is particularly true of landscape subjects, as there are only so many elements of the landscape from which to choose. If you can find subject matter in nature that hasn't already been painted a thousand times before, very soon you won't be the only artist painting it. So much work, in such a diverse variety of styles, is now available for everyone to see on the internet that nothing remains a secret for very long.

If you find it understandably impossible to produce something totally original, at least there are a few subjects that are best avoided. You may already have made a mental note of the number of times you have seen paintings of much-visited tourist destinations, so many in fact that you feel as though you have visited them already and that there is nothing else left to say. The same could be said of empty beaches with sunsets over the water, rainbows, bolts of lightning, thatched cottages with roses around the door and a stream running through the garden, a robin perched on a post box in the snow, and many other well-worn scenes. Anything that is cute and trite, and lacks artistic and aesthetic integrity should be avoided at all costs.

There is nothing inherently wrong with this kind of subject matter, but none of it is going to set the world on fire, and unless it is depicted in an entirely different way, it will be just another one of many similar paintings.

Those who aim at faultless regularity will only produce mediocrity, and no one ever approaches perfection except by stealth, and unknown to themselves.

WILLIAM HAZLITT

So what should we be striving for instead? As it is with poetry, art can invoke in others emotions that wordy explanations are incapable of doing. In poetry, words are scraped down to the bare bones in a way that encourages us to read between the lines. So much can be said with so little. And so it should be with painting. We should aim at creating paintings that contain a sense of the evocative and mysterious, to suggest that which cannot be seen or easily translated into words. We should be trying to make a statement and communicate an emotion or an idea to others. It might encourage the viewer to re-examine the way in which they perceive the environment and life forms around them. Art should be primarily about self-expression, and hopefully the product of this will be that it touches other people who have similar emotions, but perhaps are unable to verbalize them in any way. This may take the form of a simple landscape painting, but it should have a purpose, rather than just being a pretty picture.

ACKNOWLEDGEMENTS

I would like to dedicate this book to all those landscape artists, famous and not so famous, both present and past, whose work I have admired during the long process of writing this book, who have taken up their sketchbooks and paints and braved sunshine and showers, wind, rain and snow to pursue their goal of capturing their own personal record and experience of the natural world. In particular I would like to thank Antony Bridge, Roy Connelly, Anna Dillon, Douglas Fryer, Warwick Fuller (represented in the UK by Panter & Hall, London), Charles Jamieson, David Mensing, Stephen Palmer, David Sawyer, Jeffrey Reed and Deborah Tilby.

For more information on Kevin Scully and his work, visit www.kevinscully.co.uk

SUPPLIERS

Alla Prima: alla-prima-pochade.myshopify
Artwork Essentials: www.artworkessentials.com
Atlantis Art Materials & Art Supplies: www.atlantisart.co.uk
Best Brella: www.greatarttools.com
C Roberson & Co: www.robco.co.uk
Cheap Joe's: www.cheapjoes.com
Daler Rowney: www.daler-rowney.com
Eckersley's Art & Craft: www.eckersleys.com.au
Guerilla Painter: www.guerrillapainter.com
Jackson's Art Supplies: www.jacksonart.com
Ken Bromley: www.artsupplies.co.uk
L. Cornelissen & Son: www.cornelissen.com
Lawrence: www.lawrence.co.uk
Open Box M, Inc.: www.openboxm.com
Pochade: www.pochade.co.uk
SAA: www.saa.co.uk
The Art Shop: www.theartshop.com.au
U.S. Art Supply: www.usartsupply.com
Velbon: www.intro2020.co.uk
Winsor & Newton: www.winsornewton.com

CONTRIBUTING ARTISTS

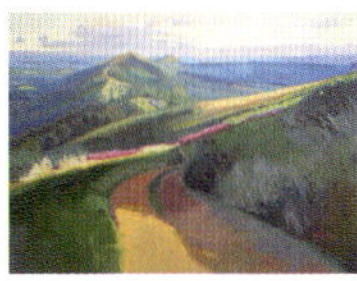

Antony Bridge
www.antonybridge.co.uk

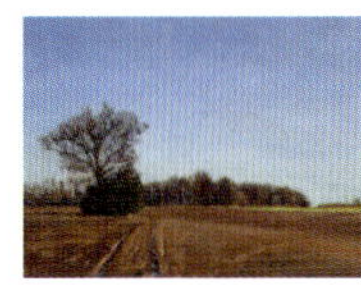

Roy Connelly
www.royconnelly.com

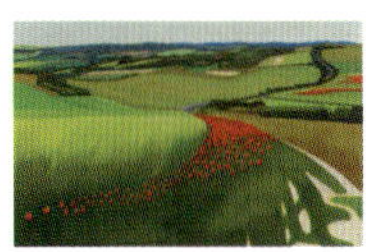

Anna Dillon
www.annadillon.com

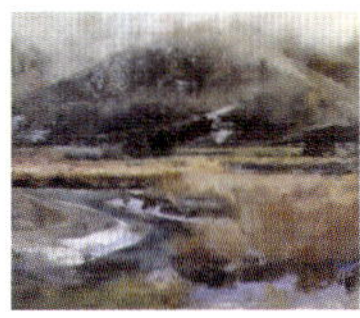

Douglas Fryer
douglasfryer.blogspot.com

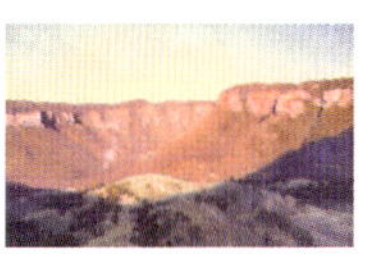

Warwick Fuller
www.warwickfuller.com

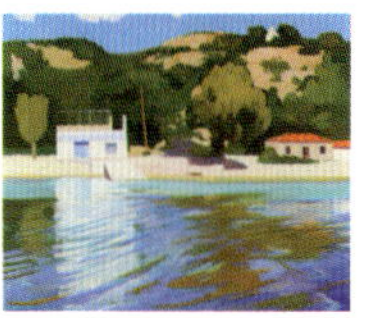

Charles Jamieson
www.charlesjamieson.co.uk

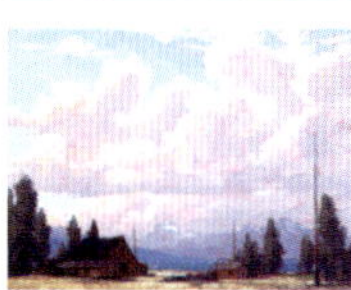

David Mensing
www.davidmensingfineart.com

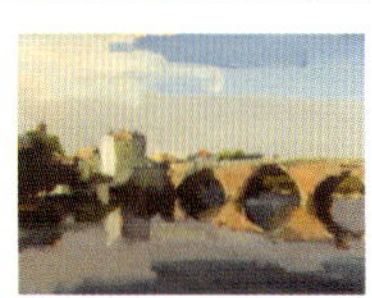

Stephen Palmer
www.stephenpalmerpaintings.co.uk

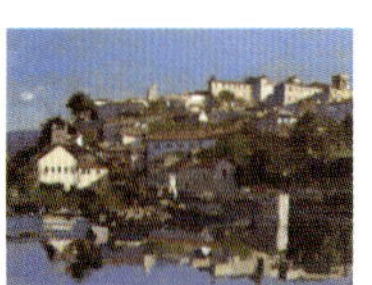

David Sawyer
www.davidsawyerrba.artweb.com

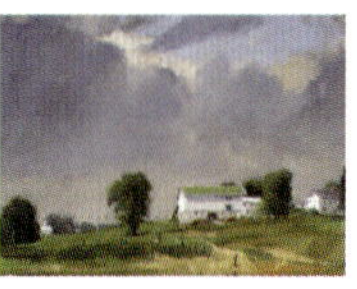

Jeffrey Reed
www.jeffreyreedart.com

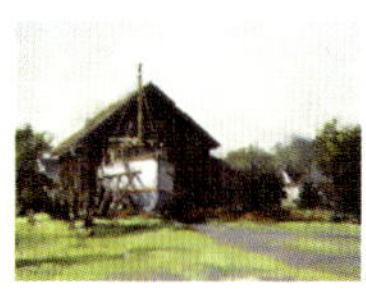

Deborah Tilby
www.deborahtilby.com

INDEX